Morris Rothenberg

The USSR
and AFRICA:

New Dimensions of
Soviet Global Power

MONOGRAPHS IN INTERNATIONAL AFFAIRS

ADVANCED INTERNATIONAL STUDIES INSTITUTE
IN ASSOCIATION WITH THE UNIVERSITY OF MIAMI

Library of Congress Number 80-67085
ISBN Number 0-933074-00-X (soft cover)
ISBN Number 0-933074-01-8 (hard cover)
© Advanced International Studies Institute, 1980

To my wife Patricia
and
in memoriam
Mildred A. Hatch
Morris Shroder

Foreword

THE MESSAGE of this book exceeds its subject matter. The book is about Soviet policies and activities in Africa over the past decade and about preparations and plans the Kremlin openly proclaims for further encroachments on that continent. But in a larger sense the book is about far more than the Soviet Union and Africa. It is about an ominous new pattern of Soviet aggressiveness toward the West and specifically the United States.

This pattern began to emerge at the beginning of the last decade. Soviet leader Brezhnev explained the circumstances in a speech delivered in June 1974:

> Having assessed the overall correlation of forces in the world, we came to the conclusion several years ago that there existed a real possibility of securing a radical turnabout in the international situation.[1]

Its point of departure was also explained by Brezhnev. In a speech in early 1970 reviewing the results of an unprecedented display of Soviet military might in the all-forces "Dvina" maneuvers in March of that year, the Soviet leader asserted:

> Today no question of any importance in the world can be decided without our participation and without consideration of our economic and military might.[2]

[1]*Pravda,* June 15, 1975.
[2]Quoted in Major General V. S. Ryabov, *Dvina: Voiskovye Manevry Provedennye na Territorii Belorussii v Marte 1970 Goda* (Moscow: Voenizdat, 1970), p. 8.

v

The new pattern dynamically developed during the course of the seventies. It was fed by an openly manifested and evidently genuine conviction of the Soviet leadership that the U.S. is undergoing a steady decline in power—in its internal social, economic and political viability, in its relations with its allies, in its ability to influence world developments, and in comparison with the USSR—and that it consequently is increasingly incapable of reacting to Soviet moves "from a position of strength." And it was powered during that decade by ever greater commitments of the Soviet leadership to the use of military force to achieve its objectives, commitments that successively involved:

• Inclusion in Soviet military doctrine of an "external role" for the Soviet armed forces, a role specifically encompassing prevention of the "export of counterrevolution," direct support of "revolutionary liberation movements," and aiding friends, allies and forces struggling for peace in resisting "imperialist aggression in whatever distant region of our planet it might occur."

• The organization and utilization under Soviet direction, and as necessary command, of surrogate strike forces manned by Cubans, East Germans and others.

• Assertion of an "inalienable right" of the USSR and any friendly state anywhere on the globe to engage in any sort of military cooperation for any purpose they might choose.

• A vast extension of the area of Soviet "security zone interests" wherein the USSR is said to have a right to resist an extension of the military presence and activities of the United States and its allies.

• Enunciation of a new Soviet doctrine of intervention that asserts the right of the Soviet Union to use military force to aid friends threatened or contesting for power in any country or region of the world.

The pattern as it has thus developed now appears on the basis of evidence supplied by the Soviets themselves to portend a persistent Soviet drive in the eighties and if necessary on into the nineties to attain the global hegemony which the Kremlin has always contended immutable natural laws plus ever growing Soviet might make inevitable for the USSR.

Africa, as Professor Rothenberg makes clear in the book, served as a key refinement point and proving ground for the assumptions and assessments that have underlain this new pattern of Soviet aggressiveness. Soviet initiatives in Africa in the seventies were qualitatively different from initiatives previously tried by the Kremlin. A striking feature of these initiatives was a willingness to directly involve the Soviet Union in situations of great uncertainty, types of situations which had previously been avoided and which risked a residue of problems that might in the future raise serious difficulties. And success with the first of these new initiatives led to the resort to others, resulting in a succession of interlocked moves in Africa ever bolder in character and ever more decisive in their effects on the overall power balance in the region.

And what was tried and proved out in Africa was immediately reflected in the broadening, deepening and hardening of the general pattern of Soviet aggressiveness. Thus, there is a direct causative relationship between developments in Soviet African policies and other displays of Soviet aggressiveness that have so startled the world in recent times, including the invasion of Afghanistan and Moscow's strident support of Iran in the hostage crisis and in its other conflicts with the U.S.; Moscow's threatening posture toward U.S. efforts to preserve its dwindling power in the Persian Gulf and even in the vast reaches of the Indian Ocean; the stationing of Soviet combat troops in Cuba and the other less heralded but more ominous military buildups on that island which make it not only a bastion of Soviet military power but a potent instrument for extending that power in ever widening directions; Moscow's welcoming of the Nicaraguan revolution in terms reminiscent of Castro's triumph in Cuba and its evident expectations that an instrument is at hand to serve as lever and spur for new revolutionary upsurges in the Caribbean "strategic rear" of the U.S.; the partnership with Vietnam in the military occupation of Cambodia.

Meanwhile, the deepening and strengthening of the global pattern of Soviet aggressiveness has had playback effects on Soviet plans and preparations for further advances in Africa, particularly in the crucial southern region of the continent, which in their turn are admittedly expected by the Kremlin to play a decisive part in finally breaking the back of the world system headed by the United States.

Altogether then, as the Soviets themselves explain the situation, "the question today" in Africa and elsewhere is not one of defensive or piecemeal actions as in the past, but one "of carrying out a total offen-

vii

sive against imperialism and world capitalism as a whole in order to do away with them."[3]

MOSE L. HARVEY, *Director*
Advanced International Studies Institute

June 1980

---

[3]Karen N. Brutents, Deputy Chief of the International Department of the Central Committee of the Communist Party of the Soviet Union, *National Liberation Revolutions Today,* Vol. I (Moscow: Progress Publishers, 1977), p. 16.

Table of Contents

The USSR and AFRICA:

New Dimensions of Soviet Global Power

CHAPTER ONE

Introduction

AFTER YEARS OF LIMITED INTEREST, Moscow has come to look on Africa as the latest, most promising arena for reducing Western and enhancing Soviet influence. Thus, Moscow's leading theoretical journal *Kommunist* at the end of 1976 declared that the prestige of the Soviet Union in African countries was continuing to grow, while that of the United States was steadily declining. Moreover, it argued that "all imperialist calculations of retaining this continent under imperialist influence are breaking down and the further growth of the confrontation between the liberation movement and imperialism here is inevitable." *Kommunist* saw an ever larger number of young African countries "longing for socialism" while "imperialism" was finding it "ever more difficult to recruit reliable allies in Africa for the ideological and political struggle in the world arena." All this, it said, was bearing out Lenin's prediction that anti-imperialist and anti-capitalist developments in what is now called the Third World would play "a far greater revolutionary role than we expect."[1] Another Soviet journal in February 1978 said with equal enthusiasm: "Africa . . . is now tackling one of the most important international tasks, the task of completely eliminating all the vestiges of colonial oppression . . . all seats of colonialism and racism."[2]

[1]L. Tamarin, "Imperialist Calculations and Miscalculations in Africa," *Kommunist,* No. 18, December 1976, pp. 96–105.
[2]Ye. Tarabrin, "The National Liberation Movement: Problems and Prospects," *International Affairs,* No. 2, February 1978, p. 61.

1

From Moscow's perspective a number of basic trends have combined to make Africa the site of increased opportunities and decreased risks; both ideologically and geopolitically it is now a more valuable target than ever before in the unending systemic contest which Moscow sees taking place in the world.

The 1973 oil embargo and its impact on the West made a profound impression on Moscow which directly affected its perceptions regarding Africa. Soviet spokesmen have been talking about the crisis of capitalism since Lenin but what previously might be dismissed as ritual clearly became operational under the impact of the energy crisis. Leninist predictions that the West could be undermined through mobilization of anti-Western actions in the colonies or former colonies at long last appeared to be coming true. U.S. and even more so Western European vulnerability was evident for all to see, not only with respect to oil but to minerals and other commodities. Europe's reliance on Africa for various specifics made the continent all the more valuable a target for Soviet activities. The ability to control Western oil routes and the sources of Western raw materials took on ever greater importance.[3] Soviet journals increasingly depicted the vulnerability of the U.S. and the world capitalist economy to developments in Africa. One called Africa a "most important reserve in the struggle to preserve the capitalist system."[4] It is no longer a case of Africa's being dependent on the West, wrote another, but of "the economy of the main imperialist powers being directly dependent on access to the fuel and raw material resources of these countries."[5]

It is hard to overestimate the impact on Soviet thinking of the fall of the Portuguese empire in 1974–75. It was another Leninist prophecy come true. Brezhnev could thus make the statement at the 60th anniversary of the October Revolution that "the colonial system of imperialism in its classical forms can, on the whole, be regarded as having been dismantled. That, comrades, is an epoch-making development."[6]

[3]For a fuller discussion of these factors, see Walter F. Hahn, Alvin J. Cottrell, *Soviet Shadow Over Africa* (Coral Gables, Fla.: Center for Advanced International Studies, 1977).

[4]G. Roshchin, "The Economic Underpinning of U.S. Expansion in Africa," *International Affairs*, No. 4, April 1978, p. 44.

[5]Ye. Tarabrin, "The Neo-Colonialist Strategem in Africa," *New Times*, No. 35, August 1978, p. 19.

[6]*Pravda*, November 3, 1977.

In another typical statement, the Soviet journal *International Affairs* noted that "under the impact of the victory of the peoples in the Portuguese colonies, . . . the national liberation struggle in South Africa, Rhodesia and Namibia has intensified" and trends set in motion "such that the collapse of the regimes of racism and apartheid and the triumph of the liberation movement in these countries can be confidently predicted."[7]

Even more important, in Moscow's view, was the next step: the shift from "national" to "social" liberation. Moscow's rising satisfaction on that score can be traced in Brezhnev's speeches between 1967 and 1977. Speaking in November 1967 on the 50th anniversary of the October Revolution, Brezhnev lumped Asia and Africa together as an area where "a number of young states have embarked on the road of non-capitalist development," a development of "great importance."[8] In the same speech, for the first time officially he used the term "socialist orientation," a concept carrying considerable ideological and political significance. In the immediate aftermath of Khrushchev's ouster in October 1964, Soviet ideologists had appeared to dampen the tendency of the early sixties to attribute socialist characteristics to Third World radical states. Brezhnev's willingness to credit them as "socialists," though tempered by the word "orientation," reflected renewed hopes in the utility of these states for Soviet policy.

Nevertheless, in his speech to the international communist conference in Moscow on June 7, 1969, Brezhnev was still cautious. While hailing the "socialist orientation" of young states of Asia and Africa as "an important achievement of the revolutionary forces and a heavy defeat for imperialism," he pointed out that the number of such states were still few and that "acute battles" lay ahead.[9] The overthrow of the pro-Soviet Keita regime in Mali in November 1968 and of Nkrumah in Ghana two years earlier (as well as of Sukarno in Indonesia, Ben Bella in Algeria) were presumably still fresh in Brezhnev's mind.

By 1971, a distinct rise in confidence was evident. In his keynote speech to the 24th Congress of the Soviet Communist Party (March 30), Brezhnev proclaimed: "Imperialism is being subjected to ever

[7]L. I. Brezhnev, *Following Lenin's Course* (Moscow: Progress Publishers, 1972), p. 46.

[8]*Pravda,* November 4, 1967.

[9]Brezhnev, *Following Lenin's Course,* p. 173.

greater pressure by the forces which have sprung from the national liberation struggle, above all, by the young independent and anti-imperialist-minded states of Asia and Africa." The main thing, he stressed, was that "the national liberation struggle" in many countries had begun to grow into a struggle against "exploitative relations." Now, he reported, "many states" in Asia and Africa were taking the non-capitalist way of development, "that is, the path of building a socialist camp in the long term."[10]

By the time of the 25th CPSU Congress in 1976, Brezhnev saw a complicated process of class differentiation under way in the Third World with the class struggle gaining in intensity. "Progressive changes have occurred in the economy and the political life of the socialist-oriented Arab, African and Asian countries," though some (such as Angola) "have come under strong pressure."

Brezhnev evinced considerable satisfaction concerning Soviet relations with African countries. Acclaiming the victory of the independence struggles in the former Portuguese colonies, he emphasized that "the CPSU has always sided with those people and rendered every possible support to the embattled patriots," support which shaped the course of relations with the USSR after independence. Brezhnev also saw "closer" relations "with our long-time friends" such as Guinea and the People's Republic of the Congo, as well as with Somalia and Nigeria.[11]

By the end of the year, Brezhnev expressed Moscow's rising sense of confidence growing out of its venture in Angola. He told a Moscow audience of an international "peace" group that:

> There has been an upsurge of the struggle of the peoples against the bastions of racism and reaction, against the stooges of world imperialism, such as South Africa and Rhodesia. The anti-imperialist forces have begun to feel more confident. We, too, could sense this when playing host in Moscow during the last few months to a number of high-ranking delegations of independent African countries, fighters for the freedom and progress of the peoples of that continent.[12]

In his 60th October Revolution speech in 1977, Brezhnev judged it of "exceptional importance" that many newly independent countries had

[10]*Ibid.*, p. 342.
[11]*Pravda*, February 25, 1976.
[12]*Pravda*, October 26, 1976.

"rejected the capitalist road of development and adopted a socialist orientation." What he had in mind regarding Africa had been spelled out by an August 1976 article in *International Affairs* which declared that "the adoption of the socialist orientation by many African countries has substantially tilted the balance of power on the continent between them and the countries still traveling the capitalist path. A most important consequence of this has been the weakening of the positions of imperialism, neocolonialism and racism on the continent."[13]

Several Soviet articles have talked to ten "states of socialist orientation," covering 30 percent of the territory of Africa and almost 25 percent of the population. Leading Soviet ideologist Boris Ponomarev characterized these states as "this historic vanguard of the peoples of the former colonies,"—vanguard in communist parlance having the function of pushing everyone else into the proper historic path.[14]

Moreover, according to a Soviet mass distribution pamphlet in 1978, "anti-imperialist potential is characteristic even of those African states which are not going along the path of constructing in the future a socialist society." These countries, it said, "come out objectively" on a number of foreign policy questions "as the allies of the countries of socialist orientation,"[15] and presumably on a number of issues with the USSR. In this connection, the pamphlet emphasized the growing weight of African countries in international organizations, noting that they accounted for 3 of 10 non-permanent members of the U.N. Security Council, 14 of 15 on the Economic and Social Council, 12 of 15 in the Coordinating Bureau of the non-aligned movement.

Moscow attributed cardinal importance to the fall of Vietnam in 1975 as an inhibiting factor on any future U.S. intervention in Third World conflicts. In his 60th anniversary speech on November 2, 1977 Brezhnev said explicitly: "The U.S. war against the people of Vietnam ended in a defeat that was too crushing and ignominious to kindle the desire to repeat such adventures."

[13]P. Grebennikov, "The Present Day Class Struggle," *International Affairs*, No. 8, August 1976, p. 24.

[14]B. Ponomarev, "The World Historical Significance of the Great October Revolution," *Kommunist*, No. 17, November 1977, p. 42.

[15]L. A. Alekseyev, *Africa: Struggle for Political and Economic Liberation* (Moscow: Znanie, 1978), p. 7.

Shortly after President Carter's trip to Nigeria, *Izvestiia* on March 19, 1978 noted that "following the failure of the Vietnamese adventure, U.S. imperialist circles are apprehensive about the consequences, for both their domestic and foreign policy, of sending their own armed forces overseas and of using them directly to extend their influence."[16] This article, written after Soviet-Cuban successes in Ethiopia, reflected the continued importance Moscow attributed to the Vietnam factor in explaining U.S. caution during the conflict in the Horn of Africa.

Soviet moves in Africa must also be seen against the background of Soviet interpretations of detente, which were, of course, quite different from those of the United States and other Western countries.

First of all, Moscow has seen detente as acceptance by the West of the changing "correlation of forces" in the world in the Soviet favor. The change from Western strategic superiority to parity brought with it steadily escalating Soviet claims of an ability and right to have a voice in all world problems. Foreign Minister Gromyko on July 12, 1969 declared that "the Soviet Union, which as a large world power has widely developed international connections, cannot take a passive attitude toward those events that might be territorially remote but that touch on our security and also on the security of our friends."[17] Then, on March 14, 1970, Brezhnev concluded the "Dvina" military exercises with a speech in which he asserted that "at the present time no questions of any importance in the world can be solved without our participation, without taking into account our economic and military might."[18]

Second, in this context, another major development influencing Soviet policy and arms in Africa has been the growth of Soviet military power. An even firmer statement was made by Soviet Premier Kosygin in his keynote October Revolution address on November 4, 1978: "The valiant armed forces of the Soviet Union have at their disposal all that it is necessary to give a crushing rebuff to any aggression against our country and against its allies and friends."[19] A 1979 article on the impact of the scientific-technological revolution on military affairs

---

[16]V. Kudriavtsev, "Gamble on Splitting," *Izvestiia*, March 19, 1978.
[17]*Pravda*, July 13, 1969.
[18]V.S. Riabov, ed., *Dvina* (Moscow: Voenizdat, 1970), p. 8.
[19]*Pravda*, November 5, 1978.

noted the "enormous increase in the possibility for immediate intervention by states in one or another potential or real military conflict, particularly by means of rapidly moving large military units and armaments over large distances." While these possibilities were said to be open to the West, the author also pointed out that never before had the "progressive" forces possessed such favorable technical possibilities for a rapid and efficient coordination of foreign policy actions for "preventing or extinguishing international conflicts at any point on the earth."[20] This is precisely the language used by Moscow to define its own and Cuban actions in Angola and Ethiopia.

Third, Soviet spokesmen interpret detente as deterring the West from supporting so-called counterrevolutions in the Third World. An article on Africa in *International Affairs* in May 1978, for example, declared that while the West wanted to mount a counteroffensive against the African liberation movements and to keep control over African mineral and manpower resources, "imperialism cannot act in disregard of the process of detente as the dominant world trend which deters the Western powers from outright armed intervention in Africa." Specifically, with respect to the United States, the same article declared that "the relaxation of tension, . . . the failure of the Vietnam venture and the realignment of forces in favor of the national liberation movements" all had compelled the U.S. to refrain from using "open armed force" there.[21]

Moscow has seen detente acting as a deterrent in two ways: (1) as a reflection of the changing correlation of forces, detente presumably also reflected reduced Western capabilities to use force to protect Western interests; and (2) Western involvement in Third World quarrels might jeopardize the detente which larger Western interests require.

Fourth, the Soviets interpret detente as allowing them a free hand to assist in any way they choose revolutionary movements—or "national liberation" movements as they like to call them—anywhere in the world. Thus Brezhnev declared at the 25th Party Congress:

[20]M. Maksimova, "The World Economy, the Scientific and Technological Revolution and International Relations," *Mirovaia Ekonomika i Mezhdunarodnye Otnosheniia*, No. 4, April 1979, pp. 23–24.
[21]V. Kudriavtsev, "Africa Fights for Its Future," *International Affairs*, No. 5, May 1978, p. 35.

Some bourgeois leaders affect surprise and raise a howl over the solidarity of Soviet Communists, the Soviet people, with the struggle of other peoples for freedom and progress. This is either outright naivete or more likely a deliberate befuddling of minds. It could not be clearer, after all, that detente and peaceful coexistence have to do with interstate relations. . . . Detente does not at all abolish, nor can it abolish or alter, the laws of the class struggle.

In the developing countries, he explained, "we are on the side of the forces of progress, democracy and national independence and "our Party supports and will continue to support peoples fighting for their freedom. . . . We act as we are led by our revolutionary conscience, our communist convictions."[22]

For its part, of course, Moscow has denied that Soviet involvement jeopardizes detente. It has insisted that detente is not "a charter of immunity for anti-popular corrupt venal regimes" and that charges that Soviet and Cuban aid to national liberation movements harms detente are totally groundless.

Meanwhile, changed Chinese policies since 1970 also have had their impact on Soviet attitudes. Chinese approaches to Africa have served to goad Soviet actions. Moscow has been ambivalent about Peking's shift to government-to-government moves rather than to support for extremist social movements as the main focus of Chinese policy. Insofar as the main thrust of Chinese efforts is to persuade the governments of the area of the Soviet danger, Soviet concern about Chinese activities has risen. On the other hand, Sino-Soviet rivalry has shifted into arenas where Moscow has major advantages, notably military aid, an advantage which Moscow has been quick to seize.

To capitalize on this confluence of favorable circumstances, basic Soviet policy can be defined as a succession of efforts to keep the pot boiling. Each advance is seen as a stepping stone to the next. What Moscow appears to be seeking is to foster situations in which Africans will turn to the USSR for support and military aid and will place the West on the other side of the barricades, preferably along with South Africa.

For a better appreciation of Soviet policy, and especially the new dimensions which characterize it, the body of this study has been divided into three sections: the first covering the major Soviet advances

[22]*Pravda*, February 25, 1976.

and attempted advances of recent years in Angola, Ethiopia and Zaire; the second, Soviet concepts on how to consolidate and capitalize on advances achieved; and the third, Soviet perspectives on future advances, especially in southern Africa (Rhodesia, Namibia and the Republic of South Africa).

The Angolan and Ethiopian adventures cannot be overestimated for the important departures they heralded in Soviet policies, not only in Africa but also generally, and for what they both reflected and stimulated in the way of changes in Soviet risk–gain calculations. Careful attention is therefore paid to Soviet relationships to the various protagonists within both countries and the factors which went into shifts from relatively limited Soviet involvement in both countries to the massive introduction of Soviet arms and advisers and Cuban troops into both, including Soviet assessments of possible Western reactions. Soviet and Cuban justifications are examined at length for what they reveal, not only about Soviet attitudes to outside reaction but in connection with emerging Soviet interventionist doctrines with respect to the Third World generally. A separate chapter is also devoted to the 1977 and 1978 incursions into Zaire for the clues they provide of a situation in which the USSR has exercised some care but also as a portent of a future Soviet objective. The final chapter in this section deals with the broad panoply of Soviet measures designed to expand the USSR's presence, particularly its military presence, not only in radical African states but throughout the continent.

The second section covers increased Soviet attention to the measures required to prevent the kind of reversals suffered in the past and to make Soviet influence permanent and to complete the elimination of Western influence in the group of states designated by Moscow as "socialist oriented." One chapter discusses Soviet pressures on these states to align themselves with the USSR and transform themselves along the Soviet model in order to insulate them from remaining ties with the West and make up for continued backwardness. Another chapter deals in detail with the specific techniques used by Moscow in Angola, Ethiopia and Mozambique with special emphasis on Soviet utilization of their security problems to bind them to the USSR, and on the new dimension which Cuban troops give the efforts both to consolidate the Soviet position in Angola and Ethiopia and to utilize this position for new undertakings.

The third section deals with the keystone southern Africa region as the climactic target to which previous Soviet efforts are leading. Chapters on Rhodesia and Namibia describe Soviet relationships with the national liberation movements, Soviet emphasis on the need for armed struggle and on attempts to discourage them from participating in Western moves to achieve a peaceful settlement on any other basis than surrender. A final chapter deals with Moscow's ultimate target, the Republic of South Africa. It discusses Soviet assessments of South Africa's strengths and weaknesses and Moscow's evident intention to use the USSR's own new status in Africa and the appearance of clients and potential clients in the neighborhood of South Africa to mount an ever growing and intensifying struggle designed to neutralize and ultimately to eliminate South Africa as a anti-Soviet power factor in the East-West struggle.

CHAPTER TWO

The Angolan Intervention

SOVIET INVOLVEMENT IN ANGOLA started cautiously but picked up momentum as the USSR began to judge the risks of confrontation with the West as minimal. Soviet aid to the Popular Movement for the Liberation of Angola (MPLA) began as early as 1961 but was modest in scope during the sixties and early seventies. While Moscow was partial to the MPLA in the three-way struggle between it, the National Union for the Total Independence of Angola (UNITA) and the National Front for the Liberation of Angola (FNLA) during 1975, the Soviets were not overtly critical of the latter two even though they were receiving Chinese and American aid. Moscow appeared to welcome the agreement reached on January 15, 1975 between the Portuguese and the three Angolan factions creating a transitional government which was to function until the proclamation of Angolan independence on November 11, 1975.[1]

Denouement of the "Liberation Struggle"

It was only after the transitional government broke down first in January and then again in June 1975 that the USSR began to pour significant quantities of aid to the MPLA. According to former Secre-

[1]This summary is based on the article by Dr. Daniel S. Papp, "Angola, National Liberation and the Soviet Union," *Parameters,* Vol. VIII, No. 1, March 1978, pp. 26–39.

11

tary of State Kissinger: "We found that between April and June something like $200 million worth of Soviet equipment was introduced on the side of Neto [MPLA's leader] which was more military equipment than all the rest of the world gave to all the rest of Africa put together.[2]

The second stage of Soviet aid came after the final breakdown of the transitional government in June 1975. According to testimony on January 29, 1976 by Secretary Kissinger to the Senate Subcommittee on African Affairs, "in August intelligence reports indicated the presence of Soviet and Cuban military advisers, trainers and troops including the first Cuban combat troops." Kissinger noted Cuban claims that a Cuban military training program had begun in June and suggested that "Cuban advisers were probably there before then."[3]

The next stage took place in October 1975 with the introduction of massive Soviet and Cuban military assistance, including the airlift of thousands of Cuban troops into Angola. At the time of this incursion FNLA forces from the north and UNITA forces from the south, aided by approximately 1,200 South African troops, had pushed MPLA forces back throughout Angola. By November 11, the MPLA controlled only Luanda and a narrow belt across north-central Angola.

Kissinger told the Senate that the U.S. beginning in October made diplomatic démarches to the Soviet Union about ceasing outside assistance. "Their responses," he reported "were evasive but not totally negative." On December 9, President Ford made a formal request to the Soviet government, and from then until December 24 the Soviets halted their airlift to Angola. However, according to Kissinger "after the Senate vote to block any further aid to Angola, the Cubans more than doubled their forces and Soviet military aid was resumed on an even larger scale. The scope of Soviet-Cuban intervention increased drastically; the cooperativeness of Soviet diplomacy declined."[4]

It was Kissinger's position that "our domestic divisions prevented us from stopping the aggressive action—as we had the capability to do." He contended that: "We were on the way to meeting the chal-

[2]"Dr. Kissinger on World Affairs, An Interview," *Encounter,* November 1978, p. 12. At a press conference on January 14, 1976, Kissinger had said that this aid had stretched over nine months and exceeded all aid to sub-Saharan Africa (*Department of State Bulletin,* No. 1910, February 2, 1976, p. 128).

[3]Statement by Secretary Kissinger, "Implications of Angola for Future U.S. Foreign Policy," *Department of State Bulletin,* No. 1912, February 16, 1976, p. 177.

[4]*Ibid.,* p. 178.

lenge and it was a manageable problem at the time of the Tunney amendment, the number of Cubans was still within proportions— capable of being resisted." Kissinger denied that U.S. military intervention would have been necessary, contending that his proposed program would have made the situation "if not untenable, then so costly for the Cubans in Angola that they would have sought a settlement."[5]

Congressional bars to aid for pro-Western factions in Angola at the end of 1975 and the beginning of 1976, despite the protests of the Ford Administration, were directly related by Moscow to Vietnam events. Two days after Senate passage of the Clark amendment to this effect on December 19, 1975, a TASS dispatch from Washington declared that the Senate's decision "banning allocations for supporting the two rebel groups reflects the deep anxiety in this country over the serious consequences of such a policy for the United States itself. Many legislators see a dangerous similarity between the present actions of the U.S. in Angola and the operations of the American military authorities in Vietnam, which in the long run landed the country in the Southeast Asian military adventure."[6]

A general survey of American foreign policy at the end of 1976 by one of Moscow's leading writers on the U.S., G. A. Trofimenko, put these Congressional actions in the context of a much broader post-Vietnam reevaluation by Washington of the "lessons of Vietnam." One of the main lessons which the U.S. leadership drew, he said, was recognition of the "disparity between the United States' extensive global military-political pretensions and its actual potential in the modern epoch." Specifically reflecting the revised U.S. calculation was the Guam Doctrine, which Trofimenko interpreted as reflecting the "realistic" premise that "not all conflicts and disputes and especially internal events in specific countries have a bearing on vitally important U.S. interests." Trofimenko saw in the Congressional actions on Angola "a desire to observe the Guam Doctrine's realistic elements at a time when the administration was seeking to violate them by its intervention policy."[7] Trofimenko was thereby suggesting that the notion

[5]Department of State Press Release, "Interview of the Honorable Henry A. Kissinger, Secretary of State, by *U.S. News and World Report,*" March 7, 1976.
[6]TASS, December 1, 1975.
[7]G.A. Trofimenko "U.S. Foreign Policy in the Seventies: Words and Deeds," *USA: Economics, Politics, Ideology,* No. 12, December 1976.

was taking root at least in the U.S. Congress that Africa was of secondary importance to the United States.

Until the massive Cuban intervention which got underway in October 1975, Moscow still interpreted events in Angola as a civil war fought basically by forces on the ground with aid, however, from the outside. The Soviet army newspaper *Red Star* on September 7 declared that "using FNLA detachments as its main instrument, imperialist reaction is attempting in the course of the civil war to physically annihilate the MPLA—the revolutionary vanguard of the Angolan people.[8] *Red Star* noted the presence of South African troops around the Cunene River hydroelectric complex as a "new phase" in the Angolan crisis, but did not dramatize South African involvement as later Soviet commentaries were to do.

Well into October, Moscow still seemed to identify the conflict as one between national liberation factions. *Izvestiia* on October 10 condemned the "perfidious imperialistic tactics of splitting the national liberation movement by planting phony organizations in its ranks" which were "disguised only superficially as fighters for national liberation."[9] While the FNLA and UNITA were already being attacked as instruments of the U.S. and/or Peking, by early November the Soviet media became increasingly laudatory of the MPLA as the "revolutionary vanguard" expressing "the will of the Angolan people."[10] As late as November 2, *Red Star* still referred to the "civil war" in Angola, noting, however, the introduction of "new reserves into the battle" from South Africa. Significantly, these forces were treated on a par with the involvement of Zaire and a motley array of foreign mercenaries also said to be operating in Angola.[11]

A little-noted aspect of the Soviet operation in Angola was Moscow's willingness to run roughshod over African apprehension about outside power involvement in African affairs. Three major elements went into this Soviet attitude. First was a Soviet estimate that the African nations would have no choice but to adjust to any settlement imposed by Moscow together with Havana. This ultimately proved to

[8]Capt. Yu. Gavrilov and V. Vinogradov, "Angola's Difficult Times," *Krasnaia Zvezda*, September 7, 1975.

[9]Papp, "Angola, National Liberation," pp. 31–32.

[10]*Ibid.*, p. 32.

[11]Capt. Yu. Gavrilov and V. Vinogradov, "Angola, At a Testing Time," *Krasnaia Zvezda*, November 2, 1975.

be correct. Moreover, the decisiveness of the Cuban victory made it possible for Moscow and Havana to portray their action as a response to the request of a legitimate, recognized government rather than intervention on the side of one party in a civil war. Second, the USSR felt it now had so much support from "countries of socialist orientation" that it could portray the issue as an African one requiring support from African moderates. Third, South African involvement also obscured the civil war features of the Angolan situation and was seized on by Moscow and Havana to garner African support first for their intervention and later for retention of Cuban troops in Angola.

Accordingly, the USSR rejected the recommendation adopted by the Conciliation Commission of the Organization of Africa Unity (OAU) in Kampala on October 24, 1975 "that no member-State should recognize any liberation movements in the event of the latter declaring unilateral independence."[12] Instead it sent two communications to Uganda President Idi Amin, then chairman of the OAU, expressing Soviet concern over developments in Angola and asking that Uganda recognize the MPLA.[13] Amin condemned the USSR for its arrogance and on November 11, 1975 broke relations, a rupture which, however, lasted a mere six days.

Simultaneously with the Portuguese independence proclamation, the MPLA on November 11, 1975 proclaimed itself the legitimate government of Angola. The USSR and its Eastern European allies immediately recognized it, as did Algeria, the Congo, Guinea, Somalia and the four former Portuguese colonies. By the time an OAU summit was convened early in 1976, 21 of its 46 member-states had recognized the MPLA, none had recognized the government proclaimed by its rival, Holden Roberto's FNLA. Nevertheless the OAU was split down the middle over the fact that the MPLA government had achieved a dominant position through Soviet-Cuban intervention. As enunciated by the Zambian government: "The MPLA victory is not really theirs. It is a Soviet-Cuban victory."[14]

In addition to the weight of military developments, what turned the tide in favor of the MPLA was the tactic of portraying the war as one of

[12]Colin Legum, Tony Hodges, *After Angola: The War Over Southern Africa* (New York: Africana Publishing House, 1976), p. 80.
[13]Radio Kampala, October 3, November 9, 1975.
[14]Legum, Hodges, *After Angola*, p. 32.

repelling South African intervention. Thus, Nigeria completely switched its stand on the issue. Whereas in November the Nigerian Foreign Minister had denounced the USSR for its intervention, in February its then head of state Gen. Murtala Mohammed saw "a much deeper danger of extra-African powers in collusion with the inhuman and obnoxious apartheid regime in Pretoria trying to frustrate the will of the Angolan people."[15] Gen. Murtala also praised past Soviet aid to liberation movements, prompting Kaunda of Zambia to counter that "assistance to liberation movements must not be an excuse for establishing hegemony in Africa."[16]

Soviet doctrine does not eschew the concept of outside intervention in civil wars. A pamphlet issued by the Soviet Ministry of Defense explicitly spells out that national liberation wars can take the form of internal conflicts as well as those of oppressed nations or peoples against their oppressors. According to the author, Col. Ye. I. Dolgopolov:

> The concept of a national liberation war is applied both to wars which take the shape of uprisings of enslaved people against their oppressors as well as wars of independent national states against the infringements of the imperialists by force of arms in order to foist or restore colonial orders. V. I. Lenin more than once emphasized the absence of any serious difference in a political sense between national wars and national uprisings, pointing out the lack of foundation of attempts to draw a line between them.[17]

As the tide of battle shifted in favor of the Cuban-MPLA forces, Soviet propaganda became more peremptory in its insistence that all African countries had to choose either victory with the MPLA or defeat with its opponents. Shortly before the OAU summit in Addis Ababa January 10 to 13, 1976, *Pravda* saw a "manifest" change "in appraisal of the real state of things in Angola even by those countries which only yesterday held a hesitant or wait-and-see position."[18] When the session split almost precisely in half between those who favored recognition by the MPLA's "People's Republic of Angola" (PRA) and those who wanted another try at a coalition government

---

[15]*Ibid.*, p. 30.

[16]*Ibid.*, p. 31.

[17]Ye. I. Dolgopolov, *National Liberation Wars At the Present Stage* (Moscow: Voenizdat, 1977), pp. 32–33.

[18]Editorial, "Concerning Events In and Around Angola," *Pravda*, January 3, 1976.

embracing all three factions, Moscow pressed even harder for the first course. *Izvestiia* attributed the position of the latter group to the fact that "the ruling clique in certain African countries is supported by foreign capital and is afraid of falling out of favor with it."[19]

For their part, the Cubans also made clear that they would disregard any OAU call for an end to foreign intervention. In an informal talk with American correspondents in Havana on January 10, 1976, Cuba's Deputy Prime Minister Carlos Rafael Rodriguez, when asked whether the Cubans would withdraw in response to an African demand, responded: "No, only if Neto says we should withdraw. We would disregard a call from the OAU."[20] Maintaining the pressure, the Soviet-dominated Bureau of the World Peace Council convening in Helsinki January 16–19 adopted a resolution denouncing "imperialist aggression" against the PRA and calling on all governments to recognize it.[21]

What was even more striking was the increasing tendency to identify the issue not as a choice between factions but between the forces of good and evil, between anti-imperialism and imperialism. As expressed by *Izvestiia* following the OAU summit:

> The independent African states are now faced with a crucial choice. . . . It is either progressive advancement along the road of uprooting the hangovers of colonialism and neocolonialism toward social progress, or the road of unjustified hesitation, marking time or retreat in the face of imperialism and racialism.[22]

Most significant of all, Soviet commentaries saw events in Angola not as an end in themselves, but as a spur to further advances in Africa. *Pravda* on February 11, 1976 stated that the Angolan "people and their legitimate government are now a major part of the national liberation movement on the African continent." Further, *Pravda* emphasized, "militarist elements" in the West were "well aware that the consolidation of the people's power in Angola will protect the natural wealth and population of that country from exploitation by the international monopolies and will represent a powerful stimulus in mounting the liberation struggle of the peoples of Namibia, the South African Repub-

---

[19]Ye. Vladimirov, "Africa Condemns Intervention in Angola," *Izvestiia*, January 27, 1976.

[20]*New York Times*, January 12, 1976.

[21]*Soviet World Outlook*, Vol. 1, No. 2, February 13, 1976, p. 3.

[22]Observer, "The Just Cause of Angola Will Triumph," *Izvestiia*, January 29, 1976.

lic and Zimbabwe, against the racist regimes." And *Pravda's* sights went even beyond southern Africa: "It will stimulate the activation of the African peoples' struggle for social and economic transformations and for the complete liberation of the continent from all that remains of colonialism and racism."[23]

Castro was particularly enthusiastic on this theme. Addressing a rally in January 1976 in honor of visiting Panamanian chief General Torrijos, Castro brushed aside the Guantanamo issue as small potatoes compared to his larger African aspirations: "Our struggle with imperialism," he asserted, "is not at the level of a small piece of Cuban territory. Our struggle with imperialism is at the world level." Emphasizing the small size of Guantanamo, Castro went on: "We love it because it is part of our fatherland. But the important thing is the liberation of the continent, the liberation of Vietnam, the liberation of Africa, the liberation of Angola."[24]

Ideological and Political Rationale

Throughout the Angolan crisis, Soviet spokesmen insisted that the USSR wanted a peaceful political solution by indigenous forces without outside interference. Protestations to this effect increased as Cuban military action intensified and apprehensions mounted about big power involvement. In this connection, the Angolan crisis provided a particularly egregious example of the perils of ascribing Western meanings to words used by Soviet spokesmen.

In January 1976, both before and after the OAU summit on Angola, as well as talks in Moscow by Secretary of State Kissinger, *Pravda* and *Izvestiia* carried articles on Soviet support for a political solution and opposition to foreign intervention which the Western press saw as the bases for a possible East-West accord on the issue.[25] Thus *Pravda* on January 3 declared: "The Soviet Union comes out firmly for the termination of foreign armed intervention in Angola. The Angolan people

---

[23]Observer, "Concerning the Situation in Angola," *Pravda,* February 11, 1976.
[24]Radio Havana, January 12, 1976.
[25]See, for example, the *New York Times* January 4, 1976 story headlined "Moscow Asks End to Intervention" and its January 30, 1976 story "Soviet Indicates Angola Political Solution."

should be given the right to decide for themselves the questions of building a new life in conditions of peace and freedom."

However, it was evident that Moscow excluded Soviet-Cuban intervention from such a ban. The same *Pravda* article emphasized that "the Soviet Union, loyal as it is to its internationalist duty, has given and continues to give moral and material support to the patriotic forces of Angola and the Popular Movement for the Liberation of Angola (MPLA) in their struggle against colonalism and makes no secret of this." At the same time, *Pravda* denied that the USSR had any ulterior motives in Angola and said assertions "about Soviet military expansion in Africa are unfounded."[26]

Then and afterwards Moscow increasingly used the Angolan situation to illustrate the qualitative difference between Soviet and Western involvement in a foreign country. Thus, *Izvestiia* wrote on January 29, 1976:

> The African peoples see the differences between real interference into Angola's internal affairs—the armed intervention by the South African regime and actions of its imperialist and neocolonialist patrons—and the disinterested aid which is given to the young national state by the Soviet Union and the other socialist countries for putting an end to the open armed interference, for securing Angola's freedom, independence and territorial integrity.[27]

Similarly, Moscow's commentaries gave a uniquely Soviet interpretation to the concept of a political solution in Angola. After stating that the USSR "has never come out against a quest for a political settlement in Angola," *Izvestiia* on January 27 immediately made clear that the MPLA's rivals, the FNLA and UNITA, were to be read out of such a process because they had "committed an act of national treachery by launching together with the imperialists and racialists an armed struggle against Angola's legitimate government." In this context, the article's statement that "the Soviet Union welcomes now too a course of action which would contribute to the consolidation in Angola of all the patriotic forces working for genuine independence"[28] meant that the USSR was looking toward proposing a post-victory consolidation of power by the Soviet-supported People's Republic of Angola under the

[26]Editorial, "Concerning Events."
[27]Observer, "The Just Cause."
[28]*Ibid.*

control of its dominant element, the MPLA. Three weeks later, *Pravda* once more welcomed "the PRA Government's efforts aimed at consolidating patriotic forces that come out for genuine independence and democratic development of their country."[29]

An interesting feature of Soviet-Cuban tactics has been the attempt to justify their involvement in terms that would make it palatable, especially to countries of the area, as well as to minimize any justification for Western counteraction. Initially, both Moscow and Havana either ignored or denied the presence of Cuban forces in Angola. Throughout the period of major Cuban involvement (from November 1975 to March 1976), Soviet media referred to the "national army" of the PRA or the "patriotic forces" of Angola. The Cuban role was only hinted at. In his keynote speech to the First Congress of the Cuban Communist Party on December 17, 1975, Castro merely talked generally about Cuban fealty to proletarian internationalism, declaring that "we are prepared to continue offering them [the Angolan people] all the necessary aid for the consolidation and independence and progress of their people."[30]

However, Castro soon dropped such pretenses. In his closing speech to the Congress five days later, he acknowledged that Cuba had sent military instructors and other personnel to Angola "from the beginning." Reviewing most recent events, he said that in response to the "unleashing" by the U.S. of South African troops in late October, Cuba and other "progressive" countries responded with aid."[31] Later, at a rally closing the Congress, he admitted that the "aid" he was talking about meant direct Cuban military participation, claiming that "we are not only a Latin American country, but also a Latin-African country. . . . We are brothers of the Africans and ready to fight for the Africans." He went on to say: "We will defend Angola and we will defend Africa. When we say we defend, we mean it. When we say we fight, we mean it. Let the South African racists know it. Let the Yankee imperialists know it."[32]

Castro's first public admission of Cuban troop involvement occurred at a press conference in Havana on January 15, 1976: "I can say that

---

[29]Observer, "Concerning the Situation."
[30]Radio Havana, December 17, 1975.
[31]Radio Havana, December 22, 1975.
[32]*Ibid.*

we have Cuban soldiers in Angola. I am not going to deny this."[33] On the following day, he told the Italian newspaper *Corriere della Sera:* "Units of our armed forces are fighting at the side of Agostinho Neto's men. I do not deny it."[34] However, these statements were not carried locally in Cuba and it was not until his annual Bay of Pigs address on April 19, 1976 that he discussed the role of Cuban troops before a domestic audience.[35]

For its part, Moscow softened Cuban pronouncements about Havana's role in Angolan events, presumably in order not to derogate from the legitimacy of the Neto government or from Moscow's contribution to its triumph. In reporting Castro's initial public acknowledgements of Cuban military involvement in January 1976, TASS avoided the phrase "Cuban troops" and adhered to the formula of Cuban "assistance to the patriotic forces of Angola." Moscow's purportedly unofficial Radio Peace and Progress on February 18, 1976 referred to "Cuba's military presence in Angola" while TASS on April 6 quoted *Granma's* praise for "Cuban fighters who fulfilled their internationalist duty" in Angola. In its report on Castro's Bay of Pigs anniversary speech, *Pravda* did not mention his statement about the dispatch of a battalion of regular troops to Angola in early November 1975 but did cite his denial that the USSR had ever asked Cuba to send "even a single Cuban soldier to Angola."[36] In June 1976, TASS, however, reported Castro's speech on the fighting qualities of troops of the Cuban Ministry of the Interior as "brilliantly displayed, in particular, in Angola." Castro was cited to the effect that this force had fought in Angola "together with soldiers of the Revolutionary Armed Forces."[37]

After the MPLA's proclamation on November 11, 1975 of the People's Republic of Angola, Soviet and Cuban commentaries increasingly justified their military involvement on the grounds that it was a legitimate response in accordance with international law to the request of a recognized government exercising its sovereignty. Thus three Soviet international lawyers wrote in January 1976:

[33]Radio Havana, January 15, 1976.
[34]Giangiacomo Foa, "Fidel Castro: This Is Why We Are Fighting in Angola," *Corriere della Sera* (Milan), January 17, 1976.
[35]Radio Havana, April 20, 1976.
[36]Foreign Broadcast Information Service, *Trends in Communist Media,* June 3, 1976, pp. 15–16.
[37]TASS, "Speech by F. Castro," *Pravda,* June 8, 1976.

"The Western press is trying to present matters as though a civil war were underway or continuing in Angola. In fact, there can be no ques-- tion of any civil war in Angola. A foreign military intervention is being conducted against the legal government of the young republic with the use, as cover, of a proposition of misled Angolans under the influence of splittist groups." In this situation, they went on, "the lawful government of the People's Republic of Angola has the full right to the support and aid of other states and international organizations in its just struggle against aggression and imperialist outside interference."[38]

But official Cuban versions make clear that Cuban intervention took place before November 11, 1975. In an informal talk on January 11, 1976 with American correspondents visiting Havana, Deputy Prime Minister Carlos Rafael Rodriguez, when asked about aid to the MPLA, replied that "we always helped them." He added that in the spring of 1975 "Neto asked us for advisers" and Cuba sent 230 military men to Angola where they set up four training centers.[39]

In April 1976, however, Castro said that "the first material aid and the first Cuban instructors arrived in Angola at the beginning of October at the request of the MPLA when Angola was being openly invaded by foreign forces."[40] On November 5, he went on, in response to South African intervention beginning October 23, "at the request of the MPLA, our party leadership decided to urgently send a battalion of regular troops equipped with anti-tank weapons to support the Angolan patriots in their resistance against the South African racists. This was the first unit of Cuban troops sent to Angola."[41] In this account, Castro did not pretend, nor did his description permit, a claim that Cuban involvement came in response to the request by the Angolan government.

Politically perhaps the major element of the case presented by Moscow and Havana especially to the rest of Africa was that Cuban intervention came in response to the involvement of South Africa. In his Bay of Pigs anniversary speech, Castro charged that "Ford and Kissinger are lying to the American people, and particularly to the black

[38]Prof. F. Kozhevnikov, Doctor of Juridical Sciences, Prof. Ushakov, Prof. I. Blishchenko, "Angola's Legitimate Right," *Izvestiia*, January 11, 1976.
[39]*New York Times*, January 12, 1976.
[40]Radio Havana, April 20, 1976.
[41]Radio Havana, November 5, 1976.

population, by hiding the fact that the fascist and racist forces of South Africa criminally invaded Angola's territory long before Cuba sent any regular soldiers there."[42]

The official American position set forth by Assistant Secretary of State William Schaufele to the Senate Foreign Relations Committee on February 6, 1976 was that "the first Cuban forces arrived in Angola in August as part of an arrangement among the Soviet Union, the MPLA and Cuba to enable the MPLA to extend its military control over all the nation." The sharp increase of Cuban troops in October was almost simultaneous with South Africa's decision to intervene militarily in the conflict. "This coincidence," Schaufele told the Committee, "plus reports from Cuban prisoners taken in Angola, indicates that the Cuban decision to intervene with combat forces was made, and forces dispatched, before the South Africans undertook their own intervention."[43]

British correspondent Colin Legum has written:

> There is little doubt that the Cubans were first brought into Brazzaville before July 1975 and it is feasible, therefore, that Cuban combat troops were later drafted in batches to Angola—these numbers increasing dramatically from the first unofficial U.S. estimates of 1,500 to 3,000 (in the middle of November) to the estimate of 12,000 in the first week of February 1976. . . . The mobilization and transport of such large numbers, both by air and by sea, would require at least six weeks from the time the decision was taken; so it is reasonable to assume that the Moscow-Havana agreement was taken at least in May 1975.[44]

Addressing the U.N. Security Council on March 31, 1976, U.S. representative William Scranton took issue with Cuba's version of its intervention. According to Scranton's chronology, "the available evidence indicates that Cuba decided no later than mid-August 1975 to commit sufficient numbers of combat troops to Angola to impose the movement they supported as the only government of Angola." He asserted that he could "state this with confidence" because "during September 1975 five Cuban vessels transported around 1,500 combat

[42]*Ibid.*
[43]Department of State News Release, "The African Dimension of the Angolan Conflict," February 6, 1976.
[44]Legum, Hodges, *After Angola*, p. 21.

troops from Cuba to Angola and that by late October at least 2,000 Cuban combat troops were deployed into Angola."[45]

Critics of U.S. policy argue that protests about Soviet-Cuban intervention suffer from their failure to take into account a long history of outside involvement in Angola. Thus a typical example:

> Kissinger's attacks on Cuban assistance to the MPLA in 1975–1976 lacked cogency and credibility, because they were made in a vacuum. By not acknowledging that the South African and Zairian regular troops, as well as assorted mercenaries from Western countries, were fighting in Angola on the side of the FNLA and UNITA, he painted a one-sided picture of the Soviet Union and Cuba attempting to take unilateral advantage of a turbulent local situation (as he told the Senate Foreign Relations Committee in January 1976).[46]

Whatever the U.S. and South African involvement, it was far outweighed by Soviet and Cuban actions in Angola. It is difficult to contradict U.S. Government claims that its actions in Angola were reactive. To begin with, there are innumerable Soviet and Cuban statements at all levels that the USSR and Cuba helped the "liberation movement" in Angola from its inception. According to Assistant Secretary of State Schaufele, "the Soviet Union began extensive rearming of the MPLA, then based in the Congo (Brazzaville) in October 1974."[47] Before that the U.S. had rejected military support to the FNLA which in early 1975 was supplied a small amount of monetary aid ($300,000).[48] After pleas from Zambia and Zaire, the U.S. on July 18 authorized the use of covert funds in order to supply military support for the FNLA and UNITA, estimated by the Select Committee of the House of Representatives at $31 million.[49]

By contrast, in January 1976 Secretary Kissinger estimated that the USSR had delivered $200 million in military equipment and supplies to the MPLA,[50] a figure which jumped to $300 million one month later.[51] According to Western sources, the Soviet Union had supplied the

---

[45]*Department of State Bulletin*, Vol. LXXIV, No. 1922, April 26, 1976, p. 560.

[46]Gerald J. Bender, "Angola, The Cubans, and American Anxieties," *Foreign Policy*, No. 31, Summer 1978, p. 12.

[47]Department of State News Release, "The African Dimension."

[48]Legum, Hodges, *After Angola*, p. 26.

[49]*Ibid.*, p. 27.

[50]*Department of State Bulletin*, Vol. LXXIV, No. 1912, February 16, 1976, p. 179.

[51]*Department of State Bulletin*, Vol. LXXIV, No. 1915, March 8, 1976, p. 285.

MPLA with over 100 T-34 and T-54 battle tanks, large numbers of PT-76 amphibious light tanks and armored personnel carriers, MIG-15 and MIG-21 fighter bombers, 122-mm rocket launchers and large quantities of light weapons, ammunition and replacement parts.[52] As pointed out in a U.S. Congressional study:

> Soviet military assistance to the MPLA was a carefully calibrated mix of weapons. It was clearly intended to insure victory for the MPLA in the Angolan civil war. Soviet T-34 and T-54 tanks, and MIG-15 and MIG-21 fighter-bombers, though not front-line equipment in the Soviet Union's own military inventory, were, nevertheless, sophisticated and supplied in sufficient numbers to insure MPLA air and ground superiority.[53]

In addition, the Soviet Union provided military advisers to MPLA forces and underwrote the Cuban involvement in Angola, ferrying Cuban troops and providing logistic support to them. According to the same Congressional study, "the cost of maintaining Cuban troops was very high."[54]

The entry of regular South African armed forces into Angola in October-November 1975 and their initial successes tended to obscure the modesty of their numbers and of their actual involvement. The MPLA Prime Minister in early December put their number at "1,000 and rising fast" while the Minister of Information estimated 5,000–6,000.[55] Soviet media also used a variety of figures in occasional references to the size of South African forces. *Red Star* on January 25, 1976 used a figure of "around 6,000,"[56] while TASS on February 4, cited a statement in the *Washington Post* by South African Defense Minister Pieter Botha to the effect that there were 4,000–5,000[57] South African troops "in the zone under their control." The latter reappeared in later Soviet articles on Angola.[58] However, Moscow did not break down

[52]*International Defense Review*, "Massive Soviet Arms Shipments to Angola," February 1976, p. 20.

[53]Report to the Committee on International Relations, *The Soviet Union and the Third World: A Watershed in Great Power Policy* (Washington, D.C.: U.S. Government Printing Office, 1977), p. 107.

[54]*Ibid.*, p. 108.

[55]Legum, Hodges, *After Angola*, p. 37.

[56]Capt. 1st Rank V. Rustov, "Patriots On the Attack," *Krasnaia Zvezda*, January 25, 1976.

[57]For example, see K. Uralov, "Angola: The Triumph of the Right Cause," *International Affairs*, No. 5, May 1976, p. 53.

[58]Johannesburg Radio, March 28, 1976.

this figure, as the South Africans did, between contingents evidently numbering 1,500 involved in an armored column which accompanied UNITA forces in a northward thrust at the end of 1975 and the 3,000 or so troops used to protect the Cunene River dam. Another version of the Pieter Botha statement in the *New York Times* reported that the 4,000–5,000 figure related to the troops "on both sides of the border" near the Cunene dam."[59] In a major article summing up Cuba's "contribution" to the Angolan victory, a Soviet scholar claimed that just before Angola's declaration of independence on November 11, 1975 South Africa had 6,000 troops in the country and that with the entry of a motorized brigade after that date, "their ground numbers rose to 12,000 men."[60]

By focusing on the South African element, Moscow and Havana sought to discredit both the United States and the enemies of the MPLA. Ignoring U.S. Government claims that it had nothing to do with South Africa's involvement in Angola, Castro in December 1975 castigated "the U.S. policy of supporting and encouraging South Africa's aggression against Angola," which, he said, made the U.S. "irreconcilable enemies of all the peoples of Africa."[61] Eighteen months later, he told Barbara Walters that he "was completely convinced that the South Africans did not launch that invasion without prior consultation with the government of the United States. I am absolutely sure of that. They would never have launched that adventure without approval from Kissinger and Ford."[62] Similarly, Soviet commentaries frequently presented as a "fact" U.S. "connivance" with South Africa on Angola.

But Moscow was obviously aware that the Soviet-Cuban actions spoke for themselves. As a pro-Western Asian told a *New York Times* correspondent: "There is nothing like raw power, readily deliverable. Moscow's military muscle and Cuban soldiery scored a brilliant victory because nobody else seems to have a thought-out policy for southern Africa at that moment—least of all the United States."[63]

[59]*New York Times*, February 7, 1976.
[60]V.B. Kokorev, "Solidarity With the Struggle of the Angolan People," *Latinskaia Amerika*, No. 6, November-December 1978, p. 130.
[61]Radio Havana, December 22, 1975.
[62]*Bohemia* (Havana), July 1, 1977.
[63]Paul Hoffman, "U.N. Aides Say Angola Debate Shows Lack of U.S. Policy," *New York Times*, April 2, 1976.

Postmortems

Angola is frequently presented by Moscow as a demonstration of the virtues of African reliance on the Soviet Union. Speaking to the Supreme Soviet Commission considering ratification of the Soviet-Angolan Friendship Treaty signed in October 1976, Soviet ideologist Boris Ponomarev hailed Angolan independence as a "great victory" which Africans "rightly regard" as "an example of what close cooperation with the Soviet Union, other socialist countries and all the world's progressive forces can produce in practice." Recalling that the USSR and Cuba came to Angola's aid when matters still hung in the balance, Ponomarev declared that "this victory convincingly demonstrated once again to the dependent countries of Africa and to the entire national liberation movement that, given the present correlation of forces in the world, they can successfully oppose imperialism."[64] A little later Soviet President Podogorny was even more categorical: "It was precisely by relying on the solidarity and fraternal aid from the USSR, Cuba and other countries of the socialist community and progressive forces in Africa and throughout the world that the Angolan people won their historic victory."[65]

At the same time, both Moscow and Havana clearly sought to avoid overplaying this theme. Long after the initial success in Angola, Castro speaking to a Brazilian journalist, explained why Cuba was reticent about its role in Angola. Apart from military security requirements, he said:

> There were, let us say, political factors as well. We did not want to draw attention to the Cuban effort; we did not want to exaggerate it, you see. It would have been wrong to make it appear to be our struggle, simply because it was basically the struggle of the Angolan people. Out of consideration for the Angolans and our revolutionary modesty, we did not want to make it appear as if we were emphasizing the role played by our country. In our relations with the Angolan people and African peoples in general, we took care to avoid this kind of thing.[66]

Colin Legum has suggested that perhaps the Sino-Soviet rivalry was the decisive element spurring Soviet intervention in Angola. In his

[64]*Izvestiia*, January 26, 1977.
[65]*Pravda*, March 15, 1977.
[66]Interview with Castro by Fernando Marais, *Veja* (Saõ Paulo), July 13, 1977.

conclusions on what made Angola unique among world crises, he put at the head of his list that "it was the first occasion when Sino-Soviet rivalry became the main determinant shaping both their policies toward a crisis in the Third World."[67] To bolster his case, he stressed the virulence of the mutual recriminations by Moscow and Peking of each other's position on Angola which "exceeded anything either might have felt about the U.S. and other Western intervention."[68]

Whether rivalry with Peking was in fact such a decisive element is open to question, especially since the Chinese in effect withdrew from the competition in mid-1975 by accepting the OAU decision at Kampala that all three liberation movements be supported. Moreover, while Chinese military aid programs had shifted during the 1970s from MPLA to the other movements, Peking had always refrained from criticism of the MPLA even for its reliance on the USSR and Cuba. Finally, Soviet discussions of Angola usually focused first on Western, then on Chinese involvement in Angola.

Nevertheless, there is no doubt that the competition with China did play a significant role in Moscow's actions in Angola. A 1978 Soviet postmortem on Peking's role in Angola noted MPLA efforts in 1971 and as late as May 1975 to secure military aid from Peking.[69] The very fact of these missions implied a rivalry between the two communist states, in which Soviet aid to the MPLA was seen by Moscow as an opportunity to take advantage first of the paucity of Chinese support for the MPLA, and then of the shift of Chinese military aid to the MPLA's rivals.

For Moscow, the coincidence of Chinese support with that given by the West and South Africa to the MPLA's opponents made the latter's triumph all the sweeter. An article on Chinese policy on Africa in the Soviet journal devoted to Far Eastern affairs expostulated in typical fashion:

> The reactionary anti-popular character of the Maoist policy was dramatically manifested during the imperialist aggression against the People's Republic of Angola in late 1975 and early 1976 when a disgraceful alliance against Angola brought together imperialism, the racist South African

[67]Legum, Hodges, *After Angola*, p. 39.
[68]*Ibid.*, p. 22.
[69]V. Sofinsky, A. Khazanov, "Angolan Chronicle of the Peking Betrayal," *International Affairs*, No. 7, July 1978, p. 65.

regime and Maoism. The defeat of the imperialists, racists and Maoists in Angola dealt a heavy blow at Peking's prestige in Africa.[70]

An added fillip to Moscow's satisfaction has been the growing sharpness of Chinese-Cuban polemics as a result of the Angolan issue, at first almost entirely on Cuba's part. Much to Cuba's annoyance, the Chinese throughout the Angolan crisis and for some time thereafter focused almost entirely on the Soviet role and dismissed the Cubans as "Soviet mercenaries." Thus when the U.N. Security Council considered the Angolan question in March 1976, the Chinese were still calling for agreement among all three liberation movements and, while approving the condemnation of South Africa, complained "that the draft resolution had failed to condemn "Soviet social-imperialism and its mercenaries for their intervention nor has it reflected the just demand for their complete and immediate withdrawal from Angola."[71] In a companion *Peking Review* article, the Chinese derided Soviet-Cuban claims that they had responded to South African action: "This is a big lie. The fact is that their armed intervention preceded the South African intervention."[72]

Who responded to whom in Angola, what the U.S. should have or could have done, whatever the validity of the positions taken, certain elements stand out concerning Soviet behavior as events in fact did unfold.

First of all, the massiveness and sophistication of Soviet military aid marked a new departure for Soviet involvement in African conflicts. When one recalls Soviet efforts at the time of Congolese independence in 1960 and then during the Nigerian civil war in 1965–68, the demonstration of Soviet power in Angola constituted a dramatic change, both in the range and quantity of sophisticated equipment that the Soviet Union was willing to supply, and in the capabilities demonstrated not only directly from the Soviet homeland but as a result of the availability of way-stations en route.

Even more significant, of course, has been the Soviet use of Cuban armed forces. Soviet reliance on proxies is not new. Bulgaria, Yugoslavia and Albania were used in this way during the civil war in Greece

[70]V. Sofinsky, A. Khazanov, "PRC Policy in Tropical Africa (1960s–1970s)," *Far Eastern Affairs*, No. 3, 1978, p. 81.
[71]"China's Stand on Question of Angola," *Peking Review*, No. 15, April 9, 1976, p. 10.
[72]"What Will Moscow Do After South African Racists' Troop Withdrawal," *Ibid.*

just after World War II. Chinese "volunteers" served Soviet purposes in Korea in the fifties. However, except for Hungary and Czechoslovakia, direct postwar Soviet military involvement in external ventures had been limited to the dispatch of advisers and in several instances of pilots (in China, Korea and the Near East). The Angolan venture marked the first time the Soviets undertook the transport of so many regular armed forces for intervention to become involved in local and regional quarrels at so great a distance.

In using Cuban troops, Moscow had hit on a technique with many advantages. It reduced the risks of American confrontation with the U.S. It took into account African sensibilities about direct involvement in big power quarrels. Much more than the Soviet Union, Cuba could profess disinterested motives or lack of intent to establish long-term positions. Yet, although Castro had his own motives, his intervention in Africa was possible only in collusion with the Soviet Union and the Cuban presence necessarily an extension of Soviet policy.

Whether or not stronger indications of possible U.S. actions might have deterred the USSR in Angola, the fact is that the basic U.S. signal to the USSR as the situation was unfolding was one of disengagement. The *New York Times* on December 25, 1975 quoted a "top-ranking Administration official" to the effect that the U.S. did not express concern about Angola until September 1975, did not formally protest the Soviet arms buildup until the end of October, and did not publicly denounce Soviet actions until late in November.

It is evident that the Soviet Union envisaged minimal risks of confrontation with the U.S. not only on the ground but at the expense of Soviet-American relations on other issues. Having correctly assessed the unlikelihood of strong U.S. counteraction, Moscow in effect ignored warnings by President Ford and Secretary Kissinger that its actions in Angola would jeopardize overall Soviet-American relations, or be linked with the solution of other issues, notably SALT. Responding to a series of statements from November 1975 onward especially by Kissinger about the long-range impact of Soviet-Cuban actions, Pravda on February 1 declared:

> The U.S. Secretary of State's logic is manifestly unsound. The whole world knows that the Soviet Union is seeking in Angola neither economic, nor military, nor other advantages. Not one Soviet person is fighting with weapons in hand on Angolan soil. Accusing our country and Cuba of

"expansion," H. Kissinger declares that this "expansion" is occuring in a place where neither the Soviet Union nor Cuba "have any historic interests whatever." As far as expansion is concerned, that is not true. And if we are to talk about historic interests, these lie not in the aspect about which the U.S. Secretary of State is thinking about in the complete and consistent support by the Soviet Union of the peoples' struggle for freedom and independence.[73]

On February 8, 1976 the *New York Times* correspondent in Moscow reported that warnings by Kissinger about the broader impact of Angola were merely electoral posturings. Soviet sources were quoted as having stated that "Angola will fade away." By the end of February 1976, Brezhnev at the 25th Party Congress, reiterated that "detente does not in the slightest way abolish, and cannot abolish or change the laws of class struggle." And with Angola clearly in mind, he went on:

> Our party is rendering and will render support to peoples who are fighting for their freedom. The Soviet Union is not looking for concessions, is not trying to gain political supremacy and is not seeking any military bases. We are acting as our revolutionary conscience and our communist convictions permit us.[74]

A few months later, a major Soviet article on the nature of detente noted that Kissinger himself had acknowledged that Moscow's support for liberation movements is an indissoluble part of Soviet ideology which it would not abandon "simply for the sake of friendly relations with the U.S."[75]

However, what this article ignored was Kissinger's follow-on argument that the United States had deprived itself both of carrots and sticks with which to deal with the Soviet Union, the carrot of credits which could be cut off (SALT being ruled out), and the stick of aid to pro-Western forces which had in fact been cut off.[76]

[73]Tomas Kolesnichenko, "International Week," *Pravda,* February 1, 1976.
[74]*Pravda,* February 25, 1976.
[75]K. M. Georgiev, "Detente: The Formula and the Process," *USA: Economics, Politics, Ideology,* No. 8, August 1976.
[76]Department of State Press Release, "Interview of the Honorable Henry A. Kissinger."

CHAPTER THREE

The Intervention in the Horn

SOVIET-CUBAN SUCCESS IN ANGOLA unquestionably led to their intervention in the conflict between Ethiopia and Somalia. And Western and African immobility in the Angolan affair obviously eased that decision. Once more there was a sudden infusion of massive Soviet arms shipments and the movement of Cuban combat troops in force at a critical point. An additional factor in Soviet calculation this time was of large numbers of Cuban troops, which despite risks and uncertainties, provided a staging area for the Ethiopian operation.

As in Angola, Moscow was slow to commit itself fully to the Mengistu regime but when it did so it sought, again with success, a rapid overwhelming victory. Although Moscow had tended to consider Haile Selassie because of his military ties to the U.S. as basically pro-Western, it had also courted him assiduously. As late as October 1973, only a few months before his powers were curbed by a military coup, the Emperor came at Soviet invitation to Moscow where *Pravda* praised him as one of the founders of the Organization of African Unity, dedicated to "full liberation of the whole African continent from colonial domination."[1] *Pravda* also recalled approvingly that he had previously visited the USSR in 1959, 1967 and 1970.

Thereafter Soviet media gave steady but low key coverage to the gradual military takeover of the reins from the Emperor to his overthrow in September 1974. While many items portrayed a process of

---

[1]*Pravda*, October 29, 1973.

34

reform, even the statement by the new leadership, the Derg, in December 1974 that their ultimate objective was socialism was only briefly mentioned in the Soviet media. Nor did the proclamation of the Derg's program in April 1976 get any immediate major accolades from Moscow.

Constraints on Soviet Policy

Several factors appear to explain Moscow's caution in its dealings with Haile Selassie's successors. For one thing, internecine quarrels within the Ethiopian military junta probably discouraged the idea of any kind of Soviet commitment. In addition, the central government both of Haile Selassie and his successors was involved in a struggle against Eritrean separatists, who had received support from Moscow and Havana either because almost all the Eritrean factions professed some form of Marxism, or as part of Moscow's overall policy toward the Arab world which included support for the Eritreans. Secondly, it was not clear for a considerable period what the relationship would be between the new regime and the United States, until then the sole source of arms for Ethiopia and still retaining its bases at Kagnew. Finally, and most important, only two months before Haile Selassie's ouster, the USSR had signed a friendship treaty with Ethiopia's arch rival, Somalia, solidifying a military relationship which afforded the USSR air and naval facilities in Berbera and other Somali ports, major installations for the USSR's new military outreach affecting the Near East and Africa, the Persian Gulf and the Indian Ocean.

Early in 1976, however, relations between the USSR and Mengistu began to gather momentum. In late January, a delegation representing the mass media led by Lt. Col. Asrate Desta visited the USSR and Eastern Europe. TASS on January 19 reported that "great importance is attached to this visit in Ethiopia." The delegation was received on January 26 by candidate member of the Politburo and Minister of Culture P. Demichev,[2] and *Pravda* on February 6, summing up the visit, reported that the delegation had "expressed a desire to develop friendly relations in every possible way between the USSR and

Pravda, January 27, 1976.

Ethiopia in various spheres of ideological, cultural and educational work."

In mid-February Moscow sent out a reconnoitering expedition of its own in the form of an "unofficial" delegation of the Soviet Afro-Asian Solidarity Committee headed by Malek Fazylov, Foreign Minister of the Kazakh Republic. Although the purported purpose of this delegation was to develop contacts "between social organizations," it in fact met twice (on February 16 and 20) with the Ethiopian Foreign Minister.[3] According to an interview in the Soviet foreign policy journal *New Times* several weeks later, the delegation came back with a mixed picture. While approving the Ethiopian regime's "progressive" measures, Fazylov also told of difficulties, "there being no progressive political party and not enough functionaries dedicated to the cause of the revolution." Making no judgment himself, he noted that "our hosts stressed that Ethiopia was firmly anti-imperialistic" and "thinks highly of the Soviet Union's foreign policy and its solidarity with the national liberation movement of the oppressed peoples."[4]

Soviet caution of Ethiopia was epitomized by the fact that Brezhnev in his main speech to the 25th Congress of the Soviet Communist Party in February 1976 did not even mention the country. Instead he singled out "strengthened" Soviet relations with Somalia, which was represented at the Congress by its President, Siad Barre. Moreover, the Derg itself was still shopping around ideologically, as indicated by the dispatch in March of a delegation led by Captain Moges Wolde-Michael to Peking where he signed an economic agreement with China.

Spurred perhaps by this development, Moscow the following July hosted a high-level delegation, also led by Wolde-Michael which was received by Soviet Premier Kosygin, Foreign Minister Gromyko and Soviet ideologist Boris Ponomarev. A communique concluding the visit asserted that "new, favorable conditions are arising for broadening relations between the Soviet Union and Ethiopia and for the development of all-round cooperation." It also reported "identity or similarity" of positions on many international questions.[5]

The constraints felt by Moscow were reflected particularly in Somali reaction to this visit. Although Siad Barre had been in the USSR in

[3]*Izvestiia*, February 17, 1976; Addis Ababa Radio, February 20, 1976.
[4]"Changing Ethiopia," *New Times*, No. 14, April 1976, p. 25.
[5]TASS, July 13, 1976.

February and March, his deputy, Deputy Minister Mohamed Ali Samantar, paid an official visit to the USSR from August 2 to 7, 1976. In casting the blame on "forces of imperialism and reaction"[6] for possible conflicts in the Horn of Africa, the communique after that visit indicated continuing differences between the two parties with respect to Somali claims against Ethiopia and how it proposed to deal with them. At the same time, it was evident that Moscow was anxious at the time to maintain and strengthen the assets it already had in Somalia.

Another possible Soviet constraint in dealing with the Ethiopians was reflected in the fate of the economic delegation. Simultaneously with the issuance of the communique, the Ethiopians announced the execution of 19 senior officials including Major Sisay Habte, considered at the time the number three man in the regime, among other reasons because he "refused to go to the Soviet Union, the founder of socialism at the head of a high-level delegation, to discuss urgent matters related to the country's urgent needs."[7] The announcement did not suggest that he opposed the mission, only that he wanted to stay in the country in order to continue his plotting. In February 1977, Asrate Desta and Wolde-Michael also were executed. Although their sins were not linked to the question of policy toward the Soviet Union, the execution of the only two members of the Ethiopian junta with whom the Soviet leadership up until then had had personal contact no doubt affected its calculations about relations with Ethiopia.

Gathering Momentum of Contacts

Nevertheless, following Wolde-Michael's visit, Moscow gave increasing treatment to the "progressive" reforms being carried out by the Ethiopian regime, and by the spring of 1977 the USSR raised its support for Mengistu several notches. Moreover, in March Castro made an official visit to Ethiopia where he pledged his full support for Mengistu, a pledge the latter must have seen as coming from the Soviet Union as well.

While Soviet President Podgorny in his trip to Africa criss-crossed Castro's only in Somalia (and not Ethiopia), a new stage opened up in

[6]*Pravda,* August 10, 1976.
[7]Radio Addis Ababa, July 13, 1976.

Soviet-Ethiopian relations with an official visit to the USSR in May 1977 by Ethiopian strongman Mengistu Haile Mariam. Between the Castro and Mengistu visits, the Ethiopian regime on April 25 closed down the U.S. station at Kagnew, expelling U.S. military aid and naval research groups as well as Western correspondents from Ethiopia. Although the regime portrayed these actions as a response to U.S. criticism of human rights violations in Ethiopia and the U.S. announced intention to reduce military aid, they also reflected the growing ties of Ethiopia with the Soviet bloc. For its part, Moscow reprinted with approval Mengistu's statement on the eve of his trip to the USSR that the closure of U.S. organizations in Ethiopia constituted "a historic achievement of the Ethiopian revolution."[8]

The Mengistu visit solidified Moscow's commitment to his regime. At a dinner on May 4, Soviet President Podgorny declared:

> The national-democratic revolution in Ethiopia opened up new opportunities for developing relations on a still stronger and broader foundation. This is only natural for the countries of victorious socialism, and the forces of national liberation are natural and reliable allies in the anti-imperialist struggle.[9]

Podgorny's "national-democratic" description of Ethiopia reflected continuing ideological caution although he also noted Soviet sympathy for the avowed Ethiopian intention "to follow the path of socialist orientation." Soviet commentaries in connection with the visit and thereafter referred to "socialist Ethiopia."

During Mengistu's visit, agreements were signed on economic-technical and cultural-scientific cooperation and on a consular convention. In addition, a declaration was signed "on the foundation for relationships and cooperation between the USSR and socialist Ethiopia." These declarations proclaimed the intent of both sides to broaden economic and cultural relations and, most important, "to have regular exchanges of opinions with each other on major international issues of mutual interest."[10]

Noticeably absent from the public documents were references to military relations. No Soviet military leaders were listed among those who participated in talks with the Mengistu delegation. However,

[8]TASS, May 1. 1977.
[9]*Pravda*, May 9, 1977.
[10]*Ibid*.

38

among those who met Mengistu and saw him off were Army General S. L. Sokolov, frequently involved in questions of military aid; more significant was the fact that Defense Minister Ustinov was among those present (along with Foreign Miniser Gromyko) when Brezhnev received Mengistu on May 6.[11] Shortly after this visit, the first Cuban military advisers appear to have arrived in Ethiopia, while Soviet military shipments, evidently inaugurated in late 1976,[12] probably increased in scope.

A major motive at the time for the USSR's rapprochement with Ethiopia was the almost simultaneous setback suffered by Moscow in May 1977 when the Sudan expelled all Soviet military advisers from that country. Almost immediately, Soviet propaganda stressed the existence of a Sudanese threat to Ethiopia.[13] New Times in May 1977 charged that "there are facts testifying to the Sudanese army's direct assistance to the anti-government forces in Ethiopia."[14] Then on June 5, TASS accused the Sudan along with "imperialism and other forces" of seeking to provoke a military conflict with Ethiopia."[15] It is quite probable that the Soviets pointed to this threat in subsequent dealings with the Somalis whose alarm obviously rose in tandem with the Soviet-Ethiopian rapprochement. Once again, Somali Defense Minister Samantar went to Moscow (May 25 to June 5, 1977), this time in a visit given little publicity.

As it has in many other areas of the world, Moscow in the months that followed continued to play both sides in the growing conflict between Ethiopia and Somalia. In arming Somalia, however, Moscow had given it the wherewithal to pursue a more aggressive policy toward Ethiopia; and in encouraging Ethiopia to drop its ties to the United States, Moscow became a victim of its own success since U.S departure from the scene removed a major constraint on Somali action.

For a number of months, Moscow attempted to prevent the Ethiopia-Somalia conflict from erupting into military action. The Castro-Podgorny forays into Africa in the spring of 1977 reflected an

[11]*Pravda*, May 7, 1977.
[12]Central Intelligence Agency, *Communist Aid to Less Developed Countries of the Free World, 1977*, ER-10478U, November 1978, p. 17.
[13]T. Yuriev, "Behind the Khartoum Smear Campaign," *New Times*, No. 22, May 1977, p. 15.
[14]*Ibid.*
[15]TASS commentary, June 5, 1977.

effort to maintain close ties with Somalia even as Ethiopia was being drawn more closely into the Soviet fold. Castro interrupted his tour in March to make an unscheduled trip to the People's Democratic Republic of Yemen (PDRY), where a year later he disclosed he had sought to reconcile the two sides.[16] Castro's visit, it may be recalled, was designed to undercut strong attempts at the time by Saudi Arabia, the Sudan and other Arab states to wean Somalia away from its Soviet ties. Podgorny in turn added an unscheduled visit to Somalia on April 1 and 2, as well as additional talks in Tanzania presumably to enlist the support of Tanzanian President Nyerere for the exercise of "maximum restraint" by both sides. Even after Somali operations began in Ethiopia in July, Moscow sought to persuade the Somalis to desist. And for several weeks before and after Somalia's actions, Moscow portrayed the major threat of Ethiopia as coming not from that quarter but from the Sudan or from "reactionary" Arab support for Eritrean separatists.

In August 1977, varying Soviet formulations appeared to reflect Soviet wavering on how to handle its dilemmas in the Horn. In the first Soviet intimation of Somali involvement, *Izvestiia* on August 2 attacked "imperialist" efforts to dismember Ethiopia which, it wrote, focused on Eritrea but "did not ignore Somalia either." However, Moscow still sought to avoid a choice as *Izvestiia* portrayed the issue as one of U.S. "imperialism" against both Ethiopia and Somalia: "The designs of the U.S. imperialists consist in splitting and thus rendering lifeless revolutionary Ethiopia and at the same time "rendering harmless progressive Somalia—if possible by its own hands."[17]

In the weeks that followed, Moscow kept changing its definition of the combatants in the Ogaden region of Ethiopia. In the first quasi-official Soviet pronouncement, the Soviet Afro-Asian Solidarity Committee issued a statement on August 6 which deplored the "alarming news" of clashes between Ethiopian forces and the "so-called Front for the Liberation of Western Somalia." Citing OAU statutes, the statement stressed the inadmissibility of efforts "to recarve existing frontiers no matter how this is justified." The statement recalled the Soviet people's "special sympathy" for both parties and urged a

---

[16]Radio Havana, March 15, 1978.
[17]V. Kudriavtsev, "Maneuver by the Colonialists," *Izvestiia*, August 2, 1977.

40

cease-fire and a settlement "in the spirit of anti-imperialist solidarity and pro-neighborliness."[18]

One week later, TASS issued a statement claiming that regular Somali army units were involved and clearly identified the problem as one between Ethiopia and Somalia. While charging that unnamed forces were attempting to "tear Somalia and Ethiopia away from their natural allies and friends," and proclaiming Soviet friendship for both sides, TASS indicated the direction of Soviet priorities by warning that these forces "are trying to strike at the progressive revolutionary forces first in Ethiopia and then in Somalia."[19]

Nevertheless, Moscow still vacillated. On August 19, *Pravda* seemed to backtrack by reporting that "Ethiopia says" regular Somali troops were involved and "Somali sources on the other hand say that the fighting is done by units of the West Liberation Front."[20] On August 22, TASS came up with still another formulation, namely, that fighting was going on between Ethiopia and the West Somalia Liberation Front among whose ranks are Somali servicemen." While *Izvestiia* reiterated this formula on August 27, on August 23 it also quoted Ethiopian leader Mengistu to the effect that the Front was a cover for involvement not by Somalia but by "certain" Arab countries.

Some of this vacillation may have been connected with a last-ditch Soviet effort to dissuade Somalia from the course it was taking. At Soviet invitation,[21] Somali President Siad Barre spent three days (August 29 to 31) in Moscow. All evidence even at the time, indicated the trip was a failure.[22] Whereas Somali sources in Cairo on the eve of the visit said that Barre would talk to Brezhnev in the Crimea,[23] a short formal announcement after its conclusion indicated that he had in fact talked only to Kosygin, Suslov and Gromyko. A terse TASS statement on August 31 that the "sides exchanged opinions on questions of mutual interest" indicated that the talks had gone badly.

From then on it was all downhill in Soviet-Somali relations. Although Moscow continued to profess goodwill toward both parties, the Soviet tilt toward Ethiopia became increasingly pronounced. Soviet

[18]*Pravda,* August 7, 1977.
[19]*Pravda,* August 14, 1977.
[20]P. Demchenko, "For a Peaceful Solution," *Pravda,* August 19, 1977.
[21]Radio Mogadiscio, August 31, 1977.
[22]*Soviet World Outlook,* Vol. 2, No. 9, September 15, 1977, p. 5.
[23]Paris, AFP, Cairo dispatch, August 31, 1977.

media steadily reported Ethiopia's side of the case and ignored Somalia's position. According to Western and Arab sources, shortly after Siad's trip, the Soviet Union stopped shipments of arms to Somalia.[24] Indeed, the Soviet Ambassador in Addis Ababa claimed Soviet arms shipments to Somalia had ceased before July 23, when the incursion into the Ogaden started.[25]

In addition to Soviet actions, the Cuban factor also began to loom more importantly in the Ethiopian-Somali dispute. Later events and circumstantial evidence suggest that an unscheduled trip by Angolan President Neto to Moscow from September 27 to 29, announced only after its conclusion, focused on Angola's apprehensions regarding the impact on it of a transfer of Cuban troops from Angola to Ethiopia. While the main thrust of Soviet attention and of Brezhnev's speech on September 18 was on the Ethiopian-Somali dispute, Neto declared that "Angola is at present at the focus of the events developing in the African continent." He said he was "very sorry" about the conflict in the Horn of Africa but thought "the revolutionary spirit" of both countries would lead to a settlement. Instead, he emphasized the "growing danger in southern Africa" which threatened "not only the progressive countries of Africa but also the whole world."[26]

Obviously Neto failed to dissuade the USSR and Cuba from the diversion of Cuban forces. The British press in September reported from Ethiopia that Cubans were said "to be arriving in droves in Addis Ababa and are assuming a combat role similar to the one they performed in Angola."[27] Somali President Barre, speaking October 21 on the eighth anniversary of his accession to power made his first charge of Cuban combat involvement, and claimed on November 1 that 15,000 Cubans were taking part. Later Western estimates, however, put the number of Cubans in Ethiopia at the end of 1977 at 1,000 and rising.[28]

Moscow reacted with relative outward calm when Somalia on November 13 expelled all Soviet specialists, closed Soviet naval bases and related facilities, renounced the July 1974 friendship treaty between the two countries, and broke diplomatic relations with Cuba. A

[24]Radio Riyadh, September 7, 1977.
[25]Belgrade, Tanjug, October 19, 1977.
[26]*Pravda*, September 30, 1977.
[27]*Daily Telegraph* (London), September 23, 1977.
[28]CIA, *Communist Aid, 1977*, p. 17.

short TASS statement on November 15 declared that "essentially behind this action lies dissatisfaction because the Soviet Union did not support Somalia's territorial claims on a neighboring state and refused to facilitate the stirring of fratricidal war in the African Horn." In a remarkably mild passage (by Soviet standards), TASS concluded that "judging from the present steps, chauvinist expansionist moods prevailed over common sense inside the Somali government," which, it added, would have to take "full responsibility" for the consequences. Nowhere in the TASS or in subsequent Soviet commentaries was reference made to the forced USSR withdrawal from its naval facilities in Berbera.

Whether Moscow expected the Somali move can only be conjectured. Almost to the very end, Moscow appeared to hope that it could maintain its foothold in Somalia despite mounting Soviet-Cuban military aid to Ethiopia and despite the failure of Soviet peace efforts. On October 4, the USSR and Somalia signed an agreement in Mogadiscio providing for Soviet aid on a water exploration project.[29] As late as one week before its announcement, Somalia sent a delegation to Moscow to take part in the celebration of the 60th anniversary of the October Revolution. It may have been Moscow's calculation that, because of Somali dependence on Soviet military equipment and replacement, the stoppage of Soviet aid would hamper Somali military operations and possibly induce Siad Barre to come to terms. It also appeared to be Moscow's estimate that Somalia would not be able to acquire sufficient aid to replace lost Soviet weaponry.

At the same time, Moscow also had prior warnings of the Somali action. A high ranking Somali military man told an Iranian newspaper on September 7 that "Soviet experts will be expelled and relations between Somalia and the Soviet Union severed if the Soviets continue to ban arms to Somalia while supporting Ethiopia with experts and weapons."[30] Siad Barre on October 21 declared that Soviet and Cuban aid to Ethiopia "would only lead to a confrontation between progressive movements in the region and the policy of socialist countries." The announcement by President Nasir of the Maldives on October 26 that the Soviet Union had offered the Maldives $1 million for a lease on

---

[29]Radio Mogadiscio, October 5, 1977.
[30]Radio Riyadh, September 7, 1977.

Gan Island suggested a Soviet effort to cast around for an alternative to its facilities in Somalia.[31] The offer was refused.

With the wraps off, the Ethiopian operation in many ways became a rerun of Angola. To counter Somali advances, Soviet deliveries of weapons and equipment expanded from a stream to a torrent. Normally, the Soviet airlift to Ethiopia went over the route from the Black Sea via Libya to Ethiopia (overflying first Bulgaria and Yugoslavia, then the Sudan). In late November and early December 1977, up to 225 air transports—about 15 percent of the Soviet military aircraft fleet—traveled simultaneously along seven different routes to Ethiopia—via Libya, Aden, and Mozambique (overflying Niger, Chad, Egypt and the Sudan). A large number of Soviet and East European cargo ships set off from Black Sea ports, and Soviet naval units in the Mediterranean were positioned to protect the transports.

In the second week of the airlift, the Soviets were reported to have drawn on stockpiles built up behind the Urals and from airfields in Tashkent and Alma Ata flown south over Afghanistan and Pakistan to Aden and Mozambique en route to Ethiopia. After flights over Pakistan, Iran and Egypt were stopped, Moscow opened an alternate route across the Dardenelles, Syria and Iraq and around to Aden. Altogether it was estimated that between November 1977 and July 1978, the USSR delivered $1 billion worth of equipment to Ethiopia.[32]

As in Angola, the massive flow of sophisticated Soviet equipment was soon followed by a large influx of the Cuban personnel to use it, transported, according to Western reports from Angola and Ethiopia, by the Ethiopian national airline and Cuban vessels.[33] According to the official Cuban postmortem in March 1978, Cuba had originally sent "hundreds of doctors" and "dozens of advisers and military instructors" to Ethiopia but, "in view of the critical situation created by the aggressors which led the Ethiopian revolutionary government to make an urgent appeal to our party, decided to send internationalist fighters, the first contingents of which arrived in December and January."[34] According to this account, the Cubans first went into battle on January 22 and included pilots, tank crewmen and armed infantry battalions.

[31]*Soviet World Outlook*, Vol. 2, No. 12, December 1977, p. 6.
[32]*Air Force Magazine*, March 1978, p. 27; September 1978, p. 33.
[33]*Air Force Magazine*, September 1978, p. 33.
[34]Havana, PRELA, March 14, 1978.

As in Angola, the Soviet-Cuban gamble paid off with a quick victory. And once more, both Moscow and Havana denied involvement until well after the fact, and then sought to play it down in order to lend legitimacy to the Ethiopian regime and later to play it up in order to show the benefits of reliance on the communist world.

Soviet and Cuban Justifications

It was an authoritative TASS statement on January 18, 1978 in which Moscow first publicly acknowledged Soviet military aid to Ethiopia, declaring that "at the request of the Government of Ethiopia, it [the USSR] is according it the requisite material and technical aid to repulse the aggression" from Somalia. TASS derided as a "fabrication" the involvement in combat either of Soviet "military personnel" or of "'thousands' of citizens of other socialist countries."[35]

In this connection, both Moscow and Havana doggedly kept denying the presence of Cuban forces in Ethiopia. In the wake of Siad Barre's initial charges on October 21 and November 1, the Cuban Foreign Ministry on November 5, 1977 declared that there was "not a single Cuban combat unit" in Ethiopia but that Cuba retained the right to provide military support to any government that requested Cuba's aid.[36] While Cuban "units" may not have been present, Cuban "advisers" and other personnel were already coming in considerable numbers.

But even after January 22, the date later given by the Cubans for the start of Cuban involvement in combat, the Soviet denials continued. Radio Moscow, in a broadcast to Africa on January 30, quoted the Ethiopian Ambassador to the USSR as saying that "there are no fighting military personnel from socialist countries or any other countries in Ethiopia." Only technical personnel and advisers were present. A *Pravda* war correspondent's report on February 15 derided Somali "fabrications" and "fables" about the participation of Soviet or Cuban units in the fighting in the Ogaden.[37] Even after Mengistu on March 2 publicly acknowledged for the first time that Cuban troops had partici-

---

[35]*Pravda*, January 19, 1978.
[36]*Granma* (Havana), November 5, 1977.
[37]V. Korovikov, "The Ogaden Front," *Pravda*, February 15, 1978.

pated in combat operations, Moscow remained aloof about this involvement. It did not report Mengistu's speech. In responding to Western criticism of Soviet-Cuban intervention, Soviet spokesmen acknowledged "military aid" in answer to Ethiopia's request but did not spell out that this aid included fighting by Cuban forces. Soviet battle reports consistently pictured advances by Ethiopian forces alone.

With their objectives obtained, the Cubans in mid-March could no longer contain themselves and sought to glorify the role of their forces in the Ethiopian conflict. *Granma* on March 14 gave a detailed account of Cuban involvement which proclaimed that "the reactionary and pro-imperialist aggressors were overwhelmingly defeated." On the following day, Castro once more went over the same ground but with some embellishments. He praised the "extraordinary effectiveness and magnificent combat qualities" displayed by Cuban forces and their ability "to march to such a far-off place and fight there as if they had been fighting in their own country."[38]

And perhaps more significantly, the intervention in Ethiopia reinforced Castro's vision of a broader role for Cuba, a role which, moreover, restored some of the revolutionary lustre lost earlier by his obvious dependence on the USSR and his defeats in Latin America. Two years earlier, in the immediate aftermath of the Angolan intervention, Castro told a rally in honor of visiting Panamanian President Torrijos that Cuban sights were set much higher than the achievement of mere national objectives such as the recovery of Guantanamo. Castro on that occasion emphasized Cuban involvement in a "struggle with imperialism . . . on the world level," in which he said his objectives included "the liberation of the continent, the liberation of Africa."[39]

Echoes of this statement reappeared in Castro's March 15 postmortem on Ethiopia. "Physical space is no longer anything for our revolution," he declared. "We feel as close, as near, as brothers of the Ethiopian revolutionaries as if they were here, beside us, in front of us . . . . For the revolutionaries of the world, distance, in effect, no longer exists."

Castro also went on to explain the discrepancy between his newfound candor and previous silence about Cuban involvement both in

[38]Radio Havana, March 15, 1978.
[39]See above, page 18.

Ethiopia and Angola. He cited security as one reason for previous Cuban silence: "If you have to carry out an operation, an operation which is complicated and dangerous, you simply have to be discreet. You cannot shout it high and low." Further, he suggested, he deferred to the Ethiopians on this subject: "As long as the Ethiopians believed that it was best to be discreet, we were discreet. When the Ethiopians mentioned it publicly, our party, too, was ready to talk of it publicly." Finally, he claimed, everybody in Cuba knew about it anyway: "We never do anything behind the people's backs. Often through party channels and mass organizations, the masses are informed of many things which are not published on the front page of the newspaper."

By contrast, Moscow sought to take credit not for the prowess of Cuban arms, but for the contribution of "internationalist aid" on the part of itself and Cuba to an Ethiopian victory. Thus, *Pravda's* version of Castro's speech did note Castro's statement that Cuban military units had fought in Ethiopia and done so as if in defense of their own land but said the bulk of his speech dealt with the background of the conflict and the "internationalist aid which the socialist countries rendered the fraternal Ethiopian people" against Somalia.[40]

Again as in Angola, Moscow pursued two lines: one, designed to garner maximum acceptance if not support from the rest of Africa, the other to reap maximum ideological and anti-American benefits from the victory of Soviet-supported forces. To justify intervention by the USSR and Cuba in Ethiopia, Soviet spokesmen emphasized first of all that they were aiding a victim of aggression at his request. Thus, the TASS statement of January 18, 1978 had declared:

> The truth is that the Soviet Union on its part has done everything possible in order not to allow the start of an armed conflict between Somalia and Ethiopia. When, however, the leaders, the leaders of Somalia, contrary to common sense and the efforts of the real friends of the Somali people began military activities against Ethiopia and Somali troops invaded its territory, the Soviet Union as always, took the side of the victim of aggression.

Moscow also took full advantage of African unwillingness to take sides in the Ethiopian-Somali dispute and underlying apprehensions about the broader implications of Somali actions. Soviet media carried

---

[40]*Pravda*, March 17, 1978.

frequent reminders that the Organization for African Unity has strongly opposed any breaches of the territorial integrity of its members. The presence shortly after Somali's actions against the USSR and Cuba of Foreign Minister J. Garba of Nigeria—a country which several years earlier had been threatened with dismemberment—was used by Moscow to elicit African understanding for its position in the Horn. Foreign Minister Gromyko at a luncheon for Garba on November 28 recalled that when the "threat of dismembership hung over Nigeria, the Soviet Union rose resolutely to the defense of the territorial integrity, existence and development of the Nigerian state." Then turning to situations in the Horn he went on:

> Take a look at what is happening at the present time in one of the regions of Africa—in the Horn of Africa. Two African countries are warring between themselves. One of them has intruded upon the territory of the other which is defending, on legitimate grounds, the integrity of its territory. It is easy to imagine what would happen on the African Continent if other African countries were to start resorting to this method of resolving disputes. It would be like a seething cauldron and human blood would flow.[41]

Although Garba expressed appreciation for the Soviet contributions to Nigeria, he made no direct reference to the Horn of Africa. Indeed, his one direct remark that "even now certain African countries are in a state of confrontation caused by outside interference" could be interpreted as a rebuke to the Soviet Union.

In this connection, the Kremlin assiduously avoided any references to the fact that it was Soviet arming of Somalia which had made possible the action against Ethiopia. Soviet media attacks on President Carter's criticism of Soviet actions in the Horn at a press conference on January 12, 1978 ignored his point that Soviet shipments of "excessive quantities" of arms to both sides had exacerbated the situation. Instead, Moscow countercharged that the U.S. ignored that Ethiopia had been the victim of aggression and even suggested that the President himself had egged on the Somalis by stating in early 1977 that the U.S. would compete for influence in Somalia with the Soviet Union. Thus, *Izvestiia* declared:

> No explanation by the U.S. State Department can refute the fact that since the Spring of 1977 Washington has been actively striving for a de-

[41]*Pravda,* November 29, 1977.

terioration in relations between Somalia and the Soviet Union. A group of editors of American newspapers invited to the White House at the time were told bluntly that the United States was "throwing down the gauntlet to the Russians in Somalia." In what way? By encouraging—even openly—Somalia's territorial claims against Ethiopia.[42]

The Soviet media then made it a major theme of their coverage of the conflict that the United States was encouraging Somalia by supplying it with weapons. Sweeping aside the fact that the U.S. had categorically barred such supplies, Moscow repeatedly charged that all this was a subterfuge with the U.S. using other countries, especially Saudi Arabia, as a conduit for U.S. arms. Taking a somewhat subtler line, *Izvestiia* implied recognition of the actual dearth of American arms by stating that "the point is not whether or not the United States began delivering arms to Somalia when the situation in this region of Africa started to become complicated, but that *promises* of such deliveries were given which rendered, as we now see, a terrible disservice to Somalia and caused bloodshed."[43]

Not unexpectedly, Moscow also overlooked its previous high praise of Somalia as a member of a select group of countries of "socialist orientation." As the quarrel sharpened, Moscow began to recall Somalia's territorial claims against Kenya and Djibouti. Soviet propagandists increasingly suggested that Somalia was falling under the influence of the U.S., "reactionary" Arab regimes and Peking. *Izvestiia's* political observer, V. Kudriavtsev, wrote in January that the "pro-imperialist features of the Somali aggressors have become visible to the whole world, particularly after they embarked on the worn-out path of anti-Sovietism."[44] Writing in his parent paper, Kudriavtsev asserted that the "imperialists are striving to use Somalia primarily to strike a blow at the national democratic revolution in Ethiopia which is being accompanied by radical socio-economic reforms."[45]

Moscow thus gradually constructed a scenario in which the Ethiopian forces, thanks to massive military aid from the USSR and Cuba, defeated Somali forces whom Moscow sought to identify with the

---

[42]V. Matveyev, "Hotbeds of Tension: Who Kindles Them," *Izvestiia*, January 24, 1978.
[43]*Ibid.*
[44]V. Kudriavtsev, "Dark Spots on the Globe," *Nedelia*, No. 4, January 23-29, 1978.
[45]V. Kudriavtsev, "Fanning the Fire," *Izvestiia*, January 29, 1978.

defeated Somali forces whom Moscow sought to identify with the West. Following Somali withdrawal, Mengistu visited Moscow in April where Brezhnev, in a telephone call from Siberia, congratulated Mengistu "and in his person the entire Ethiopian people for big accomplishments in defense of the country's revolutionary gains and sovereignty from intrigues by international reaction."[46] The precedence given by Brezhnev to "revolutionary gains" before "sovereignty" underscored the point stressed in Soviet commentaries that the main issue in the Ethiopian situation was not Somali territorial claims, but the radical turn in Ethiopian politics. What the West was seeking, according to New Times, was "to crush the revolutionary regime in Ethiopia and turn the Horn of Africa into a zone of imperialist influence, a stronghold of the Atlantic military relying for support on the reactionary regimes in this part of Africa."[47]

One of the consequences of their victory was that the USSR, Cuba and Ethiopia all hardened their bargaining positions. Moscow's initial statements called for a settlement based on mutual respect for sovereignty, territorial integrity, inviolability of borders and non-interference in each others' affairs as well as the "unconditional and immediate withdrawal of Somali troops from Ethiopian territory."[48] When the Somalis did in fact withdraw, the Ethiopians demanded, and Moscow approved,[49] that the Somalis also abandon all claims upon their neighbors and pledge not to help insurgent forces in Ethiopia. Earlier all concerned had rejected out of hand the condition that Somali withdrawal be balanced by withdrawal of Cuban forces. Pravda rejected any "attempts to link the unconditional withdrawal of Somali units to the presence in Ethiopia of military personnel invited by its government."[50]

In Ethiopia, as in Angola, Moscow saw little risk of military countermoves by the U.S. and believed it could rule out damage to Soviet-American relations. Statements by the State Department and President Carter in late February 1978 to the effect that Soviet-Cuban actions in Ethiopia might jeopardize negotiations on SALT were attacked by

---

[46]Pravda, April 7, 1978.
[47]P. Mezentsev, "Covering Up the Tracks," New Times, No. 11, March 1978, p. 12.
[48]TASS, January 18, 1978.
[49]Boris Orekhov, "The International Week," Pravda, March 19, 1978.
[50]Ibid.

Izvestiia a "highly arbitrary" and bankrupt attempt "to make the solution of the chief, most fundamental tasks dependent on a particular situation" in which Soviet "aid to the victim of aggression" was being distorted.[52]

Despite Soviet propaganda emphasis on plans by the U.S., NATO and "reactionary" Arab states to aid Somalia with weapons, it was evident that the USSR had no apprehension that this aid would come fast enough or in sufficient quantities to be of any use to Somalia. A *New Times* commentary in March 1978, moreover, once more invoked the specter of Vietnam:

> Appeals are being heard loudly in Washington now to send U.S. military advisers to Somalia "to show the Somalis how to use these weapons efficiently." But this scheme for interference would be too reminiscent of Vietnam, whose specter to this day looms over the Washington administration. A "new Vietnam" is clearly not to Washington's taste.[53]

And as time has passed, the significance of the Soviet role has become more deeply enshrined as one of the main "lessons" of both Angola and Ethiopia. Thus in 1978, *Political Self-Education,* a journal of the Soviet Communist Party Central Committee, wrote that events in the Horn "once more demonstrated the significance of the close alliance of world socialism with the national liberation movement,"[54] while Anatoly Gromyko cited both Angola and Ethiopia as examples "where Soviet and Cuban assistance foiled the aggressors' plans and compelled them to beat a retreat."[55]

[51]Georgii Ratiani, "When the Sense of Responsibility Is Lost," *Pravda,* March 2, 1978.

[52]A. Bovin, "Unconstructive Approach," *Izvestiia,* March 2, 1978.

[53]P. Mezentsev, "Horn of Africa: Covering Tracks," *Novoye Vremia,* No. 11, March 1978, p. 12.

[54]V. Popov, "The National Liberation Movement in Africa and the Plots of Imperialism," *Political Self-Education,* No. 9, 1978, p. 64.

[55]Anatoly Gromyko, "African Realities and the 'Conflict Strategy' Myth," *New Times,* No. 51, December 1978, p. 4.

CHAPTER FOUR

The Incursions into Zaire

THE INCURSIONS INTO ZAIRE first in March 1977, then in May 1978, constituted two of Moscow's boldest efforts to take advantage of its victories in Angola and Ethiopia. Soviet-Cuban dominated Angola was clearly the staging area for the invading forces on both occasions, although in 1978 the source of the infiltration was masked as a result of the movement into Zaire from Angola by way of Zambia. U.S. government spokesmen in May 1978, including President Carter, charged that the USSR was the source for the weapons and the Cubans for the training of the intruding Katangese.

Soviet Handling of the Incidents

In the months before both incursions, Soviet and Angolan media appeared to be laying the groundwork for preemptive Angolan action against Zaire. Although the main threat to Angola actually came from insurgents in the south, Angolan sources in 1977, seconded by Moscow suddenly began to insist that dissident forces were entering Angola from the north, that is, from Zaire. Soviet media on February 25, 1977 cited Angolan President Neto to the effect that a meeting of his opponents had just been held and that "military intervention against the People's Republic of Angola has been scheduled for next September-October." Thus the stage seemed set to demonstrate that Zaire threatened Angola, not the other way around, and hence to justify preemptive Angolan action.

However, the basic Soviet line which emerged was that whatever outside involvement existed came from the West since events in Zaire were portrayed as an internal uprising by dissident forces against the "repressive" regime of Mobutu. Thus Angolan Defense Minister Iko Carriera on March 11 claimed that events along the border were taking place entirely "in Zaire territory" and that "the eastern border of our country close to the Zaire province of Shaba is quiet and no movements whatsoever to or from Angola can be seen."[1] This statement was given immediate coverage in a TASS dispatch.

At a press conference on March 21 in Dar-es-Salaam, Castro declared that "not a single Cuban is involved" in what he described as an "internal problem" in Zaire which "has nothing to do with the Angolan Government either."[2] Brezhnev, in a speech to a Soviet trade union meeting on March 21, decried "the interference of NATO countries in the internal military conflict in Zaire and the new campaign of slander against the People's Republic of Angola."[3] A Soviet broadcast on March 31 sought to add verisimilitude to the line that events in Zaire were entirely internal by reporting an outbreak of revolts against the Mobutu regime in areas far removed from the Angolan border. TASS on April 12 officially denied any Soviet involvement in Zaire's "internal conflict."

This remained the Soviet-Cuban line, although after the furor over the incident died down somewhat, Castro conceded to a French leftist journal that Cubans had trained Katangese contingents inside Angola as a supplementary force to Neto's army. However, he claimed, "once Angola's war of liberation ended, we took special care not to encourage any domestic movement against the Zairian government" (which could be taken to mean that before the Angolan triumph, the training of the Katangese was for future operations in Zaire). In any case, he added, "the absolute truth is that we did not participate in either the training, equipping or formation of the revolutionary forces that began the struggle in Shaba." And reverting to the basic line he said: "Capitalist imperialism intervened in order to save Mobutu."[4]

[1]Paris, AFP, March 12, 1977; Radio Launda, March 14, 1977.
[2]Radio Havana, March 22, 1977.
[3]*Pravda,* March 22, 1977.
[4]Buenos Aires, IPS, May 6, 1977.

Meanwhile, *Izvestiia* on March 31 added another wrinkle by suggesting that the U.S. was intervening in Zaire as a move against African states spearheading the struggle against Rhodesia and South Africa. *Izvestiia* thus declared that events in Zaire should be viewed in the following context:

> The African people's national liberation movement has entered a decision period of struggle for the continent's complete and definitive liberation from colonial-racist regimes . . . The liberation struggle in the south of Africa has placed special responsibility on the front-line states— Tanzania, Mozambique, Zambia, Angola and Botswana—which are the immediate rear of the struggling peoples of the south.
>
> Under these conditions the U.S. imperialist forces, fearful of their racist allies and enormous capital investments in the Republic of South Africa, are taking all steps to complicate the position of the struggling peoples and countries bordering racist states. They are not only trying to preserve their bridgehead in the south of Africa by creating puppet neo-colonialist regimes in Rhodesia (Zimbabwe) and Namibia but are also organizing acts of sabotage in the rear of the front-line states, resorting here to the use of foreign hands—in this case to the services of the procolonialist regimes on the African continent.[5]

Soviet handling of the 1978 incursion into Zaire was almost identical to that of 1977. Throughout 1978, Soviet media had carried dispatches about alleged plans or actions against Angola from Zaire, though even more so from South Africa. Thus *Izvestiia* on March 14 charged that splinter groups "receive direct support from the South African racists who take in provocative sorties against revolutionary Angola" while "the authorities in neighboring Zaire permit territory to be used for the formation of new FNLA gangs and Zaire troops encroach into Angola."[6] *Pravda* on March 23 reported that Angola's Defense Minister had warned both "provocateurs of the firmness of Angola's borders."[7] In April, Angola sent a letter to the U.N. protesting "yet another armed attack by Zaire against Angola."[8] During the meeting on April 19 between Brezhnev and Angolan President Neto, who was vacationing in the USSR at the time, it may be presumed that the question of

[5]V. Kudriavtsev, "Zaire: Interference Continues," *Izvestiia*, March 31, 1977
[6]N. Paklin, "A Fresh Breeze," *Izvestiia*, March 14, 1978.
[7]V. Volkov, "Warning to Provocateurs," *Pravda*, March 23, 1978.
[8]Radio Moscow, April 7, 1978.

Angolan internal security was high on the agenda, possibly including the question of counteraction against Zaire.

As in 1977, Moscow and its allies took the line that the incursion into Shaba province in May 1978 was a local uprising against the "oppressive" Mobutu government with no outside involvement until the West intervened. The initial TASS dispatch on May 15 reported that "insurrectionists" had launched a rebellion in Shaba. Radio Moscow then with a report that "an uprising against the Central government has started in Shaba Province, formerly in Katanga, in the southeast of Zaire and is being led by the Congolese National Front." It claimed that foreign mercenaries were operating on the government side while "the front has denied reports that the uprising has been provoked from the outside and that there are foreign servicemen among the rebels."

Another broadcast on the same day declared: "The events in Shaba are nothing sensational. They are not intrigues by Moscow, Havana or Luanda. The protest movement against the domestic and foreign policy of Kinshasa was born before the first insurrection in Shaba and has continued since it was crushed; it has gone on virtually everywhere." TASS on May 18 charged that events in Zaire were "being used by imperialist forces to put in circulation a false version about an aggression against Zaire from the outside with alleged involvement of the Soviet Union." Soviet broadcasts dismissed charges of atrocities by Katangan rebels, especially against white Europeans, as no more than a pretext for Belgian and French intervention. Indeed, the Soviet media were filled with countercharges of wanton killings by the French Foreign Legion and by Zairian government troops.

The Cubans were even more insistent than they had been in 1977 that they were not involved in Zaire events, especially in response to statements to the contrary by President Carter. On May 17, Castro summoned the head of the U.S. Interests Section in Havana, Lyle F. Lane, in order to present personal assurances that Cuba was not involved in Zaire.[9] The Cuban government on May 20 declared that "no relations exist nor existed on the plane of military cooperation between Cuba and the forces fighting against the existing regime in Zaire."[10] Cuba denied that it had equipped or trained these forces or participated in combat operations. In mid-June Castro reiterated his position at length

[9]*New York Times,* May 18, 1978.
[10]Radio Havana, May 21, 1978.

to two visiting U.S. Congressmen.[11] In an interview with correspondents from all three major U.S. TV networks on June 16, Castro
once more conceded that Cuba had equipped and reorganized Katangan forces during the Angolan war in late 1975 and early 1976, when the
Katangese fought "at our side," but contended that since then Cuba
"avoided all forms of commitment and cooperation" with them because it did not want to cause a conflict between Zaire and Angola.[12]

In all these 1978 denials, Castro in effect undercut the Soviet, Cuban
and Angolan claims that the 1977 and 1978 incidents were totally
domestic events. According to the *New York Times* account of the
meeting with Lane, "the Cuban leader said he had explained at length
about his efforts to stop the raid by the Katangese rebels," thereby
conceding that outside forces were involved and that the movement
concerned was "Katangese" rather than a broader national opposition
movement against Mobutu.

In his American TV interview, Castro went even further in acknow-
ledging that there had been an incursion into Zaire from the outside
when he said Cuba had informed Angolan President Neto about
"rumors" that such an incursion was to take place and that "we
know" Neto spoke to the Katangese and gave orders to prevent an
incursion. However, Castro added, Neto left Angola at the time and "I
think that he, personally, was unable to insure" that his orders were
carried out. In any case, Castro also argued that Angola and Cuba had
a moral right to help the Katangese since Angola "had been invaded
from Zaire" but claimed they had not exercised that right and that
Cuba opposed doing so because it did not want to see inter-African
conflicts which would divert attention from the "fundamental problems" of southern Africa.

Logic, circumstantial evidence, and Angola's actions after its rapprochement with Zaire also tend to confirm that Moscow, Havana and
Luanda played a decisive role in the March 1977 and May 1978 incursions into Zaire. As the staging area for the invading forces, Angola
clearly had the capacity to control the actions of the Katangese on its
territory. The ease with which the situation was controlled after the
Angola-Zaire agreement of August 1978 provided *prima facie* evidence

[11]*New York Times*, June 13, 1978.
[12]As summarized in Foreign Broadcast Information Service, *Trends in Communist
Media*, June 21, 1978, pp 9–10.

that the Katangese incursion was a matter of communist manipulation in 1977 and 1978.

In calculating its risks, Moscow once more clearly counted heavily on a United States made gun-shy by its defeat in Vietnam. As Moscow has seen things, post-Vietnam United States was wary both of distant and of far-reaching military involvements, a combination applicable to all four post-Vietnam crises in Africa: Angola in 1975-76, the first incursion into Zaire in 1977, the Ethiopian-Somali war in 1977-78, and the second incursion into Zaire in 1978. Accordingly, Soviet statements were quick to warn Americans, "beware of another Vietnam" or to pick up statements to the same effect by Americans.

In mid-1978, with Ethiopia added to the list of Soviet-Cuban successes and the second incursion into Zaire underway, Moscow began to suggest that the impact of Vietnam was wearing off. A rare article on Africa in the Soviet theoretical journal *Kommunist* in June 1978 discerned a "notable change" in U.S. and NATO policy toward Africa:

> Only a short time ago, the shadow of the defeat in Vietnam appeared to them whether in Zimbabwe, or in Angola or in the African Horn, and this acted as a sobering image on the propaganda and policy of the U.S. and other countries of the West. It looks as if the sober voices, reminding about Vietnam and cautioning the governments of the NATO countries against the possibility of its repetition in Africa now have become even more drowned out by voices demanding that precisely in Africa revenge be taken for the defeat of imperialism.[13]

Moscow portrayed U.S. aid to the French and Belgians in transporting their troops to Zaire as comparable to the initial steps of U.S. involvement in Vietnam. Deriding denials to the contrary, *Izvestiia* on June 16 recalled initial U.S. aid to the French in Vietnam in 1950 and President Johnson's denials in 1964 that U.S. troops would be sent to Vietnam, and it claimed that the same "hawkish" forces had "learned nothing from the experiences of their predecessors in Vietnam" and were "trying to travel it again" in Zaire. In this connection, *Izvestiia* noted calls in Washington for removal of limitations imposed on the President by the Clark amendment.[14]

Political Self-Education wrote in September 1978 that "after the failure of the Vietnam adventure and collapse of the Portuguese colo-

---

[13]Yu. Alimov, "Relapse of Colonialism," *Kommunist*, No. 9, June 1978.
[14]V. Petrusenko, "The Hawks Set a Snare," *Izvestiia*, June 16, 1978.

nial empire, Washington strategists were forced temporarily to refrain from open military adventures in Africa."[15] The word "temporarily" implied that Western restraint had reached an end.

The straw, in Moscow's view, that broke the Western back on the question of renewed military intervention was the threat to Zaire in May-June 1978. Thus a formal Soviet government statement issued by TASS on June 23 declared that the dispatch of Belgian and French troops to counter the incursion of Katangan insurgents from Angola reflected a "transition of the leading Western powers to collective and aggressive military-political actions [which] is a new dangerous feature in Africa."[16]

Soviet Calculations

While Soviet media emphasized the U.S. role in Zaire, Moscow was of course aware that comparisons to Vietnam served propaganda and political purposes but did not reflect the actual degree of U.S. involvement in Africa. What appeared to disturb Moscow, however, was the prospect that to avoid repetition of the Vietnam experience in Africa, the United States might be succeeding in

(1) enlisting the support of its NATO allies;

(2) enlisting the support of moderate Africans;

(3) persuading some of the more radical African groups and regimes to agree to compromise solutions in southern Africa which would reduce polarizaion of the continent on a racial or ideological basis.

What troubled Moscow was that, unlike Vietnam, the United States' European allies became directly involved in repelling what was perceived as a communist threat to Zaire. While the Soviet government statement of June 23, 1978 ascribed the "guiding role" in Western intervention in Zaire in June to the United States, it also stressed that the U.S. "is making extensive use of the NATO mechanism for its aims." It should be noted that Soviet propaganda was charging that NATO was seeking to incorporate South Africa into Western defense plans, both generally and through formation of a South Atlantic Treaty

[15]V. Popov, "The National Liberation Movement in Africa and the Intrigues of Imperialism," *Political Self-Education*, No. 9, September 1978, p. 62.

[16]*Pravda*, June 23, 1978.

Organization which would include South Africa and the southernmost Latin American military regimes. Accordingly, the June 23 statement declared: "For the West the internal events in Zaire were only a pretext for switching to the formalization of long-drafted plans in NATO of cheating a mechanism for rapid reaction to changes in the African continent that are not to the taste of the Western imperialist powers."

Moscow in fact has begun to evolve theories of "collective colonialism" or "aggregate aggression" to describe the current role of NATO in Africa. *Izvestiia* on June 26, 1978 recalled NATO support for the U.S. war in Korea, the French in Algeria and Vietnam, even the United States in Vietnam, and concluded that "Zaire is new evidence of NATO's gendarme character."[17]

One of Moscow's leading military analysts, L. Semeiko, in August evolved a theory of "aggregate aggression" to describe the new situation. Semeiko began with the premise that "it is the United States that heads the forces of imperialism, racism and reaction that want, come what may, to quell the ardor of the anti-imperialist struggle in Africa and other parts of the world and not only preserve but consolidate their position there." However, he went on: "Viewing the changes in the correlation of world forces back at the end of the sixties, the United States became convinced of its inability to act alone as 'world gendarme.' For this reason, Washington decided to make the maximum use of the military manpower and economic and other resources of its allies and local reactionary regimes to attain its goals."[18]

Semeiko attributed to former Defense Secretary Laird the concept of "aggregate forces" which Semeiko claimed consisted of a trade-off in which the U.S. granted its allies nuclear guarantees and maximum technical and other aid while they in turn built up their conventional forces and were ready to deliver manpower. While U.S. allies were said to be unenthusiastic about "taking part in dangerous local conflicts for the sake of what are primarily U.S. interests," NATO's involvement in Shaba was said to have "graphically demonstrated once again that when two selfish interests of the national and transnational monopolies, which dictate their will in the world of capital, are affected, the imperialists unhesitatingly pool their armed forces for immediate collective aggressive actions."

[17]Yu. Nalin, "NATO Is Sending Legionnaires," *Izvestiia*, June 26, 1978.
[18]L. Semeiko, "Forces of Aggregate Aggression," *Krasnaia Zvezda*, August 22, 1978.

West European involvement in the Zaire affair underscores a growing dilemma confronting Moscow as it pushes its drive into Africa. Especially as it emphasizes the economic and strategic importance of Africa to the West, and the "anti-imperialist" motivation behind its efforts, Moscow has to take into account that it may be arousing anti-Soviet sentiments which could spill over into other aspects of East-West relations. Thus the Soviet government statement of June 23, 1978 emphasized "the vicious anti-Soviet campaign that has been unleashed in the leading NATO countries" in order to justify NATO intervention in Zaire. The statement also argued at length on the compatibility of detente and Soviet actions in Africa. Like many others in the past, it took the line that Soviet aid to liberation movements was a positive aid to detente because "detente would only gain if the remaining seats of racism and colonialism would be quickly liquidated in the world." The statement also reiterated the standard Soviet line that "detente by no means implies an artificial restriction of objective processes of historical development."

In emphasizing that the United States was the main culprit, Moscow was clearly seeking to mitigate the impact in Europe of Soviet-Cuban actions in Africa. The emphasis on NATO rather than on individual European countries evidently was intended for the same purpose.

The speed and decisiveness of Western counteraction in Zaire seems to have made a profound impression on Moscow. An article in the Soviet Journal *Asia and Africa Today* in September 1978 pointedly declared that in comparison to the Shaba incursion of 1977 "it is important to note that the reaction of the U.S. and other NATO countries were this time [in 1978] much swifter and harder." U.S. readiness to act in Zaire, the article went on, "shows that after a certain period of restraint and hesitation the U.S. again is gradually returning to the idea of utilization of military force in the zone of the national liberation movement, toward a doctrine of strategic interventionism."[19]

Once more, Moscow also sought to decouple Zairian events from broader international relations, with Brezhnev himself chiming in with a demurral. Speaking in Prague on March 31, 1978, he declared:

> But political circles turned up that obviously are out to frustrate the process of detente, and not only in Europe at that, and to return if not to

[19]A. Kislov, V. Vasilkov, "The Current Stage of U.S. Policy in Africa," *Aziia i Afrika Segodnia*, No. 9, September 1978, p. 6.

the cold war then at least to a "chilly" war. In the same vein are, of course, also such actions as the bloody intervention of NATO countries in Zaire, whose cynical nature they tried to conceal by a propaganda clamor over some alleged "Soviet" or "Cuban" complicity in those events.[20]

The Soviet statement of June 23 also sought to make a number of other points:

—It attempted to go on the offensive by charging that the United States was jeopardizing detente by its policy on Africa. "While hypocritically talking about the 'indivisibility of detente' and the need to spread it to all areas of the globe, the NATO countries, and first of all the United States, by their deeds in Africa are acting in a directly opposite direction."

—It indicated Soviet concern that the Shaba events not only were galvanizing the West into possible counteraction but were making the Soviet-Cuban role an issue for the Africans themselves. The West was engaged in a "vicious anti-Soviet campaign" intended "to sow mistrust in the Soviet Union and other socialist countries, to isolate Africa from its natural allies."

—It denounced as "totally groundless" contentions that Soviet and Cuban involvement in Angola and Ethiopia or aid to national liberation movements in southern Africa constituted "a threat to peace and stability in the continent." The "principled difference" between Soviet and Western aid, was that the former was designed to serve "the just cause of the liberation of peoples from racialist-colonialist slavery" while the latter constituted "armed interference in the internal affairs of Africa" by Western countries "in their narrow, selfish interests."

—It reaffirmed the Soviet position that detente could not bar revolutionary movements against regimes presumably like those in Zaire. "Detente is not a charter of immunity for anti-popular, corrupt and venal regimes, for any special rights and privileges whatsoever inherited from the colonial past or obtained under unequal deals and agreements."

—Finally, it contended that "the USSR is entirely on the side of the African peoples struggling against the further preservation in any form of the remnants of colonialism and racism in Africa, against neocolonialism."[21]

[20]*Pravda,* June 1, 1978.
[21]*Pravda,* June 23, 1978.

To underscore the message, Brezhnev told visiting President Rat-siraka of Madagascar at a banquet on June 29 that the Soviet Union "sides with the national liberation movements in Africa, as in other areas of the world for that matter. We solidarize with the just liberation struggle of the peoples."[22]

Concern Over Third World Impact

What particularly perturbed Moscow at the time was that in the wake of the Shaba events, the Soviet-Cuban role in Africa was becoming a contentious issue both in the OAU and in the nonaligned movement where Cuba was aspiring to leadership. Soviet coverage of the OAU summit in Khartoum (July 18–22, 1978) ignored the considerable dis-cussion at that meeting of the Soviet-Cuban role, especially the state-ment by Nigerian Chief of State Obasanjo warning Moscow and Havana "not to overstay their welcome" and become a "new imperial power" in Africa. The TASS account of Obasanjo's speech on July 20 focused instead on his references to the colonial past and his praise for "the countries of socialism" as the only source of effective aid to Africa in its struggle for freedom and independence. TASS on July 21 did note that "some speakers tried to discredit the policy of the coun-tries of the socialist community in Africa," but the "progressive forces" gave a "worthy rebuff to these attempts, inspired by interna-tional imperialism."

Izvestiia's postmortem on the conference was more pointed, report-ing that "an acute and protracted debate developed around the issue of the right of African countries to turn to non-African countries for de-fense aid" especially "in connection with the recent events in Angola, the Horn of Africa and Zaire." The "imperialists and their African agents" were said to have endeavored to confuse the issue of Soviet and Western aid, but said *Izvestiia:*

> The selfless aid and support given by the Soviet Union and Cuba to the national liberation in Angola or to revolutionary Ethiopia, which was subjected to aggression by Somalia, are one thing but it is something else when the imperialists send their troops to Zaire in order to suppress an

[22]*Pravda,* June 30, 1978.

uprising by the people's masses against reactionary forces that are helping the foreign monopolies to plunder the country's national wealth.[23]

Izvestiia stressed that despite imperialist "distortion of reality" and anti-Soviet slander, the OAU "did not allow itself to be dislodged from basic anti-imperialist positions." Neither *Izvestiia* nor any other Soviet source, however, reported the resolution adopted at the session urging member states to terminate "as soon as possible" any client state relationship with a foreign country which conflicted with the OAU's charter or with nonalignment.

Cuba's African role and its relationship to the USSR, to which Shaba called attention, became an especially acute issue in the nonaligned movement in view of the nonaligned summit which Havana was scheduled to (and did) host in 1979. By custom, the summit host drafts its initial documents and acts as spokesman for the movement until its replacement three years later. The Cubans, both before and after Shaba, indicated that they saw in their successes in Africa an opportunity to press their view that the nonaligned movement had an "anti-imperialist" and pro-Soviet cast. Some members of the movement—notably Egypt, Somalia and Zaire—directly questioned Cuba's nonaligned credentials while Yugoslavia, at a preliminary ministerial conference, questioned attempts to create "new forms of colonial presence or new forms of bloc dependence" in Africa.[24]

After the Shaba incident, Soviet attention to Zaire receded and at least through 1979 some of Moscow's allies moved to normalize relations with the Mobutu regime. First came Angola which established relations with Zaire on July 29, 1978. Neto and Mobutu exchanged visits in August and October 1978, while Neto made yet another trip to Zaire in June 1979. East Germany reestablished relations with Zaire on January 22, 1979, while Cuba, with an obvious eye to its role as a host for the conference of the nonaligned movement (of which Zaire is a member), re-established relations with Kinshasa in August 1979.

Moscow's first reaction to this process appeared to have been less than enthusiastic. Soviet media devoted only a few lines to Neto's first trip to Kinshasa and no press commentaries appear to have been made.

---

[23]V. Kudriavtsev, "Test of Strength: The Results of the OAU Assembly Sessions," *Izvestiia,* July 27, 1978.

[24]Excerpt from Tito's opening speech as broadcast by Radio Belgrade, July 25, 1978.

An August 17, 1978 Soviet broadcast in French to Africa commented on the establishment of relations without mentioning the Neto visit scheduled to begin that very day. The commentator welcomed this recognition of the legitimacy of "revolutionary Angola" but cautioned that "undoubtedly there still are certain influential forces in Zaire and outside that country who are not pleased by the normalization of relations with Angola." He further charged that "the NATO countries have an objective interest in prolonging the tension between Angola and Zaire" and that China also was promoting "a policy of disunity among African countries."

This broadcast suggested some Soviet uneasiness about the rapprochement between Angola and Zaire. While welcoming the opportunity which reduced threat from the outside afforded the Neto regime to strengthen its position, Moscow was probably also apprehensive that this might undermine the rationale for Angolan dependence on the USSR, especially in the military sphere. Looking the other way, Moscow may also have regretted any easing of the pressure on Mobutu or Zaire, both regarded by Moscow as extremely vulnerable.

The establishment of relations in January 1979 by Moscow's most disciplined ally, the GDR, may have heralded a change in Soviet tactics stemming from a new reading of Mobutu's attitudes toward the West. An *Izvestiia* commentary on January 27 called particular attention in this connection to a New Year's speech by Mobutu attacking U.S. "humiliating demands" on him to improve his performance on human rights as interference in his affairs. *Izvestiia* sympathetically remarked that "it is characteristic that Washington is making any aid to Kinshasa conditional on political demands that, although demogogically masked by 'concern for human rights,' are manifestly unacceptable to a sovereign state."[25]

Izvestiia also reported that "disillusionment and dissatisfaction" with Western aid "are increasingly beginning to creep into the statements of Zaire's leaders," and that "this development in Kinshasa clearly does not suit the United States, which seeks total dominion over this strategically important country." This article marked a striking change in the previous unreservedly hostile Soviet media treatment of Mobutu. Even its reference to the Shaba events of 1978 showed a

[25]S. Kulik, "In the Grip of Contradicitons," *Izvestiia,* January 27, 1979.

subtle change. While maintaining the line that what had occurred was an internal "people's revolt," *Izvestiia* attributed its suppression entirely to the "NATO power's armed aggressions," with nothing said about Mobutu's role.

Although it seemed to have ignored the development, Moscow presumably also welcomed the establishment of diplomatic relations between Zaire and Cuba as another step in Zaire's move away from the West and the removal from the lists of a major critic of Cuba's role in the nonaligned movement. As for the USSR itself, the first major move in the same direction appears to have come in December 1979 when a Soviet merchant marine delegation spent nine days in Kinshasa, and it was announced that a cultural agreement would be signed before the end of 1979.[26] According to the latter announcement, a small Soviet ballet group visited Zaire earlier in the year and the USSR awarded thirty scholarships for Zairian students in the Soviet Union.

As reflected in *Izvestiia's* reference to Zaire's strategic significance, there can be little doubt that the USSR sees it as a prime target for Soviet and bloc efforts. The constant statements about the value of Zaire to the West in terms of its mineral resources and strategic location indicates, *mutatis mutandis,* why it is of value as a Soviet objective. Virtually the only Soviet commentary of any consequence to discuss Zaire in recent years made a considerable point of the importance of Shaba province alone:

> Shaba is not only the source of the most valuable types of raw materials—copper, cobalt, uranium, cadmium, zinc, silver, germanium, platinum, palladium, molybdenum, manganese, radium, nickel, which are being extracted with the most active participation of the multinational corporations and exported by Zaire to the countries of the West. It is also an important strategic *place d'armes,* serving imperialism for the support of racist regimes in the south of Africa and on a broader plane for the preservation of its positions on the continent as a whole.[27]

Whatever its overtures to Mobutu, it was evident from this article that Moscow in mid-1979 concluded that Zaire as a whole was extremely vulnerable. The article

---

[26]On both, see Radio Kinshasa, December 13, 1979.

[27]Yu. Vinokurov, "Zaire: Fruits of the Neocolonialist Model of Development," *Aziia i Afrika Segodnia,* No. 7, July 1979, p. 10.

—noted the precarious state of the economy, compounded by natural disasters and by a scale of corruption which it doubted Mobutu would be able to curb. Despite its resources, Zaire "long has had the reputation of a country with a chronically ailing economy" which the West was seeking to prop up through loans and investments, although "without being sure of the possibility of their effective utilization."

—saw the low standard of living as the basis of "mass anti-government outbursts" and extremely firm "opposition even among higher and medium-rank officers, businessmen, and the Catholic clergy to the system of one-man rule."

—portrayed Mobutu's army as emerging from Shaba events in considerable disarray which Mobutu was trying to correct with the aid of Western and Chinese advisers, with the country meanwhile being held together through the presence of troops from the West and conservative African states.

—finally claimed that while the West wanted to give inter-African forces a permanent role in Zaire, "progressive" Africans would staunchly oppose such a suggestion.

CHAPTER FIVE

Soviet Activities Continentwide

THE MORE SPECTACULAR MANIFESTATIONS of Moscow's recent policy should not obscure its multifaceted efforts covering the entire continent. The USSR has diplomatic relations with every country in Africa except South Africa, Malawi and Swaziland. It has trade, economic and technical, cultural and scientific agreements with most of them. According to a Soviet source in 1978, the Soviet Ministry of Culture maintains contacts with 40 of 49 African countries, through formal agreements in the case of 35 of them.[1]

Radio Moscow in 1977 carried 169 hours of broadcasts weekly to Sub-Saharan Africa, Eastern Europe 235 hours, as compared to 131½ hours of weekly broadcasts to the same area by the Voice of America. Moreover, in the case of Soviet broadcasts 91 hours were in indigenous African, 78 in European languages, while in the case of the Voice of America, all but 7 hours (in Swahili) were in European languages.[2] In 1979, Moscow inaugurated a World Service series of broadcasts which increased Soviet English-language broadcasts to Sub-Saharan Africa (which was covered along with other areas) to 143½ hours (compared to 35 hours in English before that). A survey of Soviet treaty compilations also reveals that between 1965 and 1976, the USSR signed

[1]I. Bodiul, G. Mironov, "Soviet-African Cultural Ties," *Aziia i Afrika Segodnia,* No. 5, May 1975, p. 16.

[2]International Communications Agency, Office of Research and Evaluation, Communist International Broadcasting–1977, Research Report R–30–78, November 20, 1978, p. 14.

agreements with 11 African countries on the exchange of radio programs.

Focus on Influential States

Although Soviet ideologists take special comfort from the more radical regimes, Moscow is also making determined efforts to court other influential states on the continent, notably Nigeria. In addition, Moscow has sought to improve relations with countries hitherto subject to Soviet scorn such as Botswana, Lesotho and Liberia, as well as with some which had become scornful of the USSR, such as Ghana and the Sudan.

While Moscow for years called attention to its support for the Nigerian central government against Biafra during the 1967-1970 Nigerian civil war, Soviet efforts to cultivate Nigeria entered a new phase in 1975 when, in the words of Anatoly Gromyko (writing in 1979), the main emphasis in Nigerian foreign policy had shifted "from the local, though important, problems of West Africa to all-African issues" particularly the issues of southern Africa. According to Gromyko, "though relations between Nigeria and the USSR have been developing for many years, it is only of late that the cooperation has become broad and stable." The two countries, he went on, "are drawing closer together as regards the key economic and political issues of our day."[3] Some of the highlights of this improved relationship have included the signature of an agreement in June 1976 for Soviet aid in construction of an important iron and steel complex, the visit to the USSR in November of Nigerian Foreign Minister Garba, and the almost annual trips to the USSR (which began in 1972) of high-ranking Nigerian military officers.

As in the early stages of the conflict between Ethiopia and Somalia, Moscow has either maintained a low profile or attempted to keep on the good side of all parties in other inter-African quarrels, notably the Western Sahara problem from 1975 onward and the Tanzania-Uganda mini-war which led to the ouster of Idi Amin in 1979. The USSR played

[3]Anatoly Gromyko, "Nigeria In The International Scene," *Asia and and Africa Today,* No. 3, May-June 1979, p. 33.

a particularly complex game on the Western Sahara issue as it sought to reconcile conflicting Soviet interests. On the one hand, in March 1978 during the visit of Moroccan Prime Minister Osman, the USSR and Morocco signed a signficant economic agreement involving $2 billion in Soviet credits over 30 years for the development of the Moroccan phosphate industry. This will be the USSR's largest commitment to a single project in the Third World and make a significant contribution to the development of Soviet agriculture, since repayment will involve shipment of phosphates to the USSR.

On the other hand, signature of this deal came against the background of increasing tension between Morocco and two major Soviet clients, Algeria and Libya, both supporters of the Polisario Front which rejected division of the Western Sahara between Morocco and Mauritania and conducted military operations against both within Western Sahara and in Morocco and Mauritania themselves. The USSR, as a major military supplier of Algeria and Libya, which in turn were major suppliers to the Polisario Front, necessarily had a direct interest in the conflict. The Soviet problem was further complicated by increasing recognition of the Polisario Front's cause by radical African states including formal recognition of the Saharan Arab Democratic Republic (SADR) proclaimed by the Front in 1976.

Presumably because of Moscow's economic ties with Morocco, the Soviet media from 1975 to 1980 gave relatively little attention to the issue. Unlike its radical Third World friends, the USSR did not give diplomatic recognition to the SADR nor did it openly host any Polisario Front delegations in Moscow. Moscow's basic stance was that it was the friend of all parties and therefore favored a peaceful settlement to be negotiated by the parties directly or under the aegis of the OAU. In the U.N. and in joint communiques with Algeria and Morocco, Moscow generally took the position that it favored self-determination for the peoples of Western Sahara without indicating what this might mean.

Nevertheless, the few Soviet commentaries on the issue tended to tilt in favor of the Polisario Front and against Morocco. The Soviet foreign policy journal *New Times* in June 1977 noted that "most of the African national liberation movements recognize the Polisario" Front as the Western Sahara's "sole legitimate representative." It added pointedly that the USSR was "always on the side of the peoples fight-

ing for national and social liberation" and favored "complete decolonization of the Western Sahara and the right of its people to self-
determination." Accordingly, it hoped, the Maghreb countries would
"exert the maximum effort to find a way of peacefully settling the
issues and differences over the Western Sahara."[4] The "decolonization" reference clearly implied that the USSR favored the withdrawal
of both Morocco and Mauritania from the Western Sahara.

With one minor exception, *New Times* ignored the issue until August
1979 when it carried a commentary on an agreement which had just
been signed between the Polisario Front and Mauritania whereby the
latter renounced its claims to the southern half of the Western Sahara.
This agreement, it was implied, was a model for Morocco. *New Times*
praised the agreement and an earlier OAU call for a ceasefire and a
U.N.-OAU supervised referendum as "important positive moves for a
political settlement." The commentary noted Moroccan determination
to continue the struggle and attributed to the "Arab world" the conviction that it was important "to avoid any rash moves that could escalate
the fratricidal war."[5] A Soviet broadcast on August 8, 1979 noted that
the war had been a heavy burden for Morocco and Mauritania.

A gradual shift in its coverage more openly in favor of Polisario was
evident in subsequent issues of *New Times*. In October for the first
time the journal carried an interview with a member of the Polisario
Politburo, Malainine Ould Sadik, in which he set forth the Polisario
position and praised "the forces of peace and progress" for their
"moral and material support" to its cause.[6] Later in the month, a short
New Times item reported Polisario successes against Moroccan
forces.[7] In November, moreover, the USSR voted for a General Assembly resolution recognizing the legitimacy of the Polisario struggle
and the Polisario Front as the "sole lawful representative" of the
Western Sahara people.

Soviet propaganda increasingly warned about U.S. plans to support
and therefore encourage Morocco in its struggle against the Polisario
Front. Radio Moscow on August 8 claimed that U.S. military aid offers

[4]K. Andreyev, "Western Sahara," *New Times*, No. 24, June 1977, p. 25.

[5]K. Andreyev, "Difficult Search for Settlement," *New Times*, No. 34, August 1979, p. 15.

[6]"We Want Independence and Peace," *New Times*, No. 40, October 1979, p. 15.

[7]*New Times*, No. 44, October 1979, p. 11

to Morocco pursued ulterior motives. A Soviet broadcast on December 8, 1979 took Moroccan King Hassan to task for an interview he gave *Time* magazine in which he warned that the USSR was using the Western Saharan issue for expansionist purposes. The broadcast called the "alleged" statement a "brutal slander" against the Soviet Union designed "to deal a blow" to Soviet-Moroccan relations as embodied in the phosphate deal. Although the attack stopped short of criticizing King Hassan personally, it decried people who permit "exploitation of their names" for "tendentious purposes" such as those of the United States "which wants to impose on Morocco in North Africa the same role it has imposed on Egypt in the Middle East."

Moscow was even more skittish about the quarrel between Idi Amin's Uganda and Tanzania which began in late 1978 and culminated in the overthrow of Amin in April 1979. Although Soviet relations with Amin did not always go smoothly, he had been the beneficiary of considerable Soviet military largesse. For example, in 1976, the USSR had given him several MIG-21 jet fighters to replace those damaged or destroyed by the Israelis in their raid on Entebbe. As late as February 13, 1979, TASS had reported with approval criticism by one of Amin's spokesmen of the United States for its stance on the status of human rights under Amin in Uganda.

Even in its first postmortem in an article in *New Times,* Moscow took the position that the clashes between Tanzania and Amin's forces represented an unfortunate quarrel between two equally worthy countries which should have been settled peacefully. Uganda's plight was blamed principally on the West. According to *New Times:*

> The former government did not always make rational decisions in the course of socioeconomic building and often made serious errors of administration and failed to consider the interests of all groups of the population. But in evaluating what is happening in Uganda, it must also be considered the African states' economic weakness and tremendous dependence on world capitalism are still used by Western neocolonialist circles in order to undermine the national liberation movement and to continue to exploit the continent's peoples. This seems to be the main reason for the difficulties experienced by Uganda.[8]

However, the next major Soviet postmortem, a *Pravda* article on April 29, focused almost entirely on economic mismanagement under

---

[8]B. Asoyan, "The Events in Uganda," *New Times,* No. 17, April 1979, p. 14.

Amin's rule. *Pravda* noted in passing that the "security services operated arbitrarily and with impunity. Thousands of people disappeared inside barracks and prisons without trial or examination."[9] However, none of this was attributed to Amin personally.

What evidently concerned the Kremlin was that the fall of Amin meant the loss of a leader who was willing to cater to the Soviets and who continually twisted the West's tail. Initially, moveover, Moscow was apprehensive that the West might be able, in *Pravda's* words, "to use the fall of the Amin regime to retrieve and strengthen the West's position in Uganda."

After the replacement in July 1979 of Amin's successor, Yusuf Lule, by another leader, Godfrey Binaisa, the USSR appeared to see new opportunities to retrieve its position in Uganda. *New Times* attributed Lule's fall, in part, to "discontent . . . aroused by Lule's intention to open up the country to Western capital." *New Times* noted, by contrast, one statement by President Binaisa that Uganda wished to cooperate with all countries and another by Ugandan official Edward Rugumayo "that the new government will try to restrict foreign influence on the Ugandan economy and has no intention of developing a capitalist system in the country."[10]

Follow-up action was quick in coming. In July a goodwill mission headed by Ugandan Minister for Regional Cooperation A. Ejala came to the USSR where it held talks "in a friendly and businesslike spirit"[11] with Soviet Foreign Ministry officials. Ejala's mission which also stopped in every Eastern European country except Poland resulted, according to Radio Moscow on August 25, in offers to discuss trade. The bloc was also said to have offered Uganda 250 scholarships. In October, Uganda renewed an agreement between its Ministry of Information and TASS, while in December the Soviet Ambassador informed President Binaisa that relief supplies from the Soviet Red Cross society were on their way to Uganda.

In accordance with this warning trend, Soviet media belatedly began to link Amin with the Shah, Bokassa in the Central African Republic, and Macias in Equatorial Guinea among "tyrants" deposed in 1979. However, even this change appeared to come reluctantly. Moscow's

[9]V. Korovikov, "Uganda: At a Transitional Stage," *Pravda,* April 29, 1979.
[10]B. Asoyan, "Fresh Change," *New Times,* No. 29, July 1979, pp. 8–9.
[11]TASS, July 25, 1979.

last full-scale discussion of Idi Ami, which appeared in June 1979, still presented a mixed picture According to this portrayal, "Amin's complex and contradictory personality attracted and repelled at the same time. He aroused the admiration of ordinary Africans with his bold anti-imperialist actions and shook them with his unwarranted cruelty toward his political opponents."[12]

Military Ties

Overall, perhaps Moscow's most significant efforts have been those directed at establishing military ties and a physical presence throughout the continent. These efforts have included direct military aid and training, high-level military exchanges, the extension of Soviet civil air networks, a growing number of naval visits, and fishery agreements. An important element of these and other agreements is the accompanying training given African personnel in the Soviet Union and the dispatch of Soviet technical personnel and advisers to recipient countries.

The rewards of these efforts were made manifest in the Angolan and Ethiopian affairs—not only in terms of the scope of Soviet military aid but in the availability of friendly third parties as trans-shipment points for that aid, the Congo and Guinea in the case of Angola; then Angola as well as Libya, Mozambique and others in the case of Ethiopia. (By contrast, it will be recalled, Guinea refused to let the USSR use its territory as a possible trans-shipment point during the Cuban missile crisis in 1962).

The USSR has become far and away the major supplier of arms to the countries of Africa. From 1973 to 1977, for example, total U.S. arms transfers to the continent amounted to $473 million. Soviet aid was almost eight times as much, $3,645 million. Apart from Angola and Ethiopia, most notable among the recipients have been Algeria and Libya. Moscow is estimated to have sent $2.5 billion worth of weapons to Libya since 1974, thereby making the USSR an accessory in Libya's military meddling in Chad, Uganda, and other areas.

[12]B. Asoyan, "Uganda's Difficult Destiny," *Za Rubezhom*, June 21, 1979.

Soviet transfers during this period went to the following countries (in million current dollars).[13]

Algeria	470
Angola	340
Benin	10
Chad	5
Congo	30
Equatorial Guinea	5
Ethiopia	300
Guinea	40
Guinea-Bissau	10
Libya	1,800
Madagascar	5
Mali	50
Morocco	20
Mozambique	40
Nigeria	70
Somalia	260
Sudan	20
Tanzania	70
Uganda	80
Zambia	20

Annual deliveries to African countries showed a steady rise as illustrated by the following:[14]

1972	$	55 million
1973		75
1974		240
1975		635
1976		1,135
1977		1,510
1978		2,395

The sharp upsurge in 1975–1976 reflected the Angolan adventure, while in 1977, of the five clients who made up the bulk of the USSR's $3.5 billion in arms deliveries to the Third World, three were from Africa: Algeria, Libya and Ethiopia. In 1978, Africa accounted for $2.4 of $3.8 billion in Soviet arms deliveries to the Third World, Algeria, Libya and Ethiopia once more being the major recipients. Through new

[13]U.S. Arms Control and Disarmament Agency, *World Military Expenditures and Arms Transfers, 1968–1976,* October 1979, p. 157.

[14]CIA, *Communist Aid to the Less Developed Countries of the Free World, 1976,* ER 77–10296, August 1977, p. 3; CIA, *Communist Aid, 1978,* ER 79–10412U, September 1979, p. 3.

agreements in 1977, Moscow achieved almost a complete monopoly over sales of modern weapons to Algeria and was the chief supplier of arms to Libya. Algeria signed contracts with the Soviet Union doubling the amount of arms it was committed to buy from the Soviet Union. In the case of Libya, the $2.5 billion worth of weapons Moscow has supplied since 1974 is far more than the Libyans need for themselves, but useful for transfer to other Soviet clients such as Ethiopia and the Palestinian Liberation Organization. In 1978, Sub-Saharan Africa accounted for almost half of the USSR's new arms agreements in the Third World, $845 of $1,765 million.[15]

Extensive training programs for African personnel in communist countries form an important adjunct to the arms agreements. According to CIA estimates, 13,420 African military personnel were trained in the USSR from 1955 to 1978.[16] The scope of this activity is reflected by the following table.

African Military Personnel Trained In Communist Countries
1955–1978[17]

	Total	USSR	Eastern Europe	China
Africa	17,525	13,420	1,400	2,705
Algeria	2,260	2,045	200	15
Angola	60	55	5	—
Benin	20	20	0	0
Burundi	75	75	0	0
Cameroon	125	0	0	125
Congo	855	355	85	415
Equatorial Guinea	200	200	0	0
Ghana	180	180	0	0
Guinea	1,290	870	60	360
Guinea-Bissau	100	100	0	0
Libya	1,330	1,265	65	0
Mali	415	355	10	50
Morocco	145	75	70	0

[15]Data taken from CIA, *Communist Aid, 1977,* ER–10478U, November 1978, *Communist Aid, 1978,* p. 4.

[16]CIA, *Communist Aid, 1978,* p. 5.

[17]*Ibid.*

	Total	USSR	Eastern Europe	China
Nigeria	730	695	35	0
Sierra Leone	150	0	0	150
Somalia	2,585	2,395	160	30
Sudan	550	330	20	200
Tanzania	2,855	1,820	10	1,025
Togo	55	0	0	55
Zaire	175	0	0	175
Zambia	130	85	0	45
Other	1,600	1,310	230	60

A significant feature of Moscow's efforts to consolidate its military relations with the countries of Africa has been a steady exchange of high-level visits to and from key countries of the continent. The military importance of Algeria to the USSR is underscored by the number and level of Soviet visitors. Algeria hosted the now deceased Soviet Defense Minister, Marshal Grechko, in May 1974; Commander in Chief of the Ground Forces, General I. G. Pavlovsky, in November 1974; and the Chief of the General Staff, Marshal N. V. Ogarkov, in December 1977, who also went to Libya. Ogarkov, when still a Col. General and First Deputy chief of the General Staff, had also visited Algeria in 1973. Another noteworthy visit was that of the Commander in Chief of the Soviet Navy, Admiral Sergei G. Gorshkov to Tunisia in 1977, which he repeated in 1979.

The range of Soviet interests is also reflected in the several visits to Africa by First Deputy Defense Minister, Marshal S. L. Sokolov, who is reputed to play a major role in Soviet military aid programs. Sokolov has been to Mali twice (in 1972 and 1976), Nigeria (1973), Angola and Mozambique (both in 1978). Sokolov was also a member of Soviet President Podgorny's delegation which visited Tanzania, Zambia, Mozambique and Somalia in March-April 1977.

Nigeria has also been visited by Pavlovsky (1977) and by the Commander in Chief of the Soviet Air Force Marshal P.S. Kutakhov (1978), Angola by the Deputy Commander in Chief of Soviet Ground Forces,

General V. Z. Yakushin (1978). Other notable visits have included that of Grechko to Somalia (1972); Major General N. Rossikin to Uganda (1973); Major General N. Statkevich to Tanzania (1974); and the Chief of the General Staff, Marshal V. Kulakov to the Sudan (1976).

All these visits represent those announced by the Soviet media. It can safely be assumed that there were others in connection with the buildup of the Soviet position in Somalia in earlier years as well as in connection with the Soviet-Cuban interventions in Angola and Ethiopia.

Reciprocally, an even more impressive list of top African leaders have traveled to the Soviet Union in the past several years. Since 1972, these have included the Defense Ministers of Mali (several times), Somalia (before the break with the USSR, even more often), Zambia, the Central African Republic, Cape Verde, the Congo, Guinea, Guinea-Bissau, and Mozambique. The Chief of the Nigerian Air Staff came to the USSR in 1972, 1974 and 1977, the Chief of the Army Staff in 1976 and 1979, and the Navy Staff in 1978. Other high ranking visitors have come from Algeria, Tunisia, Guinea-Bissau, and Libya. As in the case of the visits by Soviet officials, these announced visits may be only a fraction of those which have actually taken place.

Not surprisingly, Soviet sources reported only the ceremonial aspects of these visits which, it may be presumed, constitute efforts of salesmanship on the virtues of Soviet armaments or actual negotiations on specific arms packages. Thus, shortly after Mali's Defense Minister visited Moscow in August 1976, his country for the first time received sophisticated Soviet aircraft.[18] Obviously these efforts are not always successful, as in the case of Soviet reversals in the Sudan (in 1977) and Somalia (in 1978), but the scope of Moscow's military diplomacy remains impressive.

To the above measures—aid, training and mutual visits—aimed at gaining friends and influence, one must add another group of measures designed as well to establish a Soviet presence in the area and either to project Soviet power or to make such projections possible. Thus, for example, Soviet deliveries of arms and equipment necessitate the dispatch of Soviet personnel to assemble and maintain the items delivered and to instruct the recipients in their use. In 1978, for example, 6,575

[18]CIA, *Communist Aid, 1976,* p. 21.

military technicians from the USSR and Eastern Europe were estimated to be in Africa for these purposes.[19] In Angola and Ethiopia, this
involved Cuban participation in combat. The following table illustrates
the scope of this activity.[20]

Communist Military Technicians and Troops in Africa, 1978

	Total	USSR & Eastern Europe	Cuba	China
Total	44,655	6,575	37,490	590
North Africa	2,975	2,760	215	0
Algeria	1,015	1,000	15	0
Libya	1,950	1,750	200	0
Sub-Saharan Africa	41,680	3,815	37,275	590
Angola	20,300	1,300	19,000	0
Equatorial Guinea	290	40	150	100
Ethiopia	17,900	1,400	16,500	0
Guinea	330	100	200	30
Guinea-Bissau	205	65	140	0
Mali	195	180	15	0
Mozambique	1,130	230	800	100
Other	1,330	500	345	485

These figures represented considerable increases over 1977. Most of
this was accounted for by the Cuban influx into Ethiopia but there were
other noteworthy increases as well in the case of Soviet and Eastern
European technicians in Algeria (from 600 to 1,000), Libya (1,000 to
1,750), Angola (500 to 1,300), and Ethiopia (500 to 1,400). Apart from
Ethiopia, the most striking increase in Cuban personnel came in
Mozambique—from 50 to 800.

Another series of measures has involved the signature of
agreements establishing air links between Moscow and individual African states. The USSR has such agreements with more than 20 African
states, most of them since 1970. Africa in fact accounts for more than a
quarter of the approximately 80 air routes the Soviet national airline
Aeroflot has worldwide. A year by year tally of Soviet air agreements

---

[19]CIA, *Communist Aid, 1978*, p. 4.
[20]*Ibid.*

in Africa since 1970 underscores the determination with which Moscow is pursuing this element of its African drive:

1970	Mauritius
1973	Rwanda
	Congo (updating a 1964 agreement)
	Equatorial Guinea
1974	Mauritania
	Chad
	Libya
	Zaire
1975	Benin
	Mozambique
	Guinea-Bissau
1976	Angola
	Cape Verde
	Ghana (reinstating the lapsed 1962 agreement)
1977	Zambia
	Madagascar
	Ethiopia
1978	Tanzania

The Soviet Maritime Presence

Finally the Soviet merchant marine, fishing fleet, maritime research teams and navy have steadily expanded their operations in Africa, the military purpose of which was enunciated by Admiral of the Fleet Gorshkov in an interview with *Pravda* on July 25, 1976: "The strengthening of naval might depends on developing all its components, including the transport, fishing and scientific research fleets, with which military sailors have had a long friendship."

Writing on Third World countries in general, a Soviet book on foreign trade emphasized the value of the Soviet merchant fleet for Soviet policy: "Taking into account the absence in the majority of these [countries] of their own merchant fleet, it [the USSR] assures delivery of goods by Soviet ships, aiding thereby the strengthening of the economic independence of developing countries."[21] Thus, as noted

[21]V. I. Klochek, B. M. Pichugin, eds., *USSR Foreign Trade: Results of the Ninth Five Year Plan and Prospects* (Moscow, Mezhdunarodnye Otnosheniia, 1977), p. 201.

by a Soviet magazine devoted to shipping problems, Soviet merchant ships are frequent callers among other places in the ports of Egypt, the Ivory Coast, Algeria, Guinea, Libya, Mali, Sudan, Togo and Tunis.[22]

The USSR has signed maritime nagivation agreements with Morocco (1971), Algeria (1973), Mozambique (1975), Libya (1976), Zaire (1976). The agreement with Algeria provides that total freightage between the two countries is equally shared by ships of both with third countries required to operate under charter by agencies of either.[23] Presumably in implementation of this agreement, a regular Soviet-Algerian shipping line was opened in 1975. The USSR also has operated a shipping line jointly with the GDR and Poland for traffic to West Africa.[24] It was also reported in late 1978 that "new [Soviet] shipping lines have been opened on the East and the West African coasts, and are set to undercut Western shipping rates so as to force them out of business."[25]

A major element in establishing the Soviet presence has been the heavy Soviet involvement in the development of African fishing which has, at the same time, aimed at facilitating Soviet long-range fishing and at creating facilities for the use of the Soviet navy.

A chronological list of these agreements underscores the Soviet drive in this field:[26]

1965	Senegal
1966	Guinea
1970	Mauritius
1971	Equatorial Guinea
1972	Somalia
1973	Ghana
	Morocco
	Mauritania

[22]Editorial, "USSR Foreign Policy and Maritime Transport," *Morskoi Flot,* No. 12, December 1978, p. 2.

[23]D. Nikolayev, "Soviet International Cooperation in Merchant Shipping," *Foreign Trade,* No. 12, 1975, p. 33.

[24]S. Lukyanchenko, "The Soviet Merchant Marine and Foreign Trade," *Foreign Trade,* No. 1, 1977, p. 23.

[25]Peter Janke, "The Soviet Strategy of Mineral Denial," *Soviet Analyst,* Vol. 7, No. 22, November 1978, p. 5.

[26]Texts of the basic agreements can be found in the relevant volume of the Soviet series of the USSR Ministry of Foreign Affairs, *Sbornik Deistvuiushchikh Dogovorov, Soglashenii i Konventsii Zakliuchennykh SSSR S Inostrannymi Gosudarstvami* (Collection of In-Force Treaties, Agreements and Conventions Concluded by the USSR with Foreign States) (Moscow: Mezhdunarodnye Otnosheniia).

1975	Gambia
	Guinea-Bissau
	Mozambique
1976	Sierra Leone
1977	Angola
	Benin
	Madagascar

Under these agreements, the Soviet fishing fleet is provided with rights to refuel and resupply, and in some cases the right to fly in exchange crews. In several, the Soviet Union in effect controls the fishing industry of the countries. In Sierra Leone, for example, the USSR serves as the chairman of a joint commission which meets annually to plan "joint ventures." In Angola the March 1977 agreement called for the establishment of a joint fishing company. The agreements generally provide for Soviet oceanographic surveys of national fishing grounds and the training of African fishermen and navigators in Soviet schools as well as on Soviet trawlers.

The Soviet Union has also undertaken to improve the port facilities in a number of countries. In Equatorial Guinea, Soviet technicians were employed to enlarge the port of Luba. The 1977 agreement with Benin called for new dock and fueling facilities. The fishing agreements with Gambia, Guinea-Bissau, and Mozambique call for Soviet construction or improvement of fishing complexes which in the case of Mozambique might in effect serve as a naval base.[27]

In accordance with a worldwide program, Africa has also been the site of an increasing number of courtesy visits by the Soviet fleet. As Admiral Gorshkov told *Pravda* in his 1978 Navy Day interview: "Ocean voyages and calls at foreign ports become ever greater in scope with every passing year. They are a visible help in strengthening our state's authority in the international arena and in strengthening friendship and cooperation with many countries."[28] These visits, Gorshkov declared two years earlier, were "of great importance" because "in these foreign ports and bases tens of thousands of Soviet naval seamen vividly demonstrate ashore Soviet ideology, our way of life, culture and discipline."[29]

[27]John Baker White, "USSR's Rewarding Fishing in African Waters," *Soviet Analyst,* Vol. 7, No. 23, November 1978, p. 3.
[28]*Pravda,* July 30, 1978.
[29]Radio Moscow, July 24, 1976.

In accordance with Gorshkov's dictum, Moscow has used port visits as display pieces for Soviet military technology. Thus, one observer reported, in the annual visits by Soviet ships to Ethiopian Navy Day festivities during Haile Selassie's reign, "the Soviet Navy attendee was normally an opportunity to show off its latest technological developments."[30] More generally, this same author noted, "the appearance in a port of a Third World country of a new Soviet surface ship, bristling with missile launchers and guns and with a wide array of electronic antennae, cannot help but impress the leaders of the visited country."[31]

Soviet port visits to Africa began in the early 1960s and increased markedly after 1968, especially in connection with Moscow's increasingly active Indian Ocean policy. Between January 1968 and November 1971, 54 visits were made to East African ports, 32 of them to Somalia. During 1970–1971, Berbera alone received 14 visits, twice as many as the entire Persian Gulf region during this period.[32]

Every year a small portion of these visits involving the presence of a Soviet flag officer is billed as a formal official visit and given a certain amount of public treatment by the Soviet press and radio. Of 17 such visits in 1976 five were to Africa (Mauritius, Tunisia, Guinea-Bissau, Angola and Nigeria).[33] A survey of these formal visits as announced in the Soviet press and radio from December 1971 to December 1979 reveals 6 to Mauritius, 5 to Tunisia, 3 to Ethiopia, 2 each to Algeria, Kenya, Senegal, Nigeria and Angola; and single visits to Sierra Leone, Morocco, Somalia, Guinea-Bissau, Mozambique and the Seychelles.

In addition to all these actions—and to a large degree because of them—the Soviet Union has also been able to engage in Africa in what naval analysts McConnell and Dismukes have labeled the "Soviet diplomacy of force."[34] The initial step, out-of-area operations by the

[30]John J. Herzog, "Perspective on Soviet Naval Development: A Navy to Match National Purposes," in Paul J. Murphy, ed., *Naval Power in Soviet Policy*, Studies in Communist Affairs, Volume 2 (Washington, D.C.: U.S. Government Printing Office, 1978), p. 41.

[31]*Ibid.*

[32]Albert E. Graham. "Soviet Strategy and Policy in the Indian Ocean" in *Naval Power in Soviet Policy*, Volume 2, p. 278.

[33]Capt. William H. J. Manthorpe Jr., "The Soviet Navy in 1976," *United States Naval Institute Proceedings*, May 1977, p. 209.

[34]James M. McConnell and Bradford Dismukes, "Soviet Diplomacy of Force in the Third World," *Problems of Communism*, January-February 1979, pp. 14–27.

Soviet Navy, first affected North Africa in the late 1950s, though Moscow's major target at the time was NATO's southern flank. In the sixties, the Soviet naval infrastructure in the Mediterranean served not only the NATO mission but Soviet involvement in the Arab world and North Africa. In 1968, the Soviet Navy moved into the Indian Ocean area, thereby impinging on West Africa, and in 1970 "the nucleus was established for what turned out to be a permanent West African patrol."[35]

As noted by McConnell and Dismukes, Moscow has demonstrated its concern over situations in which Soviet interests have been threatened or its resolve to protect these interests through changes in fleet posture or manipulation of its on-scene presence. Specifically, they list the following instances in Africa of "coercive Soviet military diplomacy" between May 1967 and February 1976 (omitting a number of other examples related to the Arab-Israeli conflict):

Date	Place	Action
January-February 1969	Gulf of Guinea	"Compellent" show of force off Ghanaian coast during negotiations on release of detained Soviet trawlers
December 1969	Somali ports	Soviet ship visits to demonstrate support for new post-coup regime in conditions of domestic tension
April-May 1970	Somali ports	USSR extends ship visits to Somali government that felt threatened by internal opposition allegedly in league with Ethiopia
1970	Sudan	Soviet helicopter pilots assist government in putting down black autonomy movement in southern Sudan
December 1970-1971	Eastern Atlantic	Soviet West Africa patrol established to deter further naval attacks on Republic of Guinea from Portuguese Guinea (Bissau)
May 1971	Sierre Leone	Soviet port-call at Freetown during period of domestic instability

[35]*Ibid.*, p. 18.

Date	Place	Action
November 1975- February 1976	Eastern Atlantic	Combatants deployed off the coast of Congo to protect sealift of military supplies to Angola
January- February 1976	Central Atlantic	Soviet anti-carrier task group deployed in connection with Angolan civil war, to counter anticipated U.S. carrier task group which did not appear.[36]

Soviet operations during the Angolan crisis deserve special attention. Initially interposed symbolically across the path of any outside intervention was a Soviet naval force composed of a Kotlin class destroyer and an LST with 100–150 naval infantrymen. As the crisis deepened, a Kresta II missile cruiser was sent from the Mediterranean, arriving in Conakry, Guinea almost simultaneously with a TASS denial that there were any Soviet ships off Angola. The cruiser replaced the destroyer off Angola in company with naval and merchant tankers and an intelligence collection ship. Other ship movements in the Mediterranean and off Portugal gave the appearance of preparations to augment the force off Angola.[37]

During the conflict in the Horn of Africa, the Western press reported that two Soviet destroyers had taken up positions off Massawa, then under attack by Eritrean forces.[38] "Government sources in Washington" were cited in late January 1978 to the effect that Soviet amphibious ships, backed by frigates, had passed through the Suez Canal and were stationed off Eritrea.[39]

The value of its acquired military positions in Africa for broader roles was illustrated by the use Moscow made of Berbera in Somalia and Conakry in Guinea.[40] Long-range reconnaissance aircraft began to operate from Somalia in 1976 and anti-submarine aircraft made several mining deployments at the same time. Somalia's expulsion of Soviet

---

[36]*Ibid.*, p. 20.

[37]Manthorpe, "The Soviet Navy in 1976," p. 207.

[38]*Sunday Telegraph* (London), January 15, 1978.

[39]Paris, AFP, January 25, 1978.

[40]Paul J. Murphy, "Morskaia Aviatsiia (Soviet Naval Aviation): Its Development, Capabilities and Limitations," in *Naval Power in Soviet Policy*, pp. 198–199.

advisers and military facilities in November 1977 put a stop to these activities, some of which may have been transferred to Aden.

In 1973, long-range Soviet TU-95s or Bears began flying in pairs from Murmansk to Conakry, whose major airfield the USSR had helped build. During 1975, Bears flying from and between Conakry and Cuba reconnoitered Soviet naval exercises. Reconnaissance deployments were made from Conakry during subsequent crises periods in Africa and the Near East. All this, however, came to a halt in 1977 as a result of disagreements between Sekou Toure and Moscow which has since acquired Luanda, Angola as a substitute.

Trade, Aid and Training of Specialists

In addition to its military aid, the USSR has also carried out a modest program of trade and aid with the countries of Africa. Trade turnover between the USSR and the continent as a whole grew from 271 million rubles in 1960 to 1,440 million rubles in 1975 but leveled off thereafter to 1,167, 1,227, and 1,339 million rubles respectively in 1976, 1977, and 1978. Moreover, more than half of this trade turnover was with Egypt, Algeria, Morocco and Libya.[41]

What it lacked in volume, Soviet trade sought to make up in breadth as the number of trade agreements rose from 6 in 1960 (all with northern African countries) to at least 38 in 1979, encompassing all parts of the continent. From 1961 to 1973, the USSR had a positive balance of trade with the continent, while from 1974 the balance has been in the other direction, reaching a high of 289.8 million rubles in African favor in 1975 but going down to only 77.9 million rubles in 1979.

Soviet commentaries acknowledge the modesty of Soviet-African trade but claim that it "is still of much importance both for the USSR and for the African countries." As with its trade elsewhere in the Third World, Moscow emphasizes the leading role played by Soviet machinery exports and especially "the large share of plant deliveries." All this, it is said, "helps to build up the material bases for the [African] developing countries' independence and strengthens their positions in

[41]Based on adding figures given in supplements of the Soviet *Foreign Trade* journals.

the struggle for equitable terms of international trade."[42] On the import side, Moscow stresses the importance of the USSR as a market for traditional African products and to a growing degree for manufactured products. Guinea in 1975 accounted for one-half of total Soviet purchases abroad of bauxite, while the future importance of Morocco for Soviet phosphate shipments has already been noted.

The Soviet picture with respect to economic credits parallels that of trade. Between 1954 and 1978, the USSR extended an estimate $3,989 million in credit to Africa, of which $2,918 million went to North Africa. $2,000 million of that sum was accounted for by the credit extended in 1978 to Morocco to expand its phosphate industry. In that same 25-year period, the USSR extended only $1,071 million to the countries of Sub-Saharan Africa (mainly to Ghana, Guinea, Mali, Haile Selassie's Ethiopia in the early sixties, Somalia and the Sudan later).[41]

Again as in other areas of the Third World, Moscow points with particular pride to specific projects built with Soviet aid. Thus, according to *Socialist Industry,* "with the help of the USSR alone more than 176 industrial enterprises and over 40 major agricultural complexes have been constructed in African countries."[44] Soviet sources cite such projects as an oil refinery in Ethiopia (producing over 625,000 tons annually), a cement plant in Mali (50,000 tons annually), a bauxite mining complex in Guinea (2.5 million tons annually) and the iron-and-steel in progress in Nigeria (1.3 million tons per annum.)[45] In connection with these and other projects, the USSR has signed economic and technical cooperation agreements with 33 African countries.[46] In addition, the USSR has agreements involving Soviet aid in evaluating, prospecting and developing the mineral resources of at least 11 African countries (Angola, Benin, Guinea, Guinea-Bissau, the Congo, Mali, Madagascar, Mozambique, Nigeria, Ethiopia and the Sudan).

---

[42]A. Skorodumov, "Soviet-African Trade," *International Affairs,* No. 5, May 1977, pp. 118–119; see also Institute of Africa, *The USSR and the Countries of Africa* (Moscow; Mysl', 1977), Chapter 11.

[43]CIA, *Communist Aid, 1978,* pp. 7–8.

[44]A. Ladygen, "Facts Versus Slander," *Sotsialisticheskaia Industriia,* October 12, 1978.

[45]B. Kozintsev, P. Koshelev, "Economic Cooperation of the USSR With the Countries of Tropical Africa," *Foreign Trade,* No. 2, February 1978, p. 26.

[46]*Foreign Trade,* No. 11, November 1978, p. 18.

As in the case of military aid, an important aspect of Soviet economic relations is the increased personal contact involved between the USSR and individual countries of Africa and the increasing possibilities for influence and indoctrination these activities permit. According to one Soviet source, 25,000 skilled workers and technicians have been trained with Soviet help in the process of construction and operation of Soviet-aided projects in Tropical Africa (presumably on the spot). The USSR has also rendered assistance in the setting up of 15 educational establishments, involving the training of 9,000 students. According to this same source, 7,000 Soviet trained specialists "are working" presumably in Sub-Saharan Africa; 8,000 from the same area "were trained" in the USSR.[47] The first figure is close to CIA figures on the number of economic technicians from the USSR and Eastern Europe in Sub-Saharan Africa in 1978; the latter is well short of the number of students from Africa in the USSR, according to CIA figures for 1978 alone.

The following table gives a breakdown of economic advisers and technicians from the USSR and Eastern Europe (taken together) and Cuba in Africa.[48] (In addition, it might be noted, China also dispatched 19,330 technicians to Africa, of which 18,615 went to Sub-Saharan Africa.)

According to the CIA, Moscow probably has spent close to a billion dollars over the past 20 years in Third World student training in the USSR.[49] In 1978, of Third World students in Soviet and Eastern European schools, almost half came from Africa. In addition, Cuba has a large and growing program for training African students. The following table provides a breakdown of the African student population in the USSR and Eastern Europe:[50]

[47]Kozintsev, Koshelev, "Economic Cooperation," p. 29.
[48]CIA, *Communist Aid, 1978,* p. 14.
[49]*Ibid.,* p. 16.
[50]*Ibid.,* pp 17–18.

Soviet Bloc Economic Technicians in Africa

	Total 55,225	USSR & Eastern Europe 43,805	Cuba 11,420
North Africa	36,615	36,165	450
Algeria	11,450	11,400	50
Libya	22,600	22,200	40
Mauritania	60	60	—
Other	2,505	2,505	
Sub-Saharan Africa	18,610	7,640	10,970
Angola	9,900	1,400	8,500
Ethiopia	1,150	650	500
Gabon	10	10	—
Ghana	95	95	—
Guinea	735	700	35
Guinea-Bissau	350	265	85
Kenya	25	25	—
Liberia	10	10	—
Mali	475	475	—
Mozambique	1,150	750	400
Niger	10	10	—
Nigeria	1,625	1,625	—
Rwanda	10	10	—
Sao Tome	160	20	140
Senegal	100	100	—
Sierra Leone	10	10	—
Somalia	50	50	—
Sudan	125	125	—
Tanzania	365	165	200
Zambia	145	125	20
Other	2,110	1,020	1,090

African Students in USSR and Eastern Europe

	Total 23,490	USSR 13,635	Eastern Europe 9,755
North Africa	3,555	2,035	1,520
Algeria	1,925	1,000	925
Mauritania	255	205	50
Tunisia	515	210	305
Other	860	620	240
Sub-Saharan Africa	19,835	11,600	8,235
Angola	815	165	650
Benin	255	235	20
Botswana	25	25	—
Burundi	250	100	150
Cameroon	155	130	25
Cape Verde	315	300	15
Central African Empire	510	260	250
Chad	410	350	60
Comoro	20	20	—
Congo	1,255	750	505
Ethiopia	2,195	1,530	665
Equatorial Guinea	250	250	—
Ghana	590	315	275
Guinea	1,160	775	
Ivory Coast	800	200	
Kenya	645	500	
Madagascar	765	605	—
Mali	490	300	250
Mauritius	145	110	105
Mozambique	360	225	1,020
Nigeria	1,950	950	1,000
Rwanda	260	225	35
Senegal	260	200	60
Sierra Leone	425	380	45
Somalia	95	50	45
Sudan	1,600	600	1,000
Tanzania	790	450	340
Togo	290	250	40
Uganda	170	140	30

African Students in USSR and Eastern Europe

	Total	USSR	Eastern Europe
Upper Volta	350	350	—
Zaire	275	25	250
Zambia	320	215	105
Other	1,640	620	1,020

CHAPTER SIX

Problems and Patterns of Consolidation

MOSCOW HAS SHOWN ITSELF JUST AS AWARE as Western analysts about the hazards of maintaining influence in Africa even in radical states. Soviet euphoria over successes has accordingly been tempered by accute consciousness of setbacks such as the overthrow of pro-Soviet regimes in Ghana and Mali; the degeneration, from the Soviet point of view, of hitherto friendly regimes in Egypt and Somalia; vacillating relations with Guinea; and occasional signs of strain even with Angola, Mozambique and Ethiopia. Soviet authors set forth a number of reasons for the setbacks as well as for continued caution about the permanence of radical orientations in states currently designated as being of socialist orientation.

Hazards of the "Socialist Orientation" Path

Thus, a leading Soviet ideologist on Third World problems, Karen Brutents, wrote in *Pravda* in February 1978:

> The strengthening of the positions of the liberated countries in the anti-imperialist struggle is closely linked with profound internal changes, which are leading to a break with the colonial past in politics and economics, in social relations and spiritual culture. This process is not occurring smoothly; zigzags and even regression are apparent in it, and it is encountering great difficulties.[1]

[1]K. Brutents, "Imperialism and the Liberated Countries," *Pravda*, February 10, 1978.

Another prestigous Soviet analyst, R. A. Ulianovskii, who is a deputy chief of the Central Committee International Section, wrote in the July 1979 issue of *Kommunist,* Moscow's principal ideological journal, that the situation in these countries is marked by "its contradictoriness, a certain insecurity and possible deviations and even sharp turns." In fact, he stated flatly, "there have been no irreversible processes here yet."[2]

The USSR sees itself severely constrained by its inability to step in as a total replacement for the West in formerly colonial countries. Almost all Soviet discussions on socialist orientation in general or of its African variant set forth as their ideal model the ethnic Soviet republics and Mongolia, that is, situations in which the entities involved were totally dependent upon the USSR and almost completely cut off from the West. These discussions, however, all concede that in Africa and elsewhere in the Third World these models are deficient, first because of the low level of Soviet economic ties with the countries concerned, and second because of the close ties remaining between these countries and the West.

Both Soviet ideologists and the Soviet government have gone on record that the USSR is not in a position, nor is it disposed (as it was in the case of Cuba), to seek to replace the West as a source of aid or even of trade with the countries of Africa, even including the "countries of socialist orientation." As far back as February 1965 the now anointed Che Guevara berated the Soviet Union during a conference in Algiers for its unwillingness to make sacrifices in order to accelerate the economic development of radical Third World states. In more recent years, Moscow has found itself the victim of its own economic boasts as Third World countries tend to link the USSR with the West in the category of "rich" countries sharing an obligation to render special economic aid to the impoverished countries of the world.

In response to more current evocations of Guevara's complaint, Karen Brutents noted that, despite the USSR's "selfless assistance to oppressed and backward nations," it "now and again has to face petty bourgeois and egoistic or, one might say, consumer views of the socialist countries' internationalist duty." Indeed, he went on, "even a

[2]R. A. Ulianovskii, "On the Countries of Socialist Orientation," *Kommunist,* No. 11, July 1979, p. 118.

section of the influential circles in the advanced national states now and again tend to take such an approach."[3]

Neither Brutents nor any other Soviet source ever mentions any examples, but there have been frequent hints during visits to and from these "advanced" states that the level and terms of Soviet aid are major points at issue with the USSR. In one of the most explicit statements on this score, President Didier Ratsiraka of Malagasy, which Moscow invariably lists as socialist-oriented, told the Italian communist newspaper *L'Unita* on March 23, 1979 that the USSR was not helping progressive countries sufficiently: "In this phase we need internationalist aid in the economic field, but it is not being granted to us. Consider the $750 million given to Egypt: Which progressive African country can say that it has received as much as that from the USSR?"

Perhaps the most striking discussion of the subordinate role of Soviet economic aid in bloc-LDC relations appeared in a 1976 Soviet book on the problems of the socialist oriented states in Africa. The key passage in this connection argued first that as a result of the changed correlation of forces in the world "imperialism lost its former influence" and prospects thereby eased in general for the appearance and development of radical states of socialist orientation. In this regard, it went on:

> The main factors, favoring such an orientation are the political, military-strategic and moral influence of the states of the socialist community, the attractive force of their example and the constantly increasing support of the liberated peoples, the affirmation in international relations of progressive principles and norms, the change of the whole international climate in a direction favorable for the peoples, etc.

And then came the punchline on the economic factor: "In these conditions material aid on the part of socialist states has ceased to be a factor directly promoting the transition to a non-capitalist path." In particular, the authors state, "the socialist states still do not have the possibilities completely to satisfy the needs of all the young states for capital, credits and technical aid."[4] Nor, according to the Soviet government do they have any obligation to do so.

In a memorandum submitted to the United Nations by Foreign Minister Gromyko on October 4, 1976, the Soviet government de-

[3]*Pravda*, October 5, 1976.
[4]N. I. Gavrilov, G. B. Starushenko, eds., *Africa: Problems of Socialist Orientation* (Moscow: Nauka, 1976), pp. 10–11.

clared that "there are and can be no grounds for making the same demands on the Soviet Union and the other socialist states which the developing countries make on the developed capitalist states, including the demand for the compulsory surrender of a fixed proportion of the gross national product to the developing countries as economic aid." The Soviet Union, the statement declared, is not to blame for the "economic backwardness which the developing countries inherited from the colonial past," and while aiding these countries as "a friend and ally in the struggle against the common enemy—imperialism, colonialism and neocolonialism," account must be taken "that the Soviet Union's potential for rendering economic assistance is not infinite" and that, "of course, the Soviet Union cannot fail to be concerned for the well-being of its own people."[5]

Other Soviet statements emphasize that the USSR merely by offering an alternative has pressured the West to give Third World countries better economic deals and sees its main functions as continuing to back Third World efforts to extract further concessions from the West. As Brezhnev told a Japanese correspondent in June 1977:

> The Soviet Union supports the demands of the developing countries for a restructuring of international economic relations on an equitable and democratic basis. This means first of all the process of the elimination of colonialism must be extended to the economic sphere and we must do away with the yoke of the multinational imperialist monopolies and the exploitation of the natural and human resources of the developing states as practiced by the capitalist countries.[6]

Meanwhile, however, the West is said to maintain considerable leverage even on radical African states. For one thing, to quote a typical Soviet source, "some socialist-oriented nations, especially those which have few profitable export commodities, urgently need external sources of finance. They are therefore compelled to maintain and even strengthen economic and financial links with the capitalist world."[7] As noted by another Soviet source, "some progressive regimes face economic difficulties which affect their political stability,"[8]

[5]*Pravda,* October 5, 1976.

[6]*Pravda,* June 7, 1977.

[7]G. Khromushin, "Ideological Struggles in Africa," *International Affairs,* No. 6, June 1979, p. 53.

[8]Alexei Kiva, "Socialist Orientation: Problems of Theory and Practice," *Social Sciences,* No. 2, 1978, p. 173.

an important element therefore justifying all measures to improve the economic situation in a given country.

This need, however, bears with it certain political dangers in Moscow's view. Thus, according to Brutents, "the prime factor which tends importantly to complicate the progressive development" of newly independent states "is the impossibility for the countries which have opted for socialist orientation not only immediately to withdraw from the world capitalist economy, but also to bring about a fundamental change in the relations with it, the necessity to carry on non-capitalist development while maintaining inequitable ties with this economy which are dangerous in socio-economic and political terms for a more or less protracted period."[9]

Or, as expressed by Anatoly Gromyko, some political forces, despite general anti-imperialist views, "are inclined at times to give in to imperialist pressure," to hesitate even on African issues as some did with respect to Angola. "Imperialism" he explained, "still has at its disposal so few possibilities for influencing many African countries, whose economies depend strongly on the world capitalist market."[10]

The continued need to rely on private enterprise is also seen by Moscow as a possible cause for backsliding by seemingly radical states. Ulianovskii notes as one of three important negative factors in the socialist-oriented state the possible "pressure on it on the part of big bourgeois and neocolonialist strata, the extensive use of private enterprise and foreign capital, tremendous corruption and the establishment of an active non-mercantile bureaucratic bourgeoisie."[11] Another frequent writer on Third World affairs, Alexei Kiva, called the question of private enterprise "a most complex question." As he notes, "the socialist-oriented countries seek to attract private capital in order to promote more rapid development of the production forces and increase employment."[12] Local entrepreneurs are depicted as often joining radical elements in opposition to foreign influence, though they may later be frightened off as revolutions move to the left. Meanwhile,

---

[9]K. Brutents, *National Liberation Movements Today,* Part I (Moscow: Progress Publishers, 1977), p. 301.

[10]A. Gromyko, "The Contemporary Stage of the National Liberation Movement in Africa," *Aziia i Afrika Segodnia,* No. 5, May 1977, p. 7.

[11]Ulianovskii, "On the Countries," p.123.

[12]Kiva, "Socialist Orientation," p. 173.

"it goes without saying that a hasty and economically ungrounded offensive on local private enterprise might cause great harm to the socialist orientation."[13]

Moscow sees other more profound domestic factors also at work. While Soviet authors suggest that the lack of well defined social groups eases the way for radical takeovers in Africa, they see the same factor as a hindrance to early transformation of these regimes into Soviet-style states and as prime sources of possible reversals. Ulianovskii explained at some length in *Kommunist* why this is so:

> The dominance of the non-proletarian intermediate strata, the influence which petty bourgeois concepts have on them, the political and economic weakness of the working class and, occasionally, its total absence, the power of feudal, semi-feudal, tribal and patriarchal conditions, the tremendous cultural backwardness, and the predominant influence of the world capitalist market which occasionally makes it necessary to take into consideration the dictate of international monopolies—all these are the real political, economic, social and ideological underpinning which sometimes give rise to deviations in the external and internal policy of the countries of socialist orientation. All this was taken into consideration by the international communist movement in working out the conception of the non-capitalist path of socialist orientation, thereby not excluding the possibility of failures, of getting stuck in the general democratic stage, of reversals to old orders under the aegis of neocolonialism, of backward movement rather than progress under socialism.[14]

Ulianovskii and other Soviet analysts also often resort to a standard Marxist-Leninist explanation that cleavages within revolutionary movements are inevitable, especially in countries which abound in non-proletarian groups who cannot keep pace with revolutionary changes. Thus, it is said, "as the revolution advanced there is a differentiation in the ranks of the revolutionary democracy" and a "demarcation into a left, revolutionary wing and a right, reformist wing."[15]

---

[13]*Ibid.*, pp. 178–179.

[14]Ulianovskii, "On the Countries," p. 118.

[15]S. L. Agayev, I. M. Tatarovskaia, "Some Problems in the Development of the Revolutionary Process in Liberated Countries," *The Working Class and the Contemporary World,* No. 5, September-October 1978, p. 52.

At the time, it was suggested, the radicals at the head of these regimes sought to push matters too far too fast. Ulianovskii stressed in his *Kommunist* article the "inadmissibility of a hasty, unprepared, 'direct transition to socialism,' and artificial acceleration of political, economic and other processes." He cautioned about the "need to outlive simplistic concepts of the transition to socialism and establishing among the national democrats a more correct approach" which "takes into consideration the relative length of the pre-socialist stage with its number of transitional steps." Ulianovskii expressed satisfaction with the attitude being taken to these questions in Algeria, the Congo, Angola, Mozambique, Madagascar and Benin which "have largely been able to avoid the errors made by the pioneers of this movement in Ghana, Mali and other countries."[16]

Moscow often notes that radical nationalist leaders are subject to a variety of influences which may come to the fore and divert them from the path of socialist orientation. Most prominently cited is nationalism, called by Brutents, "along with the 'socialist credo,' the cornerstone of the world view of the great majority of revolutionary democrats."[17] Soviet ideologies often complain that African radicals come to believe in socialism from a nationalist rather than a class position. Again Brutents: "In effect, revolutionary democrats arrive at the proclamation of socialist goals, at an orientation toward socialism, not through class negation of capitalism, but through anti-imperialist nationalism."[18]

Moscow, of course, has no objection to this and seeks to use it for Soviet purposes. But the Kremlin also expressed apprehension about "the strengthening in a number of cases of the negative sides of nationalistic ideology in emerging countries."[19] This, in Moscow's view, is what happened in Egypt and Somalia.

In this connection, Soviet analysts reject all theories of African socialism such as those espoused by Tanzanian leader Nyerere and other Africans. A Soviet book on radical African states concedes that these theories have their positive aspects because of their rejection of capitalism and their recognition of the advantages of socialism, especially for the reordering of African society. However, the authors

[16]Ulianovskii, "On the Countries," p. 119.
[17]Brutents, *National Liberation Movements Today,* Part II, p. 79.
[18]*Ibid.,* p. 82.
[19]*Ibid.,* p. 84.

stress, these theories overemphasize local peculiarities and underemphasize general laws, that is, the universal applicability of the Soviet model. Moreover, they constitute an effort "to hamper the transition of revolutionary democrats to scientific socialism, to the positions of Marxism-Leninism."[20] Or as other Soviet authors emphasize, these theories constitute an effort to find a "third road" which would keep Africa clear of Soviet (and Western influence) or constitute a vehicle for social-democrat or nationalist influence in Africa to the detriment of Soviet influence.[21]

Over the long haul, Moscow is aware of the difficulty that "revolutionary democrats" are bound to have in adopting the concept of proletarian internationalism, that is, recognition of the primacy of Soviet interests in the world revolutionary process. According to Brutents, "revolutionary democrats do not understand—we have in mind, of course, socially conditioned misunderstanding—the dialectical relationship between internationalism and patriotism. Internationalism in general, the internationalism of Communists in particular, is conceived by some revolutionary democratic circles to be incompatible with patriotism."[22]

Where communist parties exist, radical nationalists are described as considering themselves "the genuine socialist force" and as "wary of communists' links with the international communist movement, though here, without question, purely nationalistic motives also play an important role." Moreover, "of first-rate importance for relations between revolutionary democrats and communists, too, is what can be conditionally called inter-party rivalry" and the fact that "once at the helm of state, revolutionary democrats are not inclined to share *real* power with anyone."[23]

Finally, Soviet commentaries from time to time express concern about anti-Soviet prejudices lingering from the past or fanned by the "imperialists," especially in connection with such actions as the Soviet and Cuban operations in Angola and Ethiopia. Some of this anti-Sovietism Moscow equates with "class" motives or remaining

[20]Gavrilov, Starushenko, eds., *Africa: Problems of Socialist Orientation,* p. 44.
[21]See, for example, Khromushin, "Ideological Struggles in Africa," p. 53.
[22]Brutents, *National Liberation Movements Today,* Part II, p. 199.
[23]*Ibid.,* pp. 199–200.

bourgeois elements even in radical African states, some to the "nationalist narrow-mindedness of some leaders." Some is attributed directly to propaganda by the West and by the Chinese against Soviet actions and intentions in Africa. And some Moscow sees as suspicion of the USSR as a great power. Accordingly, *New Times* wrote, one of the motives for the USSR's signature of friendship treaties with Angola and Mozambique was to make it "harder for imperialism and Maoist propaganda to implant anti-Sovietism on the African continent by ascribing to Soviet policy something utterly alien to it—hegemony."[24] In addition, Soviet spokesmen including Brezhnev incessantly emphasize that the USSR has no ulterior motives or selfish aims in Africa.

To deal with these problems, Moscow has adopted both short-term and long-range policies. In the first instance, southern African issues have provided Moscow with the most obvious potential for identifying with African nationalism and for putting a premium on political-military arenas best suited to give the USSR sources of influence and leverage. In addition to other issues, such as support for a new economic order, Moscow has also sought to ride with nationalist currents in general as long as they are directed against the West.

Thus an article on ideological currents in Africa, while stressing Marxist opposition in principle to nationalism, emphasized the need to differentiate between bourgeois and petty bourgeois, between reformist and revolutionary, between narrowly interpreted and non-isolationist nationalisms providing for alliances with "progressive" forces. Thus, it concludes, "the conditions of anti-imperialist struggle and national revival in formerly colonial countries dictates the need to combine criticism in principle of nationalist and petty bourgeois ideology with the ability to conduct a struggle on the soil of nationalism, to support progressive revolutionary-democratic nationalism (with the clear realization of its social and historical limitation) against reformist, national-bourgeois nationalism. In the radical, consistently anti-imperialist and democratic nationalism of oppressed nations, reflecting the longings of the popular masses, communists see not only an ally in the struggle for independence and social progress,

---

[24]V. Sidenko, "The Truth Versus Lies," *New Times,* No. 19, May 1977, p. 20.

but that environment from which true adherents of scientific socialism have emerged and will emerge."[25]

What has particularly encouraged Moscow about Africa is that the process of attaining political independence has often been linked with the need to achieve economic independence and that has meant rejection by African leaders of Western economic forms and ties. According to one Soviet journal:

> The very logic of life has led the peoples of the liberated countries toward an understanding of the truth that the national-liberation revolution cannot be completed with the attainment only of political independence and that the final liquidation of the survivals of colonialism is impossible without tearing out its roots.[26]

And in the African context, these roots are identified as the capitalist system in general and the position of capitalists, either foreign or domestic. Soviet sources emphasize that radical Africans identify the West not only with colonialism, but as the cause of African backwardness. One Soviet Africanist thus noted that in the early stages of independence in a number of countries, "subjective rejection of capitalism" marked the attitudes of the leaders who linked capitalism "with economic oppression and political inequality."[27] In many instances, he noted, "the concepts of capitalism and colonialism were equivalent" with many arguing that capitalism was alien to national traditions.

Moscow has seen in their far-reaching reforms important steps in the limitation of Western influence and in the possible transition to Soviet-type and, it is implied, Soviet-dominated states. All Soviet authors attribute particular importance to the emergence of radical leaders in these states, the "democratization," i.e., the increasing leftist dominance of the state apparatus, the priority given to the public as opposed to the private sector, state regulation of the economy, agrarian reform, initial steps toward cooperative forms of agriculture, fostering of

[25]O. Martyshin, "On Certain Ideological Tendencies in Contemporary Africa," *Aziia i Afrika Segodnia,* No. 4, April 1978, p. 25.

[26]J. K. Shirokov, A. M. Khazanov, "The Soviet Union and the National Liberation Movement," *Narody Azii i Afriki,* No. 1, January-February 1978, p. 7.

[27]Yu. Gavrilov, "Ideological-Political Development of Contemporary National and Revolutionary Democracy," *Aziia i Afrika Segodnia,* No. 1, January 1979, p. 26.

"anti-imperialist" ideology.[28] All put particular emphasis on the elimination or at least strict control of foreign firms and of local private enterprise.

Participants in an international communist symposium on African socialist-oriented countries concluded that "the essence of non-capitalist development" consisted in the "uprooting of survivals of feudal and semi-feudal relations and containment of the growth of capitalism by means of revolutionary reforms [which] will introduce anti-capitalist elements into public life, create transitional relations which under certain political conditions can quite quickly become relations of a socialist type."[29]

Soviet Third World authority, R. A. Ulianovskii, in an article in *Kommunist,* declared:

> The content of socialist orientation is defined as a course of internal and external policy, directed toward anti-imperalist, anti-feudal and partially anti-capitalist reforms, the aim of which consists in the creation of state-political, socio-economic and scientific-technical prerequisites for the gradual approach in the future toward socialism.[30]

For Soviet theoreticians, the key problem is political. If the leadership of a Third World country is sufficiently tempered ideologically and politically, they seem to say, then economic ties with the West and fostering of a certain amount of private enterprise can be turned into an asset, enabling socialist-oriented regimes to consolidate their positions while maintaining their "anti-imperialist" (i.e., anti-Western) stance in foreign policy and their "anti-capitalist" aspirations at home. Brutents thus approves the analysis of a fellow Soviet author who, he said, did not "make the attainment of economic independence *directly* contingent on a break between the developing countries and the capitalist system." Indeed, Brutents says, "such independence is largely possi-

---

[28]For fuller discussions, see Gavrilov, Strarushenko, eds., *Africa: Problems of Socialist Orientation;* A. Shin, "The Great October and Contemporary National Liberation Movements," *Aziia i Afrika Segodnia,* No. 8, August 1977; "The Revolutionary Process in African Countries of Socialist Orientation," *Problems of Peace and Socialism,* No. 1, January 1978; S. P. Nemanov, "Parties of the Vanguard Type in African Countries: A Socialist Orientation," *Narody Azii i Afriki,* No. 2, March-April 1979; Ulianovskii, "On the Countries"; Anatoly Gromyko, "Socialist Orientation in Africa," *International Affairs,* No. 9, September 1979.

[29]"The Revolutionary Process," p. 63.

[30]Ulianovskii, "On the Countries," p. 119.

ble even *before withdrawal* from the world capitalist economic system provided, of course, that an anti-imperialist policy is pursued."[31]

Moscow's basic model in this regard is its own early history during the New Economic Policy (NEP) period when the Soviet regime turned to the outside world for help while holding fast to its ultimate objectives. Thus, B. G. Gafurov wrote: "The experience of NEP, whose main feature was the utilization of private enterprise on conditions favorable to Soviet power, under strict state control and with preservation of the commanding heights in the economy in the hands of the state has fundamental significance."[32]

Noting that radical states faced a dilemma between their current needs and their ultimate ideological objectives, Alexei Kiva suggested the following solution:

> The tendency is that while attracting foreign investments the socialist-oriented countries try to establish strict state control over them: mixed enterpises are founded in which the controlling packet of shares belongs to the national state. And it is stipulated that the foreign companies concerned should help train local managerial personnel. The young national states hope ultimately to take over the enterprises built by foreign capital.[33]

Importance of the "Vanguard Party"

Over the long term, Soviet writers have identified two characteristics of the socialist-oriented states as particularly crucial: the formation of Marxist-Leninist vanguard parties which will increasingly come to resemble orthodox communist parties and growing ties between the countries concerned and the Soviet-led "socialist community."

Moscow sees as an encouraging starting point the tendency throughout Africa, but especially in the radical states, toward one-party rule. One of the more sophisticated Soviet writers on Africa, Vladimir Kudriavtsev, noted the impact of tribalism in this connection:

[31] Brutents, *National Liberation Movements Today,* Part I, p. 170.
[32] B. G. Gafurov, "The Banner of Struggle for the Liberation of Peoples," *Narody Azii i Afriki,* No. 5, September-October 1977, p. 9.
[33] Kiva, "Socialist Orientation," pp. 178–179.

Actual experience has shown that pluralism in the African context nearly always resolves itself into a system of parties representing either tribal interests or the views of certain individuals, ultimately laying the groundwork for dictatorial rule. On the other hand, the development of social relations on the continent has shown the vitality and great political advantages of a one-party system, provided it reflects the anti-imperialist and anti-colonial mood of the people and makes progressive changes in the interests of the working masses.[34]

Soviet and communist analysts occasionally suggest that the model being followed by Moscow is that of Cuba where an initially non-communist group, in Soviet parlance "revolutionary democrats," launched the revolution but voluntarily transformed itself into a communist party organized along orthodox Soviet lines. Thus one of the participants in the international communist symposium on African socialist-oriented states, a Jordanian communist, noted that the "subjective political factor is of exceptionally great significance in Africa" because of the low level of socio-economic development and the "instability of political leadership" on the continent. As a result and because of the "growing influence" of the Soviet bloc, the possibility of the evolution of radical into Soviet-type states "is much more favorable than in the past. Cuba is a classic example," the speaker said, and "comparable processes are taking place in Angola, Mozambique, the Congo, Algeria."[35]

No Soviet source has similarly named specific countries, but other leading Soviet ideologists have also suggested Cuba as a model for African political development. Karen Brutents thus wrote: "The 1960s provide examples of political evolution toward the left, toward Marxism-Leninism, among forces and organizations that were at first basically revolutionary democratic. We refer above all to the path trod by Cuban revolutionaries."[36]

The basic problem from the Soviet point of view, however, is that unlike Cuba, few African countries have communist parties whose members can be infiltrated into radical nationalist movements. Moscow accordingly has evolved the notion of transforming existent political organizations into "vanguard parties." Soviet theoreticians over

---

[34]V. Kudriavtsev, "Africa Fights for Its Future," *International Affairs,* No. 5, May 1978, p. 32.
[35]"The Revolutionary Process," p. 57.
[36]Brutents, *National Liberation Movements Today,* Part II, p. 217.

and over again emphasize that without such parties, socialist orientation cannot become true socialism. Thus, one of the Soviet Central Committee journals declared in September 1978 that "the understanding is growing that a new society can be built only under the leadership of a revolutionary party basing its activity on Marxist-Leninist theory."[37]

Although several parties in Africa have declared their adherence to Marxism-Leninism (Angola, Mozambique, the Congo, Benin), this is not enough for Moscow. Thus wrote Ulianovskii:

> The creation of a really vanguard party, gravitating toward Marxism-Leninism and in the conditions of a post-colonial but still extremely backward society in socio-economic relations, is an extremely complicated process. It cannot be reduced to the approval and proclamation of a program of scientific socialism which, it seems, is not so difficult to do taking into account the authority and influence of basic Marxist-Leninist propositions. It is significantly more difficult to master scientific socialism genuinely in all links of the party, to place it at the foundation of its practical activity, to attain the creation of a social, ideological-political, organized structure of a vanguard party in accordance with the tasks of moving the majority of the popular masses in the direction of socialism.[38]

In the fullest discussion of the "vanguard party" in the African context, S. P. Nemanov (identified as an instructor at Lumumba University who specializes in national liberation movements) notes that the process of forming a vanguard party differs from one country to another. In some of them it is a matter of transforming the broad coalitions which featured the struggle for independence into elite parties. Angola, Mozambique, Tanzania, and Guinea are cited as examples. Other variants have included the creation of parties from scratch or through combining several organizations into a single party.[39]

Whatever the process, according to Nemanov, "an important peculiarity of the countries of socialist orientation of tropical Africa in politi-

---

[37]V. Popov, "The National Liberation Movement in Africa and the Intrigues of Imperialism," *Political Self-Education*, No. 9, September 1978, p. 65.

[38]Ulianovskii, "On the Countries," p. 120.

[39]Nemanov, "Parties of the Vanguard Type," p. 16–28.

cal terms is the fact that they practically lack an organized communist movement. The working class movement here has not yet attained the level of maturity when it becomes dominating in the revolutionary process.'' Accordingly, even the vanguard parties at the present stage would be a bloc of various classes united by ''consistent anti-imperialism—the struggle against the remaining dependence of the countries that have liberated themselves of the imperialist powers, their neocolonial policy, which is aimed at keeping the liberated countries in the sphere of the world capitalist economy as agrarian and raw material appendages.''

To begin with, Moscow believes a proper vanguard party must purge its ranks of pro-Western or pro-capitalist elements. According to Nemanov, ''it is precisely with the determination of class composition that this formation of vanguard revolutionary parties begins. This finds expression, in particular, in the removal from the ranks of the elements that have become bourgeois in their orientation, as well as people subject to bourgeois influence.'' By incorporating this into their statutes, these parties are said to establish their difference ''from the bourgeois and pro-bourgeois parties, which conceal their class essence in every conceivable way, taking refuge in 'all-popular' and 'all-national' slogans.'' Like the Soviet Communist Party, these parties devote ''paramount attention'' toward admitting ''the most advanced and conscious elements from among the workers'' as well as toward establishing transmission belt organizations. But most important, Nemanov wrote, was the ''gradual transition, in the process of the formation of the vanguard parties, of the foremost representatives of revolutionary democracy from the ideology of nationalism and various currents of 'African socialism' to scientific socialism, thus turning to the Marxist/Leninist teaching on the paths to the revolutionary reorganization of society.''

Anatoly Gromyko also suggested as another possibility the formation of communist cells in the African trade union movement:

An important role in the spread of the ideas of scientific socialism is also being played by the revolutionary wing of the trade union movement which is organizing the struggle of the working class not only to satisfy its essential economic demands, but also for the realization of progressive, socio-economic transformations. The working class undergoes a political education schooling and the cadres of the most conscious part of the working class—the supporters of Marxism-Leninism—are formed in them.[40]

According to Gromyko, there are at present only ten communist parties in all of Africa, five in the north (Algeria, Morocco, Tunisia, the Sudan, Egypt), two in the south (South Africa, Lesotho), two in the West (Senegal, Nigeria) and one other (Reunion). Hints of things to come may have been contained in the announcement by *Pravda* on August 26, 1978 of the "recent" meeting of communist and workers parties of tropical and southern Africa. The site of the meeting was not mentioned, nor was any list given of the countries represented. Whatever the reason (to hide the small number of parties or to avoid revealing the existence of underground parties), the very announcement of the meeting and the summary in *Pravda* of its appeal to all of Africa appeared designed to stake out an independent role for existent African communist parties and for African communists operating within radical parties in Africa south of the Sahara.[41]

In this connection, Alexei Kiva reflects Soviet caution on attributing too much to ruling radical parties at the current stage by suggesting that a distinction should be made between vanguard and proletarian, i.e., orthodox communist parties. He said that radical African leaders began to talk about establishing vanguard parties and pro-Soviet Marxists went along with the designation, though strictly speaking this was not "scientifically" correct. However, he said, the term "has long entered into common usage and it is hardly worthwhile rejecting it." Yet, he cautioned, "one must only keep in mind that we are speaking about a vanguard revolutionary-democrat and not a Marxist-Leninist party."[42] To go from one to the other, a party must accept Marxism-Leninism (i.e., as defined by Moscow), proletarian internationalism (i.e., loyalty to Moscow), democratic centralism, parties organized on production-

---

[40]Anatoly A. Gromyko, "Tendencies of Development of the Working Class in African Countries," *The Working Class and the Contemporary World,* No. 5, September-October 1978, p. 115.

[41]For a full text of the communist "Call to Africa," see *The African Communist,* No. 75, Fourth Quarter, 1978, pp. 5–33.

[42]A. Kiva, "Revolutionary Democratic Parties: Some Development Tendencies," *Aziia i Afrika Segodnia,* No. 3, March 1978, p. 32.

territorial lines (i.e., class or economic rather than national or tribal lines).[43]

There is thus an implication in all Soviet writings that eventually the vanguard parties in radical African states will necessarily become communist parties not only in function, but in name as well. *Asia and Africa Today* in August 1977 noted that for "objective reasons" in a majority of African and Asian states no communist parties existed or existing parties were "still not ready" to fulfill their mission to lead the "broad toiling masses." However, it went on, "undoubtedly this situation is temporary, historically transitional." As these countries develop, the necessities of a socialist order "will inevitably push the communist movement to the fore as the leading socio-political movement." The author suggests this will happen in one of three ways: through the gradual transformation of "national-democratic" into Marxist-Leninist parties; through the rise to the top of existing communist parties as working classes increase; or through the unification and merger of communist and national-democratic parties into a single Marxist-Leninist party.[44]

The USSR as a Model

In emphasizing the need for a vanguard party, the USSR clearly is setting itself forth as a model for radical African states to follow, which in turn will facilitate the consolidation of Soviet influence on how to make the model work. Supplying the guidance involves constant exchanges of publications and personnel with endless opportunities to indoctrinate local populations and to build up a Soviet-trained and Soviet-oriented lobby within African ruling elites.

Soviet authors indicate that Moscow attaches great importance to a purposeful effort to indoctrinate African leaderships from the top down in the validity of the Soviet model for the solution of African problems. Nemanov pointed "to the enormous significance of the establishment of durable contacts between the parties of the countries of socialist orientation and the world communist movement, and in the first place, with the ruling parties of the countries of the socialist commonwealth.

[43]*Ibid.*, p. 34.
[44]Shin, "The Great October," p. 3.

Such intercourse gives the revolutionary democrats the possibility to study in depth and to utilize creatively the rich experience of the communist parties applicable to their conditions." Nemanov noted that "comprehensive links between communist and revolutionary-democratic parties are at the present time developing successfully and fruitfully" in the form of delegation exchanges, consultations on various questions, participation in perspective congresses.

Karen Brutents, discussing radical countries throughout the Third World, added two other points. First, he called attention to the "great significance to the evolution of revolutionary democracy [of] the personality of the leader of the revolution, of the revolution's most influential figures," factors whose impact he described as "especially great in developing countries." Second, he emphasized the importance of the generational change, the replacement of old guard leaders by "younger cadres who did not grow up in the atmosphere of colonial domination and are free of the political and psychological complexes associated therewith, who are often more familiar with socialist ideas, with Marxist literature and have not infrequently been educated in socialist countries."[45]

From a doctrinal view, what all this is taken to mean is that the Soviet input makes up for the institutional weaknesses in African countries. According to the journal of the Institute of the International Working Class movement, the ties between communists and Third World radical states are a new form of political solidarity between the world communist movement and revolutionary democracy which "facilitates the strengthening socialist tendencies in the zone of national-liberation revolutions."[46]

Brutents goes even further, declaring that "together with the international communist movement, the socialist system now has the function of *proletarian vanguard on a worldwide scale,* including the countries delivered from imperialist oppression, the peasant and semi-proletarian masses, and all the intermediate strata in the former colonies and semi-colonies, thus helping to compensate—only to some extent, of

[45]Brutents, *National Liberation Movements Today,* Part II, pp. 222–23.
[46]G. F. Kim, A. S. Kaufman, "The October Revolution and the National Liberation Movement," *The Working Class and the Contemporary World,* No. 6, November-December 1977, p. 45.

course—[for] the weakness and inadequate organization and influence of the working class in some countries."[47]

All Soviet theoreticians insist that it is obligatory for socialist-oriented states to establish even closer ties with the Soviet Union and its allies. "And this is natural," explained a Soviet book on USSR relations with Africa, "because without solidarity and cooperation with the world system of socialism there can be no progressive policy really responding to national interests and consequently successes in the struggle for political and economic independence, for renovation of the forms of social life."[48] Or as Soviet theoretician B. G. Gafurov expressed it: "Life itself convincingly confirms that real movement along the path of democratic and socialist reforms is possible in our times only with maximum reliance on the international labor and communist movement and its glorious offspring—the world socialist commonwealth."[49]

As a starting point for earning the designation of "socialist orientation," Moscow requires not only an anti-Western foreign policy but strongly pro-Soviet positions on most if not all important international issues. The full length Soviet book on African socialist-oriented states noted that "from the first day of their arising these countries invariably support all basic foreign policy actions of the Soviet Union, of the other socialist states, directed toward the affirmation of the principles of peaceful coexistence in international relations, the repulsing of imperialist aggression, the struggle against colonialism and neocolonialism, for relaxation of world tension."[50]

The authors cite in particular African willingness to support the USSR on non-African issues especially in the U.N. A Soviet Institute of Africa analysis of votes in the General Assembly from 1960 to 1972 was said to show that socialist-oriented states voted with the USSR on 69 percent of the issues, against Soviet-supported resolutions only 9 percent of the time. By contrast, they noted, these countries voted with

[47]Brutents, *National Liberation Movements Today*, Part I, p. 311.

[48]Ye. A. Tarabrin, ed., *The USSR and the Countries of Africa* (Moscow: Mysl', 1976), p. 4.

[49]Gafurov, "The Banner of Struggle," p. 13.

[50]Gavrilov, Starushenko, eds., *Africa: Problems of Socialist Orientation*, p. 419.

the U.S. only on 24 percent of the issues, against the U.S. on 49 percent.[51]

In an echo of past Soviet pronouncements that the test of true communists is their unconditional loyalty to the Soviet Union, Karen Brutents, looking at the need in the future for strengthening the alliance between the Soviet bloc and the anti-imperialist national liberation movement, remarked: "Nor is there any doubt that the attitude to this alliance is an important indicator of the progressiveness of political forces, movements, regimes and organizations in the developing countries."[52]

Contrariwise, R. A. Ulianovskii emphasized in *Kommunist,* "Any manifestation of lack of faith, and more than hostility toward the world of socialism, any manifestation of an inclination toward conciliation with respect toward imperialist policy, toward the neocolonialists, to the newly appearing 'Greeks bearing gifts,' usually serves as a signal of a retreat from the principle of socialist orientation."[53]

Indeed, the concluding section of a Soviet book on Soviet-African relations declared that the problem of these relations for the foreseeable future "can even be formulated as follows: friendship and cooperation with the USSR, other socialist states, reliance on their support for the strengthening of independence or orientation toward international capital which inevitably will lead to a repetition of dependence and exploitation."[54]

In their discussion on bloc-LDC ties, Soviet theoreticians make it clear that they mean political and military rather than economic support, although more grandiose Soviet statements seek to give the impression that all are on a par. Thus, *International Affairs* in August 1977 claimed that the "Soviet Union is the key economic, political, ideological and military factor in the national liberation revolutions and in the successful struggle of the newly free states to consolidate their political independence by achieving economic independence and resist all forms of neocolonialism and imperialist pressures."[55]

[51]*Ibid.,* pp. 419–20.

[52]K. Brutents, "The Soviet Tension and the Newly Independent Countries," *International Affairs,* No. 4, April 1979, pp. 12–13.

[53]Ulianovskii, "On the Countries," p. 122.

[54]Tarabrin, *The USSR and the Countries of Africa,* p. 400.

[55]G. Kim, "World Socialism and Present Day National Liberation Movements," *International Affairs,* No. 8, August 1977, p. 74.

Particularly in the light of Angolan and Ethiopian events, Moscow has been emphasizing its constant readiness to provide military support to radical regimes that want it and claiming that the specter, not to mention the reality, of such support serves to deter the West from forceful action against socialist-oriented states. Citing Angola as a prime case in point, a Soviet pamphlet declared: "The economic, political and military might of the Soviet Union, the countries of the socialist commonwealth is the main deterrent factor to neocolonial strivings of imperialist states, their expansionist encroachments."[56]

[56]L. A. Alekseyev, *Africa: Struggle for Political and Economic Liberation* (Moscow: Znanie, 1978), p. 62.

CHAPTER SEVEN

Consolidation in Mozambique, Angola, Ethiopia

WHILE WELCOMING ALL COUNTRIES of "socialist orientation," the Kremlin has clearly put primary emphasis on consolidating its positions in those countries—specifically Angola, Ethiopia, Mozambique—where Soviet leverage is already great and which are of great strategic value in themselves and as springboards for future undertakings. In all three cases, Moscow worked first to tie their regimes to the Soviet Union in foreign affairs, and then to guide their internal evolution in directions which Moscow hopes will maximize its influence and leverage.

The sequence in all three countries was almost the same, although their starting points were different: Neto in Angola requiring Soviet-Cuban intervention to consolidate his power over internal rivals, Machel in Mozambique and Mengistu in Ethiopia having come to the fore at home by their own efforts, with the latter requiring Soviet-Cuban aid against external enemies. The first stage consisted of high-level vists to the USSR culminating not only in specific economic agreements, but in the signature of political documents emphasizing the coincidence of the foreign policies of the USSR and the countries involved, and establishing the basis not only for state-to-state but party-to-party ties.

Mozambique: A Network of Contacts

The process began first with Mozambique which achieved independence before Angola. The initial step came there with the signature on

February 12, 1976 of a series agreements on economic and technical cooperation, merchant shipping, fisheries, civil aviation, trade, and the stationing of trade representatives in both countries.[1] Despite the political importance of these agreements, they do not appear to have been reported at the time by the Soviet media and only briefly by Maputo.[2] Nevertheless they appear to have set the stage for the next step in consolidation of ties, the pilgrimage to Moscow by Mozambique chief Samora Machel two months later during which a cultural and scientific agreement was added to the roster and a joint statement issued which solidified Mozambique's shift of allegiance from Peking to Moscow.

The joint statement asserted that "during the exchange of opinions the sides noted the Soviet Union and Mozambique act from common positions in the struggle against imperialism and colonialism. They noted a coincidence of views on a wide range of international problems under discussion." Of particular satisfaction to Moscow, the statement proclaimed that "a guarantee of the success of the anti-imperialist, anti-colonial struggle of the peoples of Africa, Asia and Latin America lies in their unity of action with the socialist countries and other progressive forces of the world." It urged that "the united forces of reaction be countered by the powerful alliance of revolutionary forces—the world socialist system, the international workers movement and fighters for the peoples' national and social liberation." Specifically it called for "regular consultations at various levels" on both bilateral and international issues.[3]

A second major element at this stage was the strengthening of ties on the party level. The invitation to Machel was tendered both by the Soviet Communist Party and the Soviet government. Probably expressing more a Soviet than a Mozambique assessment, the joint statement noted that "the sides attach great significance to the development of cooperation between the CPSU and FRELIMO" (Front for the Liberation of Mozambique). Both sides were said to deem it "expedient" that

---

[1]For texts of these agreements, see USSR Ministry of Foreign Affairs, *Sbornik Deistvuiushchikh Dogovorov, Soglasheniii Konventsii Zakliuchennykh SSSR S Inostrannymi Gosudarstvami,* Vol. XXXIII (Moscow: Mezhdunarodnye Otnosheniia, 1978), pp. 241–250, 476–483.

[2]Paris, AFP, February 18, 1976.

[3]*Pravda,* May 24, 1976.

there be "joint elaboration and coordination of annual plans for party ties" and expanded relations between "mass public organizations."

At the same time, there remained a striking disparity between Machel's definition of the nature of Mozambique and Soviet descriptions. On the eve of his visit, TASS quoted Machel to the effect that "we have made our choice for socialism" and "have been guided by the theory of Marxism-Leninism."[4] In his major Moscow speech, however, he indicated that Mozambique was at a preliminary stop: "We have established a people's democracy and the power of a worker-peasant alliance in our country,"[5] This toned-down definition undoubtedly reflected the caution of his Soviet hosts about Mozambique's ideological status. Soviet President Podgorny, speaking on the same occasion as Machel, completely omitted any reference to the question. Brezhnev, during his audience with Machel, expressed Soviet solidarity "with the struggle of the People's Republic of Mozambique against imperialism for the consolidation of the people's democratic order and construction of a new society."[6] The concluding joint statement reflected Soviet caution citing Machel's aim at "building a society free from man's exploitation by man" and Soviet good wishes to Mozambique "in the struggle for the consolidation of political and economic independence, the social renewal of their country, and the consolidation and development of the people's democracy."[7]

During 1977, two developments signaled an even closer relationship between the USSR and Mozambique. The first was the holding in February of the first FRELIMO Congress since the attainment of independence during which FRELIMO formally proclaimed that it intended to be a vanguard party guided by Marxism-Leninism. The second was the visit to Mozambique in March of Soviet President Podgorny and the signature of a Soviet-Mozambique Friendship Treaty. Podgorny's rhetoric reflected the ideological upgrading in Moscow's eyes of Mozambique. Speaking at a dinner in his honor, Podgorny declared that Mozambique had an "honored place" among African states "which have not only proclaimed the building of socialism as their goal but have also actually entered on the path of transition to

[4]TASS, May 15, 1976.
[5]*Pravda,* May 18, 1976.
[6]*Pravda,* May 19, 1976.
[7]*Pravda,* May 24, 1976.

socialist tranformations." Specifically, he emphasized, "the creation at the recent third FRELIMO Congress of a vanguard party of working people guided by the principles of scientific socialism was a historic event for Mozambique and, I dare say, for the whole of Africa."[8]

At the same time, Podgorny emphasized the difficulties that lay ahead and prospective "clashes with the intrigues of imperialism, with its aggressive actions and attempts to intimidate and split the progressive forces." What he appeared to be saying was that anti-Westernism and the Soviet example were the cement which would bind the USSR and Mozambique together rather than any large-scale Soviet aid. Thus he cited Brezhnev's statement at the 25th Soviet Communist Party Congress that it is the "real and fundamental community of interests in the struggle against imperialism that creates a reliable basis for lasting state relations and mutual understanding between the liberated countries and the socialist community." In opting for Marxism-Leninism, Podgorny stated, "you have a chance to use the experience accumulated by other socialist countries and to lean on them for support." But he told a Maputo rally on March 31 not to expect too much economic support, because of the number of those competing for Soviet aid and the limits on Soviet resources: "We are giving no small economic aid and support to tens of states of Asia, Africa and Latin America, although frankly speaking we do not have excessive means."[9]

The signature on March 31, 1977 of the Soviet-Mozambique Treaty of Friendship and Cooperation constituted an important milestone for Moscow in the solidification of Soviet relations with the Machel regime. The conclusion of this treaty against the backdrop of increasing raids against Mozambique by Rhodesian forces underscored Soviet intention to exploit the military vulnerability of Mozambique as a conduit for Soviet influence through the supply of military aid. And in fact Article 4 of the treaty provided for continued cooperation in the military sphere "in the interests of reinforcing defense potentials" of the two parties.[10]

But beyond that, the treaty provided the formal basis for relations on an ideological plane as well. Article 1 calls for cooperation "in every way" in order to preserve and deepen "social and economic gains."

[8]*Pravda*, March 30, 1977.
[9]*Pravda*, April 1, 1977.
[10]*Pravda*, April 4, 1977.

Article 3 calls for expanded links between their "political and public organizations, enterprises, cultural and scientific institutions." Article 7 calls for continued cooperation "in supporting the just struggle of peoples for freedom, independence, sovereignty and social progress" and the struggle by both "against the force of imperialism." Article 8 calls for consultations on bilateral and international affairs, while Article 9 calls for contacts "to coordinate their position" should situations arise "that threaten peace or break the peace."

An important element which facilitated Soviet efforts in Mozambique was the role the USSR played in the FRELIMO struggle against the Portuguese. Constant reminders of this role have appeared in speeches by Soviet leaders, by those of Mozambique, and in their joint statements. During his 1976 visit to Moscow, Machel thanked the Soviet people for its "sacrifices" and "contribution to our victory,"[11] and Brezhnev directly "for the all-round assistance and support for Mozambique's struggle for national independence."[12] Podgorny, in turn, also recalled that "at that difficult time for the people of Mozambique [the USSR] invariably gave them assistance and all-round support in word and deed." Moreover, he added, such support reflected "one of the fundamental principles of the Soviet Union's Leninist foreign policy" and would "also determine the relations between our peoples in the future."[13]

Similar statements were made during Podgorny's visit to Mozambique in March 1977. At a March 31 rally, Machel recalled that the Soviet Union "from the first days after FRELIMO was established actively and unconditionally helped the people of Mozambique in their just liberation war," while Podgorny stressed that current relations "are based on the firm foundation laid in the years of the hard selfless struggle of the people of Mozambique against the colonialist yoke."[14] The Friendship Treaty in its preamble similarly recalled "the relations of friendship and cooperation that formed in the difficult years of the people's war for the liberation of Mozambique and that consolidated after the formation of the People's Republic of Mozambique."[15]

[11]*Pravda*, May 18, 1976.
[12]*Pravda*, May 19, 1976.
[13]*Pravda*, May 18, 1976.
[14]*Pravda*, April 1, 1976.
[15]*Pravda*, April 4, 1976.

In stressing this theme, the Soviets obviously were seeking to reinforce Machel's sense of gratitude and to indicate that military aid is the kind of support which the USSR is still most willing to give. Machel, in turn, has sought to emphasize the Soviet commitment to his regime which he presumably hopes will deter Rhodesia and South Africa from military actions against it. Accordingly, he frequently reiterates, as he did before the non-aligned conference in Havana in September 1979, that "the socialist countries are a reliable rear guard for the victory of our liberation struggle" and "are the natural ally for the defense of our political and economic independence which are the foundations of nonalignment."[16]

Angola: Security Problems Dominant

The process of consolidating the Soviet position in Angola has taken a course superficially similar to that of Mozambique, although the differing situations in both countries give different significance to Soviet actions. Soviet leverage has been incomparably greater in Angola, first, because Neto and the MPLA were so much more beholden to the USSR and Cuba for their victory, secondly, because the continued threat to the MPLA, especially from UNITA, limited the domestic base of the Neto government (and presumably its successor) and left it dependent on Soviet and Cuban support for survival. The continued presence of a Cuban expeditionary force clearly gives Moscow and Havana a decisive role in Angolan affairs for the indefinite future. At the same time, these uncertainties together with past indications of factionalism within the MPLA mean that the USSR has become enmeshed in a highly fluid situaiton, thereby belying the frequently portrayed image of Soviet caution. While the very uncertainty gives Moscow leverage in the short run, it also prevents the long-term consolidation toward which Soviet policy aims in all its client states.

The consolidation process in Angola began virtually concurrently with that in Mozambique. Two days after Machel left the USSR, Angolan Premier Lopo do Nascimento made his appearance in Moscow and within a few days combined some of the features noted both before and

---

[16]Radio Havana, September 5, 1979.

during Machel's visit. The Nascimento visit brought the conclusion of agreements on trade, trade representatives, cultural and scientific cooperation, fishery, merchant shipping, and a consular convention (a civil air agreement having been signed earlier). In addition to the usual communique concluding the visit, Moscow trotted out another device, a Declaration of Basic Principles to guide relations between the two countries, a device the USSR had previously used in its relations with the West.

As in the Mozambique case, the joint statement concluding the visit emphasized the "coincidence of views" between the two sides "on the most important problems of the international situation." In a position undoubtedly drafted by the Soviets, the statement also declared that "in the face of the combined forces of international reaction, they consider it necessary to unite still more closely the alliance of revolutionary forces—the world system of socialism, the international workers movement and fighters for the peoples' national and social liberation."[17] In addition, agreement was recorded on several specific issues.

Again, as in the case of Mozambique, the joint statement reported agreement "on certain measures aimed at rendering the PRA assistance in strengthening its defense capacity." Beyond this, the Declaration of Principles pledged "comprehensive cooperation" in a variety of fields and "mutual consultations at various levels on all important international problems of mutual interest and on questions pertaining to their bilateral relations."[18] The joint statement also echoed its Mozambique counterpart on the need for "unity of action" between Africa and the USSR.

In accordance with the actual course of events, expressions of Angolan gratitude for Soviet and Cuban aid as well as Soviet responses were more far-reaching than those in the case of Mozambique. Nascimento in his keynote speech during his visit said "it should be especially noted that the Angolan people's successful struggle was made possible "because of the combat solidarity" with Angola by the socialist countries and world "progressive" movements. He specifically noted the "tremendous assistance" which "manifested itself in the sending of people and provision of arms by the Soviet Union, Cuba, Guinea-

[17]*Pravda,* June 1, 1976.
[18]*Ibid.*

Bissau and the Republic of Guinea." Moreover, he underscored, "we do not conceal the fact that we needed international solidarity, particularly when we were waging the armed struggle for our liberation."[19]

On the Soviet side, Kosygin emphasized the USSR's responsiveness to the call of duty in Angola:

> The Soviet people have always displayed solidarity with the struggling patriots of Angola and other African countries. Following its international duty, the Soviet Union, at the request of the PRA, rendered it political and economic aid and assistance for the defense of the Angolan people's achievements against the armed intervention of the South African regime and the actions of its imperialist patrons.[20]

Soviet-Angolan party cooperation and the formulations on Angolan domestic affairs indicated that the Kremlin gave the Neto regime a higher ideological status than Machel in Mozambique. Whereas Machel's visit appeared to set the stage for talks about party ties, during Nascimento's trip it was announced that "a plan of party ties and contacts between the CPSU and MPLA was agreed upon."[21] Although Soviet ideologists did not yet regard the MPLA as a true "vanguard" party, Kosygin declared that he was greeting the Nascimento delegation as representative of the "military vanguard of the Angolan people and their revolutionary-democratic organization," the MPLA.[22] In the same speech, Kosygin credited the Angolan regime with directing the country "along the path of profound socio-economic transformations . . . having as their final aim the builidng of a society on the principles of socialism." Kosygin expressed confidence that because of Angola's resources, the Neto regime, "having chosen the correct road and right methods," would achieve Soviet-approved ends.

In October 1976, the visit to Moscow by Angola's top leader, Agostinho Neto enhanced the consolidation of Soviet relations with Angola in several new and important respects. First and most important, the Soviet Union and Angola signed a treaty of friendship and cooperation. Indicative of the importance Moscow attached to this treaty was that it was the first one of the series to be signed by Brezhnev (earlier such treaties with Egypt, Iraq, India, Somalia, and the later one with

[19]*Pravda,* May 25, 1976.
[20]*Ibid.*
[21]*Pravda,* June 1, 1976.
[22]*Pravda,* May 25, 1976.

Mozambique were signed for the USSR by Podgorny, Kosygin and Gromyko, subsequent pacts with Vietnam, Ethiopia and Afghanistan by Brezhnev, who then had become Soviet President).

The treaty signed on October 8, 1976 by Brezhnev and Neto was almost identical with the one signed by the USSR with Mozambique six months later. It emphasized the struggle against "imperialism," and the need for bloc—Third World unity and cooperation, and it called for further Soviet military aid to Angola, and for closer ties in all other fields. It contained the same article as in the Mozambique treaty on contact between the two sides in case of a threat to peace and spelled out in more detail than its Mozambique counterpart the multilateral and bilateral issues on which the two sides would "regularly exchange opinions."[23] These same themes were reiterated in the joint statement issued at the conclusion of Neto's visit.[24]

Even more than in the case of Mozambique, Moscow has put Angola's treaty into the context of the East-West struggle. Speaking during the ratification process in January 1977, Soviet ideologist Boris Ponomarev said the treaty reflected "common aims in the joint struggle against imperialism." It also reflected, he contended, a "natural law" of the "world revolutionary process" according to which "countries which have achieved political independence and chosen the path of progressive socio-economic development seek to establish multifaceted relations with the Soviet Union and to give them a sound treaty basis."[25]

Unlike Machel, Neto on his visit also criticized the Chinese for their policy in Angola and Africa. At a Kremlin dinner in his honor soon after arrival, he deplored China's "alignment with the forces of imperialism" in Angola and its "naked anti-Sovietism" in Africa. However, he expressed the conviction that China "still has a possibility to free itself of its pseudosocialist society."[26] The failure of the final documents to mention China further suggested that Neto still sought to keep his options open and to avoid excessive involvement in the Sino-Soviet dispute.

[23]For a text of the treaty, see *Pravda,* October 9, 1976
[24]TASS, October 13, 1976.
[25]*Izvestiia,* January 26, 1977.
[26]*Pravda,* October 8, 1976.

Maintaining the trend demonstrated during the Nascimento visit, Moscow continued to give high ideological marks to Angola. Brezhnev, at the Kremlin dinner for Neto, was confident that Angolan people supported "the program of profound socio-economic transformation leading to the liquidation of all exploitation, including that by capitalism, which the MPLA has put forward."[27] The joint statement declared that the "adherence of both parties and governments to the ideals of peace, freedom, international solidarity and socialism were and still are the foundation" of relations between them.

And underscoring Soviet-Angolan ideological affinity, Brezhnev and Neto signed a separate formal agreement on cooperation between the Soviet Communist Party and the MPLA.[28] The agreement called for inter-party contacts "at all levels" to include systematic mutual consultation, contacts between the media and "public organizations" of both countries, and the drawing up annually of plans for party cooperation. The agreement also called for cooperation "in the training of party cadres" and the conduct of "joint research into urgent problems of contemporary social developments," clauses which would appear to give the USSR broad avenues for building a pro-Soviet lobby among the Angolan elite and influencing domestic Angolan policies over the short and long run.

It appears less than coincidental that within days after his return from Moscow, Neto told an Angolan trade union conference that the "immediate task" in Angola was to transform the MPLA into a workers' party to lead Angola to socialism.[29] Shortly afterward, the MPLA Central Committee met to work out the guidelines for this transformation, announcing that a party congress to implement the changes would be held in the second half of 1977. This development was duly reported and praised by Soviet dispatches and articles.[30]

Precisely what role Moscow had in an attempted coup in May 1977 which Neto put down with Cuban aid is far from clear. The leader of the coup, Nito Alves, was considered by many outside observers to

[27]*Ibid.*
[28]TASS, October 13, 1976.
[29]Radio Havana, October 19, 1976.
[30]*Pravda,* October 23 and November 2, 1976; V. Volkov, "Angola: A Year's Independence," *Pravda,* November 11, 1976; Yu. Tsaplin, "The Path of Creation: The People's Republic of Angola Celebrates Its First Anniversary," *Sovetskaia Rossiia,* November 11, 1976.

have close relations with the Soviet Embassy in Luanda. The confession by one of the "splittists", Ruiz Jose Coelho, indicated that one complaint of the rebels was that "the movement was led by right-wing forces, anti-Soviet forces." Furthermore, he said, he and his colleagues felt the MPLA "should be linked to the USSR," presumably more tightly. They were "convinced," he said, "that there was a great deal of anti-Sovietism within the movement and the government."[31]

To judge from Neto's speeches following the coup attempt, the Alves group was pressing for divesting the MPLA of more moderate, less "proletarian" elements, a course which would appear more consistent with Soviet pressure for transformation of the MPLA into a vanguard "workers party." In some respects, the situation was reminiscent of earlier phases in Cuba when a pro-Soviet faction led by Anibal Escalante sought to dominate the Cuban party, only to be purged by Castro. Whether Moscow was directly involved, or whether the people involved took advantage of their ties with Moscow to act independently, is not known. In both instances, however, the Kremlin stuck with the winners, the Soviet press faithfully reporting Neto's version of events,[32] including his denials that either the USSR or Cuba had been involved. A later Soviet commentary claimed that the main pretext for the coup attempt was the charge by its perpetrators that the MPLA leadership was excessively mulatto, an emphasis which would presumably give verisimilitude to claims that the USSR was not involved. The same commentary also charged that the rebels had resorted to "demagogic ultra-left slogans," a charge usually meant to suggest a pro-Chinese orientation.[33]

Whatever the case, the Neto regime satisfied Moscow's views on how to proceed in December 1977 when the MPLA became the MPLA-Party of Labor. Underscoring the importance attached by Moscow to this event, the Soviet delegation to the MPLA Congress was headed by A. P. Kirilenko, Soviet Politburo member and Party Secretary. By contrast, mere Central Committee members headed the Soviet delegations to the FRELIMO Congress in Mozambique and TANU (Tanganyika African National Union) conference in Tanzania

---

[31]Radio Luanda, June 10, 1977.

[32]*Pravda*, May 29, 1977; TASS, May 31, 1977.

[33]A. M. Kazanov, "Angola On a New Path," *The Working Class and the Contemporary World*, No. 5, September-October 1977, p. 145.

earlier in 1977 when they similarly proclaimed the transformation of their organization into vanguard parties.

In his speech to the meeting, Kirilenko called the Congress "the greatest political event in the establishment of a new Angola," in which "at the center of your Congress' attention lies the question of transforming the MPLA into a vanguard party armed with the theory of scientific socialism." According to Kirilenko, "the creation and strengthening of such a party is undoubtedly the most important link in the whole set of problems on strengthening the new power and the country's development along the path of socialist orientation." Kirilenko saw this action as part of an "historic reorientation of the development of a sizeable group of African states" as well as reflecting a situaiton in which "the CPSU and the MPLA have every reason to consider themselves comrades in arms in the joint struggle for the victory of the ideas of peace, national liberation, democracy and scientific socialism."[34]

Neto's speech on this occasion, it should be noted, put Angolan action within a global context familiar to Soviet readers: "Socialism or capitalism? There is no other third way and this, comrades, is what determines our strategy and our revolutionary tactic." Angola, he said, had "opted for socialism" and "this option of ours determines our positions and our relations with the socialist states. They are our natural allies in the struggle for the construction of the socialist society, in the front against imperialism."[35]

As explained by Soviet sources, the creation of a vanguard party marked the shift of the MPLA from the kind of mass movement required in the fight for independence into an elitist organization destined to steer the country into the Soviet version of socialism. This vanguard party, wrote one article, would be guided by "Marxist-Leninist principles of leadership by revolutionary classes" which would unite all representatives of workers, peasants and intelligentsia "who are dedicated to the cause of the proletariat." The current stage is described as a "revolutionary-democratic dictatorship directed against internal and external reaction, creating the conditions for establishment of a dic-

[34]*Pravda,* December 6, 1977
[35]*Granma* (Havana), December 15, 1977.

tatorship of the proletariat at this stage of the construction of socialism."[36]

This same article made clear that the creation of such a party is not a single step, but a "long and complicated process" because of the low state of literacy in Angola, the predominant role still played by the peasantry, and the small number of industrial workers, all this against the background of a continuing civil war, economic difficulties and external threats. Neto also told a Soviet journal that the party-building process "will take up several years."[37]

One of the most striking features of Soviet involvement in Angola (as later in Ethiopia) has been Moscow's willingness to commit itself so deeply to a regime still beset by so many uncertainties and so far from being consolidated. To some degree, of course, it is these very uncertainties which serve Soviet purposes. Insofar as its problems are still military, Angola remains dependent on Soviet and Cuban military support. Like Mozambique, Angola's function as a "front-line" state against Rhodesia and South Africa keeps the focus on Angolan military needs, especially because Angola has been subject to reprisals for its harboring of SWAPO (South West African Peoples' Organization) guerrillas. Even more important, the military dimension has remained central in Angola because of the continued insurgencies in Cabinda and by UNITA forces in Angola proper. These military uncertainties, both external and internal, also provide a continuing rationale for the presence of the Cuban expeditionary force which provides Moscow with an important level to steer Angola in "proper" directions.

Another striking feature in Soviet coverage of Angolan developments has been the constant emphasis on the continuing security problems confronting the Angolan government. During the Soviet-Angolan treaty ratification process, Ponomarev emphasized that this document "acquires all the more significance because at the present time a dangerous hotbed of tension has still not been liquidated in southern Africa, in immediate proximity to Angola, and acts of aggression are frequently undertaken against independent African coun-

---

[36]L. Fituni, "Angola: Struggle and Triumphs," *Aziia i Afrika Segodnia*, No. 4, April 1978, p. 4.

[37]*New Times*, No. 48, November 1978, p. 10.

tries."[38] At a later stage of the same process, Foreign Minister Gromyko declared:

> One cannot but see that the situation in and around Angola remains quite complex. The reason lies in the fact that the imperialists and neocolonialists are not abandoning their attempts to interfere in Angola's internal affairs and are still dreaming of regaining their former dominion in order to continue to plunder and exploit the Angolan people.[39]

These outside forces, Gromyko went on, sought revenge "if not with the aid of military intervention, then by means of intrigues and plots." As a result, the Angolans "must still repulse the provacative attacks of the imperialist forces which are guiding and financing the subversive actions, diversions and sabotage from the counterrevolutionary groups they feed." Accordingly, Gromyko stressed, "the Soviet Union will continue to be on the side of the Angolan patriots. It has rendered and will continue to render the PRA government diverse aid in reinforcing its independence and sovereignty."

When Neto visited the USSR for three days in September 1977, Brezhnev excoriated imperialist sponsorship of "acts of banditry by splitter groups, attempts to kindle in every way conflicts in some countries."[40] However, he gave even more emphasis to the growing conflict in the Horn of Africa which was to involve a transfer of some Cuban troops from Angola to Ethiopia. Brezhnev's statement that "we have fulfilled and will unstintingly fulfill the commitments the Soviet Union has undertaken" under the friendship treaty and economic agreements, suggested an effort to reassure Neto, who appeared to be arguing with the USSR to give priority support to Angola's needs. Angola, Neto told Brezhnev, "is at present at the focus of the events developing in the African continent" which "is now becoming the hottest spot of the struggle between the forces of imperialism and the forces of progress." He said he was "very sorry" about the conflict in Somalia and Ethiopia, but expressed the belief that the "revolutionary spirit" of both would enable them to achieve a peaceful settlement. Meanwhile, he stressed, there was a "growing danger in southern Africa" which threatened "not only the progressive countries of Africa

[38]*Pravda,* January 25, 1977.
[39]*Pravda,* March 15, 1977.
[40]*Pravda,* September 30, 1977.

but also the whole world." This area, by implication, was where he thought the USSR should put its prime efforts.

As subsequent events demonstrated, Neto's appeals failed to divert the USSR from its adventure in the Horn, but Moscow continued to emphasize its commitment to Angola and its recognition of Angola's unresolved security problems. To further implement the friendship treaty, an intergovernmental commission on economic, scientific-technical cooperation and trade was agreed upon during Neto's visit. In his speech to the MPLA Congress, Kirilenko noted that Angola "has many friends on whose support it can rely, but it also has enemies, internal and external."[41] Following the successful Soviet-Cuban intervention against the Somalis in Ethiopia, Neto once more went to Moscow "on vacation." Once more Brezhnev pledged "every kind of support" to Angola and Neto expressed his "profound grati-tude" for Soviet aid in "stengthening the defense potential and eco-nomic development of the PRA."[42]

Throughout 1978 and 1979, Soviet media portrayed an uneasy An-gola still beset by security problems, internally and externally. A two-part series on Angola in Moscow's Afro-Asian journal in late 1978 described allegedly successful operations during March 1978 against UNITA bands infiltrated "with the aid of the South African racists." The author told of captured weapons bearing a "made in China" label. This same article also suggested the existence of an internally gener-ated opposition:

> The people's power also has to encounter the intrigues of internal coun-terrevolution which often resorts to economic sabotage, spreads provoca-tive fabrications and rumors with the aim of destabilizing the situation in the country (incidentally these rumors are picked up readily by Western propaganda).[43]

In July 1979, Angolan Foreign Minister Paolo T. Jorge told the Soviet journal *New Times* that Angola was subject to "increasing ag-gressive attacks" by South Africa which included "constant provoca-tions of various kinds from air raids to the smuggling of small armed groups to create tension in our towns and villages or cause damage to

[41]*Pravda,* December 6, 1977.
[42]*Pravda,* April 20, 1978.
[43]N. Paklin, "Angola: The Step of Revolution," *Aziia i Afrika Segodnia,* No. 10, October 1978, p. 20.

the economy." Apart from this, he said that Angola, "giving preference to ties with socialist countries," had made a "clear political and ideological choice, taking the road of a socialist society."[44]

Havana and Moscow have continuously changed their justifications for the failure of Cuban troops to leave Angola. Since the original explanation for their entry was to help Angola repel a South African invasion, South African withdrawal in March 1976 presumably removed this pretext. And indeed, for a brief period the Cubans sought to give the impression that in fact their mission was completed and they would be withdrawing. In a letter to Swedish Premier Olaf Palme on May 21, 1976, Castro was reported to have said that Cuba had already begun or would shortly begin to withdraw 200 men a week, with the implication that it would continue until the withdrawal was total.[45] An Angolan government spokesman on May 25 declared that "the People's Republic of Angola appealed to Cuba for help against the South African invasion last fall and has now decided that the situation is sufficiently under control that the Cuban troops can withdraw."[46]

Neither Moscow nor Havana mentioned the Castro letter to Palme and it was not long before it became clear that the terminal date for Cuban withdrawal was vague and open-ended. In his first public statement on withdrawal, a speech in Havana on June 6, 1976, Castro said it was "absurd to think that when our fighters left for Angola it was with the idea of remaining indefinitely in the country. They went with the idea of remaining there at Angolan request as long as there was an invader in the territory of the sister state of Angola." Referring presumably to the departure of South African forces, Castro went on to say that "their task having been concluded, under the agreements between the governments of the People's Republic of Angola and Cuba, our military personnel are gradually being withdrawn."[47]

In this same speech, however, Castro supplied the qualifying conditions making possible an indefinite stay in Angola. Bringing up the question of a withdrawal timetable, Castro replied that Cuban troops would stay as long as "strictly necessary to support the Angola people's defense against any foreign aggression while the Angolan

[44]*New Times*, No. 31, July 1979, p. 23.
[45]*New York Times*, May 26 and 28, 1976.
[46]*New York Times*, May 26, 1976.
[47]Radio Havana, June 7, 1976.

People's Army is organized, trained and equipped." He went on to say that the Angolan "people" had requested Cuban aid "when they saw they had been invaded by mercenaries everywhere but mainly by South African troops." Subsequently, however, "we, along with the Soviet Union, are helping to organize the Angolan army" and "we are sure that Angola will have a magnificent and great army which at some time will not require Cuban regular units to defend its country."

Havana sharply attacked a Chinese article which made the point that this formulation provided no timetable for final withdrawal, but once more stated that this withdrawal was being managed so that "when it ends Angola will have military forces, trained, organized and qualified to defend and maintain the national boundaries which are still surrounded by enemies."[48] Castro repeated essentially the same formula in his annual July 26 speech but suggested that the main problem was no longer the threat of external attacks but the actions of "counter-revolutionary groups" like the FNLA and UNITA who, however, he claimed "are totally demoralized and will never rise up again."[49]

When he visited Angola in March 1977, Castro once more said the Cubans would remain as long as "necessary" and envisaged that "the day will come when the Angolan people will not need our military collaboration and will have enough units, tanks, planes, artillery and soldiers to face the imperialist acts of aggression." Moreover, he declared that "what weapons and how many Cubans combatants are going to be in Angola and for how long have been agreed upon by the governments of Angola and Cuba." Moreover, he emphasized that this could not be a subject of negotiations with the "Yankee imperialists."[50]

Since 1977, there have been virtually no further references by either Moscow or Havana about the possibility of Cuban withdrawal. As noted above, continued references to external and internal threats presumably still provide a rationale for the Cuban military presence, although both Moscow and Havana also claim that these threats are well in hand and Angola's main problems are political and economic development. Little is said, moreover, about whether Angolan armed forces are reaching the point where they can take care of Angolan security

---

[48]Editorial, "Escalation of Infamy," *Granma* (Havana), July 6, 1976.
[49]Radio Havana, July 26, 1976.
[50]Radio Havana, March 29, 1977.

needs unaided. Castro in his March 1977 speech in Luanda did acknowledge that the Angolan army "is growing" and said that it was capable, along with "Cuban combatants and arms," of crushing any aggression.

Similarly vague references to the Angolan armed forces have appeared in a few later Soviet commentaries but none of these have linked these references to Cuban withdrawal. Thus a Soviet commentary in October 1978 stated that "in the circumstance of increasing armed attacks and provocations, the people of Angola are increasing their revolutionary vigilance, creating a modern army whose growing might the bandits are feeling on their own skin."[51] And in an interview with *New Times* in July 1978, Angolan Foreign Minister Jorge described "increasing aggression" against Angola from its neighbors which "compels us to pay serious attention to the strengthening of our defense potential,"[52] presumably therefore insufficient.

The death of Agostinho Neto in September 1979 (perhaps fittingly in Moscow) marked the third and most important test in the Soviet campaign to establish relationships with socialist-oriented states aimed to outlive any specific leader. The assassination of M. Ngouabi of the Congo in April 1977 and the death of H. Boumedienne of Algeria in December 1978 provided the first two, though they involved countries where Soviet leverage was less than in Angola. The transition in all three instances appears to have been made without a ripple as far as the USSR was concerned.

Scarcely three months after Neto's death, his successor, Jose Eduardo dos Santos headed a large delegation to Moscow where the main lines of the relationship worked out between the USSR and Neto were reaffirmed and strengthened. Dos Santos in his major public speech on December 21, 1979 as carried in all Soviet papers the next day, spelled out two major elements of that relationship. First, he noted, his visit would give "greater dynamism" to bilateral relations, especially in broader economic ties which he called a "vital necessity" for Angola. Accordingly, during his visit a series of agreements were signed covering economic and technical cooperation, Soviet geology and mining

---

[51]Palkin, "Angola: The Step of Revolution," p. 20.
[52]*New Times*, No. 31, July 1979, p. 23.

aid, telecommunications, exchange of books, and Soviet construction of a satellite observation station.

Of particular satisfaction to Moscow was dos Santos' affirmation that Angola would not turn inward but do its international duty in furthering the communist cause in southern Africa. Dos Santos in his December 21 speech thanked the Soviet Union and "Cuba's heroic internationalists" for their contribution to Angola's victory and pledged that "despite tremendous sacrifices, the People's Republic of Angola will not give up assisting oppressed peoples," especially in southern Africa. Gromyko in his speech on the same occasion said that Brezhnev was "satisfied" with "very substantial" results of dos Santos' trip and declared that Angola had achieved a "worthy place in the ranks of the independent progressive countries of the world."

The joint statement concluding dos Santos' mission which was carried by the Soviet press on December 24, 1979 declared that the Soviet side "evaluated highly the internationalist support which Angola gives to the cause of liberating Namibia and achieving the full independence of the peoples of the African continent." It also proclaimed Soviet support for "the Angolan state's legitimate right to use all means to defend its territory against aggression by the South African racist regime," a formulation justifying not only past Cuban involvement but the continued presence of Cuban forces in Angola. The joint statement reaffirmed that both sides supported the "cause of liberation" of Namibia, Zimbabwe and the Republic of South Africa and declared "their solidarity with the struggle being waged in the Republic of South Africa under the leadership of the African National Congress to liquidate the shameful apartheid system."

Ethiopia: Reliance on the Military Component

The same general process of Soviet consolidation which took place in Angola and Mozambique was repeated in Ethiopia despite the significantly different situation in that country. Moscow did not have the head start in Ethiopia of aiding Mengistu to come to power. Moreover, the domestic situation within the group that had overthrown Haile Selassie was so chaotic that any Soviet involvement may have been constrained. For a time, Moscow may also have been uncertain about the new Ethiopian regime's attitude to the United States especially in view of Carter Administration efforts to preserve previous U.S. positions in Ethiopia. However, after Mengistu emerged as the number one leader in February 1977 and took a strongly anti-U.S. position, highlighted in the spring of 1977 by the expulsion of U.S. cultural and military missions and the closing down of the U.S. base at Kagnew, Moscow obviously felt the time propitious for and the Ethiopians receptive to an increased Soviet presence.

The highlight of this phase was Mengistu's visit to the USSR from May 4–8, 1977. In his major speech, Mengistu was enthusiastic in his praise of the Soviet Union and its world significance in the "global struggle between imperialism and working class revolution,"[53] Mengistu attacked "reactionary Arab ruling classes" for their support of Eritrean separatists and charged that "the guardian, coordinator and leader of these reactionary forces is the sworn enemy of the oppressed peoples—imperialism, especially U.S. imperialism." Podgorny, in his speech on the same occasion, said that "the national democratic revolution in Ethiopia opened up new opportunities for developing relations between our countries on a still stronger and broader foundation." He called this trend "only natural, for the countries of victorious socialism and the forces of national liberation are natural and reliable allies in the anti-imperialist struggle."[54]

The documents concluding the visit were designed to solidify the growing relationship between Moscow and the Mengistu regime. On the practical side, a protocol on economic and technical cooperation, a cultural convention, and an agreement on cultural and scientific cooperation were signed; but more important were the political documents—the joint communique and a declaration on bilateral relations. According to the joint communique, "the sides were gratified to note that the talks were held at a time of considerable development of Soviet-Ethiopian relations" made possible by "the progressive transformations and changes in Ethiopia [which] created new opportunities for the emergence of a new quality in Soviet-Ethiopian relationships."[55] The communique denounced "the imperialist powers and the

[53]*Izvestiia*, May 6, 1977.
[54]*Ibid*.
[55]*Pravda*, May 7, 1977.

racist regimes" for their policies in southern Africa and set forth Soviet-Ethiopian agreement on a variety of other issues. The declaration proclaimed the intention of both sides to strengthen political and economic relations and "cooperate with each other and with other peaceful states in supporting the just struggle of peoples for sovereignty, freedom, independence and social progress."[56]

The declaration also provided that the two sides "will strive to have regular exchanges of opinion" on bilateral and international issues, less than the mutual commitment to hold such exchanges in the Soviet-Angolan declaration and reflecting constraints then still operating on the USSR because of its continued relationship at the time with Ethiopia's arch rival, Somalia. In this connection also, neither Podgorny's speech nor the final documents mentioned or even hinted at the possibilitiy of Soviet military aid to Ethiopia.

Moreover, although the Mengistu regime referred to itself as "socialist Ethiopia," Soviet spokesmen remained cautious about the status of Ethiopia's ideological development. During his audience for Mengistu, Brezhnev was reported to have congratulated the Ethiopian leadership and people for their "reconstruction of the old, historically outlived order, the consolidation of their independence and the creation of necessary conditions for building a new society."[57] In his banquet speech, Podgorny welcomed Ethiopia's statement of socialist goals but warned that "from the experience of our revolution we know that winning power is but the beginning of a long and difficult road."[58] In the final communique, the Soviet side welcomed the "progressive transformations" in Ethiopia while the Ethiopians were said to be determined "to defend the gains of their revolution" and to pursue an "anti-imperialist and anti-colonialist" foreign polciy.[59]

During the next several months, Soviet commentaries welcomed the closer ties with Ethiopia but also emphasized the continued uncertainties facing the Mengistu regime. An article in the journal of the ideologically significant Institute of the International Workers' Movement made it quite clear that Soviet attitudes toward Ethiopia hinged on the extent to which the Mengistu regime was willing to tie itself to the

[56]*Ibid.*
[57]*Pravda*, May 7, 1977.
[58]*Izvestiia*, May 6, 1977.
[59]*Pravda*, May 9, 1977.

Soviets. Citing a statement by Mengistu that the Ethiopian revolution was going from the defensive to the offensive, the article commented:

> The ability of Ethiopian revolutionary democrats to come out as the leading force of social progress depends on the link of the Ethiopian revolution with other, socially more mature detachments of the world revolutionary process, exerting a profound influence on its contents and perspectives. This is not simply a question of Ethiopia's foreign relations, but a question of the degree to which the progressive forces of Ethiopia, relying on world socialism, enriching themselves with its theory and practice, uses the unfolding international situation in the interests of further revolutionary struggle.[60]

Explaining that what it had in mind was the ability of the Soviet camp to "paralyze" imperialist intervention, the article asserted that "this is why the support which friendly countries and in the first place the countries of the socialist community rendered it has important significance for the further fortunes of the Ethiopian revolution."

As events later showed, the Ethiopians proved more than willing to rely on the support of the "socialist community" which in turn, was more than willing to render that aid even at the expense of a hitherto strong Soviet position in Somalia. Following the Soviet-Cuban intervention and repulse of the Somali invasion of Ethiopia between November 1977 and February 1978, the process of consolidating the Soviet position in Ethiopia went into its next phase, highlighted by Mengistu's second visit to the USSR in April 1978. By this time, Soviet sources were putting Ethiopia in the main stream of Soviet-type revolutions, one of them stating, for example, that the "development and character of events in Ethiopia in one or another measure recalls at times individual features of the three Russian revolutions."[61]

The joint communique concluding Mengistu's three-day "working" visit to the USSR in April 1978 recalled that agreement had been reached on extending ties between state and public organizations, on creating a Soviet-Ethiopian intergovernmental commission on economic, scientific and technical cooperation, on trade, and on holding regular consultations on international questions. A few weeks later,

---

[60] A. G. Kokiev, "Socio-Economic Reforms in Ethiopia and the Workers' Situation," *The Working Class and The Contemporary World,* No. 4, July-August 1977, pp. 82–83.

[61] G. Galperin, "The Revolution in Ethiopia: Peculiarities of Development," *Aziia i Afrika Segodnia,* No. 3, March 1978, p. 9.

Mengistu also visited Cuba. And five months later (September 10–20) a Soviet delegation led by candidate Politburo member V. V. Kuznetsov attended festivities in honor of the fourth anniversary of the Ethiopian revolution where, according to the final communique, "the Soviet delegation affirmed that the USSR considers the Ethiopian revolution an integral part of the word revolutionary process."[62] Further agreements were concluded on economic and technical cooperation and on the establishment of an intergovernmental commission. In addition to the standard roster of international issues on which agreement was proclaimed (southern Africa, Near East, disarmament), the communique lined up Ethiopia more strongly then ever before in condemnation of the "expansionist policy and the hegemonist stand pursued by the Chinese leadership."

Simultaneously with Kuznetsov's visit, Fidel Castro also came to Addis Ababa not only to participate in the anniversary festivities but to become the star attraction at a "conference of solidarity of the African-Arab peoples against imperialism and reaction." In addition to being a kind of victory celebration for the Cuban-Ethiopian duo and an inspection trip for Castro, it also marked an effort by the communist world to take advantage of Addis Ababa's central position in Africa as the site of the OAU.

In November 1978, the USSR went through the last preliminary phase of its consolidation process by concluding a treaty of friendship and cooperation with Ethiopia. Brezhnev on behalf of the USSR signed the treaty, which was the high-water mark of Mengistu's third visit to the USSR. Like the USSR's other treaties, this one formalized the commitment of both parties to strengthen relations in all fields, called for consultations on international questions and contact "with a view to coordinating their positions" in case of a threat to or breach of international peace (Article 7).[63]

As in the case of Angola and Mozambique the military component remained the major element in the cementing of Soviet-Ethiopian relations. Unlike previous Soviet-Ethiopian documents, the treaty was explicit about military cooperation between the two countries, Article 10 providing that such cooperation would continue. For Moscow, the main rationale for this aid was the continuing threat to Ethiopia from

[62]*Pravda,* September 21, 1978.
[63]*Pravda,* November 21, 1978.

Somalia. "We know," Brezhnev told Mengistu "that the situation in the Horn of Africa still remains complicated" and that "imperialist circles are using the tension persisting there to serve their own purposes."[64] At the time of the treaty's ratification in February 1979, USSR deputy Foreign Minister N. P. Firyubin said the document "assumes particular importance as a factor for stability and peace in the Horn of Africa where a political settlement has still not been reached and imperialist and reactionary circles are continuing their provocative, subversive actions against progressive forces."[65]

The joint communique, however, also implied an offensive thrust to Soviet-Ethiopian cooperation, stating that the treaty would serve not only as a "firm foundation" for relations in general but for the "strengthening of their solidarity in the joint struggle against imperialism and colonialism."[66] Mengistu, in his major speech during the visit, linked Soviet aid generally to "an internal and external offensive coordinated by imperialism" against Ethiopia and foresaw the day when his country "will make its internationalist contribution and become a reliable bulwark for the Asian, African and Latin American countries fighting oppression and exploitation. Proletarian internationalism is the basis of our revolution and of the international progressive forces' struggle and we will implement it consistently."[67]

Mengistu's aspirations to play a wider international role have been articulated with increasing frequency especially since the Afro-Asian conference in September 1978 which may, in part, have been a Soviet effort to satisfy these aspirations. As he did two months later in Brezhnev's presence, Mengistu in his speech to the conference also expressed a desire to have Ethiopians play an "international" role like his friend Castro. Thanking the Soviet Union and Cuba for their aid to Ethiopia, Mengistu declared: "Cuba is an example of struggle of oppressed masses. We solemnly pledge to pay our debts, through resolute proletarian internationalism for the help extended to us."[68] When Castro visited an Ethiopian air base, the Ethiopian Air Force Commander, Col. Fanta Belay, expressed gratitude for Cuban "combat support"

[64]*Pravda*, November 18, 1978.
[65]*Izvestiia*, February 8, 1979.
[66]*Pravda*, November 21, 1979.
[67]*Pravda*, November 18, 1979.
[68]Radio Addis Ababa, September 12, 1978.

and declared that "we intend to follow their path and be ever more ready to defend other revolutions in other places in like manner."[69]

Throughout 1979, Mengistu continued to suggest his desire to emulate Cuba. On May Day, he stated that although Ethiopia still needed outside aid, "we must be internationalists capable of helping the oppressed people of the world struggling for independence and be capable of discharging our internationalist obligations."[70] On June 29, he was more specific, declaring that "efforts are being made to look into the possibility of the Ethiopian people discharging their own internationalist obligation by giving what support they can to the liberation fronts in southern Africa."[71] In September 1979, Raul Castro, during a visit to Ethiopia, suggested a joint "internationalist obligation to those who are suffering under colonialism, imperialism, fascism and Maoism."[72] On the practical level, what all this appeared to mean as of the close of 1979 was that Ethiopia was providing the site and possibly participating in the training, under Soviet and Cuban tutelage, of Rhodesian guerrillas. However, the suggestion is there of Soviet development of new proxies for intervention in Africa and elsewhere.

The Eritrean Problem

While anxious to exploit the role played by Soviet and Cuban military aid in Ethiopia's struggle against Somalia, both Moscow and Havana have carefully avoided any suggestion that they might become directly involved in Ethiopia's campaign against Eritrean nationalist rebels. Two specific elements of the Eritrean situation have complicated matters for the two communist states. First, as in the case of Somalia, support for the central government marks a shift from the support, especially by Cuba, for the Eritrean secession movement when its opponent had been the government of Haile Selassie. Secondly, Moscow in particular has had to tread softly on the Eritrean issue because of the support for the Eritreans by significant parts of the Arab world, including countries such as Libya and Iraq who themselves have been the subject of Soviet wooing.

[69]Paris, AFP, September 16, 1978.
[70]Radio Addis Ababa, May 1, 1979.
[71]Radio Addis Ababa, June 29, 1979.
[72]Radio Addis Ababa, September 3, 1979.

In the immediate postwar period, the USSR strongly championed Eritrian independence during U.N. consideration of the future of all the former Italian colonies (Libya, Somaliland and Eritrea). In 1949, Andrei Gromyko, then the USSR's U.N. representative, proposed that a U.N. trusteeship be established over the three areas under a Trusteeship Council Administration and an advisory committee on which the USSR would be included. He also proposed that the Security Council designate and set aside strategic areas in Eritrea for international security purposes.[73] In the following year, the USSR modified its proposal on Eritrea calling for immediate independence, British withdrawal within three months and the cession of enough of Eritrea to give Ethiopia an outlet to the sea through the port of Assab.

In support of their positions, Soviet representative Arutiunian argued in 1950 that, contrary to Western and Ethiopian contentions, "it was an undeniable fact a national consciousness did exist among the Eritrean people and that it was constantly growing."[74] He also contended that "a large part of the population opposed federation."[75] Accordingly, the Soviet bloc voted against the General Assembly resolution in 1950 which approved Eritrean incorporation into Ethiopia as an autonomous unit.

In the years that followed, Moscow was quiescent on the question, especially following the death of Stalin when both the Khrushchev and Brezhnev regimes sought to establish good relations with Haile Selassie and to support OAU views opposing movements aiming to dismember entities formed during the colonial period. Nevertheless, during the sixties, the Soviets and Cubans covertly supported Eritrean secessionist movements with arms and training. As Cuban leader Carlos Rafael Rodriguez told the London *Observer* in 1978, "We helped the Eritreans in their fight for self-determination from the time of Haile Selassie onward."[76]

As relations improved between the USSR and the post-Selassie regime, Moscow increasingly supported the idea of political solution of

---

[73]United Nations, *Official Records of the Third Session of the General Assembly, Part II,* First Committee, Summary Record of Meetings, 5 April–13 May, 1949, pp. 23–24.

[74]United Nations, *Official Records of the Fifth Session of the General Assembly,* Ad Hoc Political Committee, October-November 1950, p. 221.

[75]*Ibid.,* p. 335.

[76]*Observer* (London), February 26, 1978.

the Eritrean issue. The Soviet media gave enthusiastic approval to Ethiopian government offers in April-May 1976 to negotiate with Eritrean "progressive groups and organizations" on a peaceful settlement based on autonomy for Eritrea.[77] The joint communique following the first major visit to the USSR by an Ethiopian official, Capt. Moges Wolde-Michael, in July 1976 reported that the Ethiopian delegation had informed the Soviets "of the actions taken by the government to get a peaceful settlement of the Eritrean problem"[78] but made no references to a Soviet response. Nor did Soviet accounts of a Kosygin audience or Gromyko banquet contain any allusions, even indirect ones, to the Eritrean problem.

This comparative reticence probably stemmed from Soviet realization of the complexities of the Eritrean issue. A major Soviet article on Ethiopia in early 1977 noted the "great difficulties" confronting the Ethiopian government on the question which it attributed to the policy of "forced Amharization" conducted by the Haile Selassie regime. According to the article, "under the monarchic regime repressions had been constantly conducted there, giving rise to the movement for the separation of Eritrea." The new government was said to be "making efforts to settle this serious conflict, which has become detrimental to the country's unity, by peaceful means," but despite some "positive results," the article concluded, "a final settlement of the conflict in Eritrea has not been achieved."[79]

During Mengistu's first visit to the Soviet Union in May 1977, Soviet support for his Eritrean policies was considerably more forthright. Speaking at a dinner in Mengistu's honor, then President Podgorny remarked that "we regard with understanding the intention of the PMAC (Provisional Military Administrative Council) to resolve this question on a democratic basis,"[80] while the final communique proclaimed Soviet support for PMAC moves "for the democratic solution of national problems."[81] Moscow carried Mengistu's banquet speech which charged that "imperialism and reactionary Arab ruling classes,

[77]See, for example, *Pravda,* May 22, 1976; Radio Moscow, May 23, 1976.
[78]*Pravda,* July 14, 1976.
[79]V. Korovikov, "A New Life Comes to Ethiopia," *International Affairs,* No. 3, March 1977, pp. 132–133.
[80]*Pravda,* May 6, 1977.
[81]*Pravda,* May 10, 1977.

in particular, the ruling class of the Sudan, having united the reactionary separatist elements of Eritrea, are now waging armed aggression more intensively than ever against our country in the hope of wrenching Eritrea from Ethiopia and establishing full strategic control over the Red Sea."[82] Soviet spokesmen, however, did not talk about the Sudan's role, while Podgorny blamed Saudi Arabia "first of all" for "imperialist" efforts to control the Red Sea, the difference presumably attributable to renewed Soviet efforts to improve relations with the Sudan at the time and a calculation that support for Eritrean separatism by more radical Arab states might be weakened if it were identified with Saudi Arabia.

Necessarily subordinate to the Ethiopian-Somali conflict in late 1977 and early 1978, the Eritrean conflict appears to have become a major bone of contention between Ethiopia and its Soviet-Cuban allies. Buoyed by the defeat of Somalia and the clearing of the Ogaden front, Mengistu evidently hoped for maximum Soviet-Cuban participation in Eritrea. Both Moscow and Havana appeared to reemphasize the need for a political solution. Carlos Rafael Rodriguez in February told the London *Observer* that Mengistu had no authority to use Cuban "specialists" to put down the Eritrean rebellion; "there have got to be talks between the Eritreans and the central government."[83]

As later revealed by various Ethiopian officials, the Soviet bloc made an intensive effort during this period to negotiate a settlement of the Eritrean question. Mengistu on June 6, 1978 in announcing the opening of a new military campaign against Eritrean rebels, reported that "we have made a number of attempts to open the door, through some socialist countries, for negotiations."[84] He also disclosed that Ethiopian delegations had fanned out first to the Sudan, Lebanon, Syria, Iraq and Egypt, then to Libya, Algeria, Saudi Arabia, Kuwait and North and South Yemen to plead the Ethiopian case.

Another Ethiopian offical, Major Berhan Baye, member of the PMAC in charge of foreign affairs, a few days later implied that the Arab visits came somewhat earlier and also that the USSR, Cuba, the GDR, the PDRY, Libya and the Palestine Liberation Organization had all tried to bring the parties together but failed "due to the arrogance,

[82]*Parvda,* May 6, 1977.
[83]*Observer* (London), February 26, 1978.
[84]Radio Addis Ababa, June 7, 1978.

narrow nationalism and unacceptable demands" of the Eritrean movements which thereby "revealed to the progressive world" their "reactionary character."[85] In another talk, Baye specified that the Yemeni effort had taken place in 1975, the Cuban in 1976 and the Libyan in early 1978. He then disclosed that an Ethiopian delegation and leaders of one Eritrean organization (the Eritrean People's Liberation Front) had met in Berlin under East German auspices on February 1, March 22 and June 11, 1978—again to no avail.[86]

In addition, Western sources were also claiming that the USSR had gotten into the act. An Arabic-language journal in Paris reported that Soviet officials had met Ethiopian and Eritrean officials in Paris, presumably in May 1978,[87] while Reuters cited African sources to the effect that Ahmed Nasser of the Eritrean Liberation Front Revolutionary Council had gone to Moscow from Algiers in the second week of June.[88]

Whatever the truth of these reports, there can be little doubt that the Eritrean issue was high on the agenda when Mengistu in April 1978 went to both the USSR and Cuba. According to the communique concluding Mengistu's "working visit" to Moscow, the Ethiopians informed the USSR of their struggle "to defend the revolutionary gains and territorial integrity of their motherland," a phrase applicable both to the Ogaden and to Eritrean problems.[89] The Eritrean issue came out even more pointedly during Mengistu's Cuban visit. In his speech at the inevitable rally, Castro compared the issue to the U.S. Civil War and said that Cuba advocated "just political solutions, based on Leninist principles, to the problem of nationalities within a revolutionary Ethiopian state, which preserves as an irrevocable right its unity, its absolute integrity and sovereignty."[90] Mengistu, by contrast, appeared to make a bid for more direct Cuban involvement in Eritrea. Stressing that "numerous reactionary forces" from outside the country were involved on the Eritrean side, Mengistu said Ethiopians know "that in their struggle against the current danger they can count on

[85]Radio Addis Ababa, June 22, 1978.
[86]Radio Addis Ababa, June 26, 1978.
[87]*An-Nahar Al-Arabi Wa Ad-Dawli* (Paris), May 27, 1978.
[88]London, Reuters, June 22, 1978.
[89]*Pravda*, April 7, 1978.
[90]Radio Havana, April 26, 1978.

internationalist support" and specifically that "the Cuban masses will be alongside us"[91] in an intensified drive against the Eritrean rebels.

Later events suggested that the compromise reached called for Ethiopia to continue its efforts to achieve a political settlement along with Soviet and Cuban logistic aid for an intensified Ethiopian military effort against the Eritrean rebels. Shortly before the new offensive, the Cubans appeared to make a special effort to let it be known that they did not intend to become directly involved. Thus Osman Saleh Sabbe, one of the leaders of a group which according to Sabbe had "long-standing relations" with Cuba, told a London interviewer that Castro had informed both Dr. George Habash of the Popular Front for the Liberation of Palestine and Libyan leader Kaddafi that Cuba would not become militarily involved in Eritrea.[92] Sabbe speculated that Castro did not want to get involved in a long drawn-out war and was responding to pressures from Arab countries. At the same time, Cuban forces, by holding positions elsewhere in Ethiopia, freed Mengistu's forces for operations in Eritrea, and Soviet-Cuban involvement continued in the form of training and arms supplies.

Soviet uncertainties may well have been reflected in an unusual Hungarian Radio commentary on August 11, 1978 which took the position that both sides were to blame for a lack of a settlement in Eritrea. On the one hand, the commentator declared, "the group of progressive officers in Addis Ababa was too late in offering peace and a wide measure of the right of self-determination to Eritrea." On the other hand, the Eritreans were faulted for continuing their struggle which "with the support of the Arab countries became harmful from an historical perspective." Crediting the Eritrean forces with control of over 90 percent of the province when Ethiopian forces were diverted to the Ogaden, the Hungarian claimed the Ethiopian offensive begun in June had achieved significant successes. However, he concluded, "even in the event of the complete victory of the Ethiopian Army the bloodshed that has been going on in Eritrea for a decade and a half will not suddenly come to an end."

Nevertheless, both Moscow and Havana by the fall of 1978 appeared to believe that a turning point had been reached on the Eritrean issue enabling a change in focus by Ethiopia from security to economic

[91]*Ibid.*
[92]*Ad-Dastur* (London), 12–18 June 1978.

reconstruction and long-range political consolidation. The presence in September 1978 of Castro and candidate Politburo Member V. V. Kuznetsov at festivities in honor of the fourth anniversary of the Ethiopian revolution, as well as the holding of an African-Arab solidarity conference in Addis Ababa, both reflected this increasing confidence in the Ethiopian regime. Brezhnev and Kosygin, in a message to Mengistu on September 11, said the USSR viewed "with pleasure" Ethiopian successes in maintaining their independence and territorial integrity.[93] Mengistu proclaimed that the "oppressed people of the Eritrean Administrative Region are being liberated and they have started breathing the air of peace."[94] Castro in his speech expressed "certainty that the leaders of Ethiopia will find just, revolutionary and Marxist-Leninist solutions to their problems" and that they would - "maintain the territorial unity of Ethiopia."[95] The final communique reported that the Cuban side had expressed "unswerving support for the revolutionary measures taken to strengthen the revolution and territorial integrity of socialist Ethiopia" and "reaffirmed its absolute opposition to any kind of secession."[96] The conclusion of a number of economic agreements during the Castro and Kuznetsov visits was clearly designed to reflect the favorable trends seen in Ethiopia.

Two months later, Mengistu came to the Soviet Union to sign the treaty of friendship, epitomizing Moscow's confidence in the Mengistu regime. Brezhnev was almost categoric in his statement that Ethiopia's military trials were over. He said that the Ethiopian people had "courageously repulsed foreign invasions and upheld the gains of the revolution and the territorial integrity of their homeland" and were now "faced with the immense tasks of peaceful construction."[97] Mengistu, presumably still wanting a high level of Soviet military aid, emphasized that operations were still going on in Eritrea in which "imperialism and the region's reactionary states are weaving a conspiracy, utilizing groups of renegades for their own purposes."[98]

By the Ethiopian regime's fifth anniversary in September 1979, both parties exuded equal amounts of confidence on the state of affairs in

[93]*Pravda,* September 12, 1978.
[94]Radio Addis Ababa, September 12, 1978.
[95]Radio Addis Ababa, September 14, 1978.
[96]Radio Addis Ababa, September 21, 1978.
[97]*Pravda,* November 18, 1978.
[98]*Ibid.*

Eritrea. Mengistu told a press conference that "great and encouraging improvements have been noted in the current Eritrean situation as opposed to the situation that has existed since the problem started."[99] *Za Rubezhom* portrayed continuing military actions in Eritrea virtually as mopping up operations against "remnants of the separatist groupings."[100] Neither the visiting Kosygin nor Mengistu mentioned the issue even indirectly, focusing instead on other political and economic problems that lay ahead.

There were other subtleties during 1979 which also reflected growing Soviet satisfaction with the course of events in Eritrea. For one thing, Soviet commentaries began to emphasize the alleged Chinese role in Eritrea both to add to the list of Chinese misdeeds and to Chinese setbacks. Thus a Soviet military journal in January 1979 juxtaposed claims that Chinese military instructors were active in Eritrea with accounts of Ethiopian military successes especially in connection with the capture of the Eritrean stronghold of Keren.[101]

In addition, Soviet analysts began to spell out more openly the change in Moscow's line on the Eritrean issue. In a notable instance, *New Times* engaged in a polemic with a Moroccan journalist who had evidently taunted the Soviets on their change in position. What may have irked the Soviets in particular was that the Moroccan was reacting to an article which had evidently been carried only in the Russian-language edition of the journal and had been omitted in other language editions (a relatively rare occurrence, it might be noted).[102]

The Soviet demurral, in addition to denying that the USSR had ever favored "the separation of Eritrea and dismemberment of Ethiopia," reaffirmed the Russian version of the article, which spelled out two essential elements in the current Soviet position. Putting Eritrea in quotation marks, it declared (contrary to Moscow's postwar position in the U.N.) that " 'Eritrea' is not a national concept; it is a purely geographical and administrative concept developed by the Italian col-

[99]Radio Addis Ababa, September 19, 1979.

[100]Vadim Lobachenko, "Ethiopia Five Years After the Fall of the Monarch," *Za Rubezhom,* 7–13 September 1979, p. 13.

[101]Yu. Irkhin, "Ethiopia on the Path of Socialist Orientation," *Kommunist Vooruzhennikh Sil,* No. 2, January 1979, p. 84.

[102]The initial article is by G. Galperin, "The Eritrean Problem—Facts and Fabrications," *Novoye Vremia,* No. 5, January 1979, pp. 26–28; the second by G. Tanov, "At Odds With Logic," *New Times,* No. 8, February 1979, p. 14.

onialists.'' Further, the population of the area is a conglomeration of numerous nationalities and races. The article cited as authority the *Encyclopedia Britannica* (1976 edition) to bolster the current Soviet case.

The second argument, cited as ''perhaps the main point,'' posed the question, ''self-determination and secession for what reason, in the interests of what classes, social groups and political forces?'' In other words, self-determination against a capitalist state is legitimate but not so against a communist or pro-Soviet state. Applying this to Ethiopia, *Novoye Vremia* declared:

> The question today is as follows: either a historically established state splits up and numerous ''emirates'' and ''republics'' dependent on imperialism form in its place, or a socialist-oriented multinational state is strengthened.

The *New Times* rejoinder to the Moroccans put the issue even more succinctly: ''Can the struggle against British colonialism and imperial satraps be equated with subversive activity against the popular revolution, the working people and their social gains?''

The fact that most of the Eritrean secessionist groups profess to be Marxist or Leninist was dismissed by *Novoye Vremia* with the charge that they have degenerated: ''Under the conditions of the Ethiopian people's heroic struggle to strengthen their revolutionary gains, Eritrean separatism, originally an objectively progressive—anti-feudal and antimonarchy—movement, turned into an elitist, narrowly nationalist current.''

The same point was made even more sharply by the same author, G. Galperin, in a later article which said that the Leninist thesis that self-determination is subordinate to communist ends explains ''the progressive direction of the Eritrean movement in conditions of national oppression under the feudal-monarchist regime and its reactionary degeneration in the period of the Ethiopian revolution.''[103] Galperin conceded that the Eritreans might with some justification consider the first phase of the Ethiopian revolution as no more than a conventional military coup and their opposition therefore presumably justified. However, he argues, they should have recognized the merits of the reforms undertaken by the Mengistu regime and rallied behind it.

---

[103]G. Galperin, ''Ethiopia: Certain Aspects of The National Question,'' *Aziia i Afrika Segodnia,* No. 8, August 1979, pp. 23–26.

At the same time, this article was notable for its sober appraisal of the whole complex of national, tribal and religious issues lying ahead for the Mengistu regime. Galperin stated that "the factors making up a nation have not yet achieved sufficient development" and the "ethno-centrifugal forces" in Ethiopia, although localized mainly in the Ogaden and Eritrea, are still "extremely significant." Moreover, he noted, in addition to local nationalism, one must take into account "an opposite tendency, the long time cultivated chauvinist strivings of the Amhara, their intolerance toward certain small peoples," above all in Eritrea. While praising efforts of the new regime to correct these tendencies, Galperin said the "leadership and revolutionary aktiv of Ethiopia nourishes no illusions about an easy solution of the national question. The process is long and extremely complicated and painful."

Galperin sees many similarities between Ethiopia and the Soviet Union in its early years and says the USSR serves as a model for the future Ethiopia which he envisages combining political and economic centralization with grants of regional autonomy based as much as possible on ethnic grounds. There is even a hint of an eventual larger entity based on the same principles and encompassing the entire African Horn, presumably including Somalia and Djibouti. Thus, Galperin notes that Ethiopia comprises 83 percent of the population of the Horn and that its solution of the national question "cannot with time fail to influence the ethno-political problems of this entire troubled region, cannot fail to facilitate the liquidation there of the still very dangerous source of tension." What he may have in mind is the kind of solution Castro proposed in March 1977, a federation of Ethiopia, Eritrea, Somalia, and Yemen.

Following Ethiopian military successes, Moscow may have encouraged one more serious effort by Sudanese President Nimery at a negotiated settlement in Eritrea. In February 1979 under OAU auspices, Nimery and Mengistu met in Freetown, Sierra Leone on the Eritrean issue. Following his return from what proved to be an unsuccessful effort, Nimery said, "I had in mind the support I received from the Soviet Union"[104] for reaching a peaceful settlement. It should be noted that this support accorded with the improvement of Soviet-Sudanese relations following the low point of June 1977 when the

---

[104]Radio Addis Ababa, February 26, 1979.

Sudan expelled Soviet military advisers, reduced the Soviet Embassy staff, and closed down a Soviet cultural center. Throughout the rest of 1977 Soviet propaganda accused the Sudan of malevolent intentions toward Ethiopia. In May 1978, however, the Soviet Ambassador to the Sudan returned after a year's absence, and during the next year relations between the Sudan and the USSR (as well as the latter's clients) began to improve. On September 2, 1978, for example, TASS and the Sudan News Agency signed a formal agreement on exchange of information. In June, Cuba and the Sudan established diplomatic relations. The Mengistu-Nimery meeting in Freetown fitted into this same pattern; despite its failure, relations between Ethiopia and the Sudan do not appear to have deteriorated greatly. Soviet-Sudanese relations seemed to go into a holding pattern not only because of the Sudan's continued nervousness about the Soviet-Cuban presence in Ethiopia, but because of rising tensions between the Sudan and radical Arab regimes, notably Iraq, over the Sudan's support of the Camp David accords between Egypt and Israel.

Pressure for a Vanguard Party

Meanwhile, a key element in Moscow's solution for the Eritrean and other Ethiopian problems is the creation of a Soviet-type party transcending all nationalities. According to Galperin, "it is understood in Ethiopia that the complete effective solution of the national question is impossible without the organizing, guiding activity of a vanguard party of scientific socialism" which he saw as near to formation. "Only such a party," he went on, "a party of internationalists, free of nationalist limitations, localism, armed with an advanced theory is up to a really socialist solution of the national question . . . . Only it is capable of consistently, creatively taking account of local conditions to transfer onto Ethiopian soil the tremendous experience of solving the national question in the countries of socialism, especially in the USSR."

Moscow, in fact, has been exerting pressure on the Ethiopian regime since the beginning of their relationship to create such a "vanguard party." Dickering on this question may have taken place well before Mengistu took over completely. According to Castro, the Cubans had been a contact with Mengistu even before the creation of the revolution and the Ethiopian state in February 1977. "From very early when you were not yet Chief of State, fraternal relations were established between you, as a genuine representative of the Ethiopian revolution and the Cuban revolution."[105] One may assume that Moscow also had established "fraternal relations" with Mengistu in the earlier period.

Mengistu's emphasis since 1976 on his intention to form a vanguard party has appeared as part of his bargaining for Soviet support. As early as April 1976, the PMAC announced in a proclamation of its plans for the future of Ethiopia that the government would give "special support" to groups and individuals "who make efforts to establish a workers' party built on the ideology of socialism."[106] Shortly afterward a Provisional Bureau for the Organization of the Masses and an Ideological School were established. The first major Ethiopian delegation to visit the USSR in July 1976, while ostensibly a governmental delegation, had also been received at the Central Committee of the Soviet Communist Party where, it may be presumed, the question of a vanguard party was thoroughly aired.[207] In the first article by a member of the Ethiopian junta to appear in the international communist journal *World Marxist Review,* the author Berhan Baye (sometimes spelled Bayith, Bayit, Bayeh) appeared to be arguing against immediate establishment of a single party. Baye suggested that in the immediate future, "there will probably be three or four political parties" united in a National Front because "the peasants are not yet prepared to join a Marxist-Leninist Party," nor were "certain intellectual groups."[108] Moreover, a Soviet commentary on the eve of Mengistu's first visit to Moscow acknowledged that "the formation of a leading political party is no simple matter" because in Ethiopia "the progressive forces still have neither enough experience of political struggle nor mature and united organizations."[109] During his visit, Mengistu noted the difficulties involved in uniting the various groups in Ethiopia, and the final communique did not refer even indirectly to the party question.

Nevertheless, the Soviet leadership appears to have persisted in their insistence on the need for such a party. Brezhnev, in his audience

[105]Radio Havana, April 23, 1978.
[106]Radio Addis Ababa, April 21, 1976.
[107]*Pravda,* July 14, 1976.
[108]Berhan Baye, "Feudalism to People's Democracy," *World Marxist Review,* No. 8, August 1976, p. 114.
[109]V. Korovikov, "A New Life Comes to Ethiopia," *International Affairs,* No. 5, May 1977, p. 132.

for Mengistu, was reported to have "emphasized the role and significance of the Communist Party of the Soviet Union as the leading and organizing force of Soviet society in the accomplishment of all the tasks of socialist and communist construction."[110] The lesson for Ethiopia was clear.

It appears less than fortuitous that one month after Mengistu's return from Moscow, in June 1977, the five major Marxist organizations agreed to establish a united front on the basis of a common action program. Before that (in January) a national trade union organization had been established and afterward (in September) a national peasants group. Throughout 1977, measures were taken in Ethiopia to propagate Marxism-Leninism Soviet-style with its emphasis on the role of a single ruling party. *New Times* in May noted the expanding dissemination of Soviet political literature and introduction of courses and seminars in Marxism-Leninism in secondary and higher educational establishments.[111]

However, the pressure to unite the evidently sharply disparate groups appeared instead to have the effect of sharpening their divisions. As explained by Berhan Baye in the international communist journal *World Marxist Review,* one of the five Marxist-Leninist groups, the all-Ethiopian Socialist Movement (Meison) "decided it was the strongest and aspired to subordinate the other groups."[112] In the summer of 1977, the PMAC, meaning probably Mengistu, cut the Meison down to size. The ruling junta dismissed or executed several Meison leaders who had had leading positions in the government, while one of their number, Negede Gobezie, who had been in Paris when the situation came to a head, stayed there as an exile.

Although the Meison was said to have had close ties to Moscow, Soviet commentaries after their purge increasingly expressed confidence that progress was being made in the formation of a "vanguard party." *New Times* in August 1977 said that "work to accomplish the [PMAC's April 1976] program's main aim of setting up a Marxist-Leninist working class party—the leading political force of society—is

[110]TASS, May 6, 1977.

[111]A. Nikanorov, "The People Have Made Their Choice," *New Times,* No. 20, May 1977, p. 6.

[112]Berhan Baye, "The Ethiopian Revolution: A Hard Period," *World Marxist Review,* No. 4, April 1978, p. 61.

being pursued with increasing vigor."[113] A TASS dispatch in *Pravda* on October 12 reported the statement by a "recently created" Ethiopian revolutionary information center that "the Ethiopian working people are in acute need of the creation of a Marxist-Leninist party." Radio Moscow on October 18 said "the process of creating a vanguard proletarian party had entered its concluding phase."

Nevertheless, Soviet sources were soon explaining once more difficulties holding up the process. A leading Soviet writer on Ethiopian affairs (Georgi Galperin) explained in March 1978 that "many tactical disagreements" still divided Ethiopian leftist groups. Galperin noted that many of them thought that rather than forming a party, it was necessary only to strengthen the trade unions and governmental organs.[114] In his *World Marxist Review* piece at about the same time, Berhan Baye explained that suppression of the leftists under the monarchy had left a heritage of weakness which was still impossible to overcome. To do so, he explained, the regime had invited Ethiopian students abroad "who had accepted the ideas of Marxism-Leninism" to come home to form the backbone of a party only to find that "these people were members of various groups."[115]

Only indirectly hinted at in Soviet discussions was the problem of the relationship of a party to the military junta which had overthrown the monarchy and carried out the revolution. Radio Moscow on October 18, 1977 described the prospective party as the body "to which the military revolutionary government intends finally to hand over power." No Soviet discussion dealt with the willingness of the Ethiopian military to make the transfer, but sporadic references to why the revolution was led by the military hinted at the existence of a military-civilian problem. In the only discussion of any length on this question, Georgi Galperin in March 1978 noted that "in the absence of a vanguard party, in conditions of a very difficult armed struggle against internal counterrevolution and external enemies, the concentration of power in the hands of the military became inevitable."[116] According to

[113]G. Galperin, "In and Around the Horn of Africa," *New Times,* No. 32, August 1977, p. 22.

[114]Galperin, "The Revolution in Ethiopia, p. 12.

[115]Baye, "The Ethiopian Revolution," p. 60.

[116]Galperin, "The Revolution in Ethiopia," p. 12.

Galperin, military revolutionary democrats regard their ruling position as a temporary, transitional phenomenon, though the "main thing," he said, was that the military "revolutionary democrats" were leading the drive toward formation of a party. However, during his trip to the USSR in November 1978, Mengistu appeared to be explaining that military rule was "a particularly historical feature" of Ethiopia and that the PMAC (i.e., the Ethiopian military) was "fulfilling the task entrusted to it by history" of "rallying the entire people on the basis of the revolutionary policy line which it has elaborated."[117]

During 1978 and 1979, the sequence of Mengistu visits to the USSR appears to have been repeated twice followed by new steps toward formation of a party, then new evidence that the process was foundering. Although Mengistu's visit to the USSR in April 1978 evidently focused mainly on Eritrea and Soviet press accounts did not broach the party issue even indirectly, only a few months after Mengistu's return from the USSR (and Cuba), the PMAC Fourth Congress in June-July 1978 announced a new drive for the establishment of a Marxist-Leninist party. While Mengistu was in Cuba at the end of April, Western sources reported that Negede Gobezie had been smuggled into the Cuban Embassy and the USSR had sought to persuade Mengistu to reinstate Meison. Mengistu reportedly refused and Negede allegedly left, along with the Cuban counselor whose recall was said to have been requested by Mengistu.[118]

When Mengistu next came to the USSR in November 1978, his major mission, the signature of a friendship treaty with the USSR, obviously took precedence over the party issue which did not figure either in Brezhnev's one reported speech or in the final communique. Mengistu assured the Soviet leaders that he realized the need for a vanguard party but portrayed the process as an unfinished task. He declared that the PMAC "has attempted to unite and rally Ethiopian Marxist-Leninists" and that "we have no doubt" that the "elements comprising" the alliance of Marxist-Leninist groups "will make the transition to the stage of complete amalgamation and will create the basis of a working people's party."[119] However, he gave no indication when he

---

[117]*Pravda*, November 18, 1978.

[118]*Economist* (London), June 3, 1968; see also Hamburg, DPA, May 25, 1978; *Sunday Telegraph* (London), July 30, 1978.

[119]*Pravda*, November 18, 1978.

expected this to be done. Moreover, in a speech shortly after his return from Moscow, Mengistu declared (as reported in a Soviet journal) that "the Marxist-Leninists must purge their ranks of pseudo-revolutionaries and bourgeois elements as soon as possible and step up their efforts to merge their organizations." Evidently reflecting new Soviet patience on the issue, the same article declared:

> The creation of a party based on Marxism-Leninism is not easy in a country where the working class is inexperienced, while the peasants and the progressive wing of the intelligentsia are still strongly influenced by petty-bourgeois sentiments. The Marxist-Leninist organizations themselves have little experience of work with the masses, some of them are sectarian, and views and sentiments alien to Marxism-Leninism have not been completely eradicated.[120]

When Soviet Premier Kosygin visited Ethiopia in September 1979 to attend festivities in honor of the fifth anniversary of Haile Selassie's ouster, Mengistu once more announced a step toward the long-awaited party, this time the formation of a commission under Mengistu's personal chairmanship which is to be responsible for the formation of a party. In an address to the nation on September 13, 1979 with Kosygin present, Mengistu announced that the commission "will soon start its work officially."[121] Kosygin emphasized that "the creation of such a party is decisive for consolidating the political, economic, social and military victories secured in the past and for leading the struggle which is to come."[122]

However, the fact that Mengistu announced a commission rather than the actual formation of a party indicated continued resistance within the ruling groups toward a party. In his September 13 speech, Mengistu admitted that "the problems we have faced with regard to the question of a party, which is a key issue, have not been easy to overcome" and described the commission as the vanguard of the vanguard party to come. At a press conference six days later, Mengistu avoided a direct answer as to the composition of the commission and said "it is very difficult for me to predict when the party will be set up."[123]

---

[120]S. Sergeyev, "Ethiopia Starts A New Life," *International Affairs,* No. 5, May 1979, p. 18.
[121]Radio Addis Ababa, September 13, 1979.
[122]*Pravda,* September 13, 1979.
[123]Radio Addis Ababa, September 19, 1979.

While the successes against Somalia and Eritrea, the moves toward establishment of a political party, and the increasing emphasis on economic development all suggested growing confidence in the Ethiopian regime by its own leaders and by the USSR, there was no suggestion that these favorable trends would make possible the withdrawal of Cuban troops from Ethiopia. Unlike the case of Angola, Havana and Moscow have never linked Cuban withdrawal directly with any specified conditions in Ethiopia (such as an agreement with Somalia or Ethiopian attainment of a certain level in its armed forces).

Moscow and Havana first ignored, then brushed aside President Carter's calls on March 2 and 9, 1978 that the USSR and Cuba withdraw militarily from Ethiopia. Both initially merely cited an Ethiopian statement of March 11, 1978 which called attempts to link Somali withdrawals "with the presence of military personnel invited by the Ethiopian government" as "tantamount to interference" in Ethiopia's internal affairs.[124]

The basic Soviet-Cuban line then and since is that Cuban troops will remain as long as Cuba and Ethiopia agree upon their presence— presumably until Ethiopia no longer feels threatened. When Castro made his first public acknowledgement in March 1978 that his troops were in Ethiopia, he suggested that the only rationale for the Cuban presence was the "Somali aggression."[125] Now, he flatly declared, "the war is over," and "I do not think that the Somalis are tempted to commit the stupidity of launching an attack." However, he left himself an out by suggesting that Somalia's alleged patrons, "reactionary countries, NATO countries and imperialism," might goad Somalia into another attack.

One month later, Castro was more categoric in his rejection of the notion of a Cuban withdrawal. Following Somalia's defeat, he declared during Mengistu's visit to Ethiopia, "imperialism and its reactionary allies madly demanded the immediate withdrawal of Cuban combatants from Ethiopia."[126] However, he went on, "anyone can understand that this also means the immediate initiation of new acts of aggression." Rejecting the idea that this was an issue which he would ever discuss with the United States, Castro then declared that "Cuban mili-

---

[124]TASS and Prensa Latina, March 12, 1978.
[125]Radio Havana, March 15, 1978.
[126]Radio Havana, April 26, 1978.

tary personnel will be in Ethiopia for whatever time is agreed on by the Ethiopian and Cuban governments to support the Ethiopian people against any aggression,'' thereby leaving open-ended the time and circumstances of withdrawal.

Pravda, in its weekly review of foreign affairs on March 19, 1978 took much the same position:

> Ethiopia rejects any attempts by the U.S. Government and its allies to interfere in the solution of problems which are exclusively under Ethiopian jurisdiction, particularly attempts to link the unconditional withdrawal of Somali units to the presence in Ethiopia of military personnel invited by its government. It is obvious that this question can only be resolved by Ethiopia and the corresponding sides.

As far as the Somali salient was concerned, all three parties (Moscow, Havana, Addis Ababa), especially in the immediate aftermath of the Cuban military victory, appeared to take the position that they would consider Ethiopia secure only if Somalia accepted Ethiopian demands that Somalia unconditionally renounce its territorial claims not only against Ethiopia but against Kenya and Djibouti, ''pledge to observe strictly the principle of non-interference in the internal affairs of other countries and renounce the use of force in resolving international disputes.''[127] The Castro-Mengistu communique in September 1978 declared that the mere existence of the Greater Somalia idea was ''tantamount to being a permanent threat of aggression'' and therefore presumably a permanent pretext for the Soviet and Cuban military presence.

While clearly convinced that the Siad Barre government in Somalia was unlikely to agree to Ethiopian terms, Moscow and Havana evidently once considered that because of defeat in Ethiopia, Siad Barre might be overthrown and presumably replaced by a more amenable regime. Castro was almost open about this in his March 15 speech. Claiming that it was only a ''rightist faction'' which had suffered defeat in Somalia, he pointedly noted that ''there was also progressive, leftist forces in Somalia. Let us wait for the coming weeks to see what happens.'' Of course, he hastened to add, this was ''totally up to the Somalis.''[128]

---

[127]See *Pravda,* March 19, 1978; *Granma* (Havana), March 14, 1978.
[128]Radio Havana, March 15, 1978.

In October 1978, Soviet commentaries once more took up the theme. A TASS dispatch from Washington carried in Pravda on October 6 reported that "the movement against the military dictatorship of Siad Barre, who.e adventurist course has led the country into an impasse and put it on the verge of economic collapse, is growing wider in Somalia." The dispatch cited one of the alleged leaders of this movement to the effect that it had "resistance echelons" throughout the country, including within the Somali armed forces. Radio Moscow on October 11 in a broadcast to Africa repeated this item which thereupon was dropped.

Another possibility broached in the West has been a possible rapprochement between Somalia and its communist antagonists. Low-level Soviet broadcasts on January 30 and 31, 1979 noted statements at the Congress of the Somali Revolutionary Socialist Party ten days earlier that Somalia wanted good relations with the USSR and Ethiopia but made progress in the direction contingent upon Somali changes. "It wasn't the Soviet Union that cancelled the Soviet-Somali treaty," said the January 30 commentary. "It is quite possible to restore fruitful Soviet-Somali relations but not at the expense of a new aggravation of the situation in that part of the world" through "claims to vast territories of neighboring states under the guise of support to movements for self-determination." Continued Somali reports of actions in Ethiopia by the Western Somali Liberation Front, including sporadic claims that Cuban and Soviet personnel had been killed, indicated that any moves toward improved relations were stillborn at least as of the end of 1979.

Neither Moscow nor Havana has suggested, as they have in the case of Angola, that the Cubans might withdraw once the training and equipment of Ethiopian armed forces has attained a sufficiently high level. Paradoxically, Castro has been much more enthusiastic about Ethiopian fighting abilities and military potential than in the case of Angola. In his March 15, 1978 speech, Castro noted that Ethiopia "is a big country with a large population and it has soldiers, very good soldiers." He suggested that Cuban soldiers had been dispatched to Ethiopia because the threat from Somalia was immediate and Ethiopian troops, hitherto armed with American weapons, did not have the time to assimilate the influx of Soviet weapons they were getting in order to fight the Somalis. In his closest approximation of a statement linking the Cuban presence to the question of training the Ethiopians, Castro said: "We thought it would be only a matter of time to help them train their army. When the Ethiopian Army is trained and well-armed, no one will be able to meddle with it."[129] When visiting Ethiopia in September 1978, Castro once more praised the "combative, courageous and heroic soldiers" of Ethiopia but said nothing beyond that.

In connection with the fifth anniversary of Haile Selassie's overthrow in September 1979, Soviet commentaries suggested that Ethiopian armed forces were now able to handle current security tasks but did not link this in any way with the suggestion of Cuban withdrawal. *New Times* in its major commemorative article stressed the defeat of Somalia and the pushing back of Eritrean rebels to "only" the northern part.[130] In an interview in the next issue of the journal, Mengistu declared that "after five years of bitter struggle we can confidently say that the Ethiopian revolution and the country's unity are generally safe and secure." However, he said, "we are confident that the Soviet Union and the other socialist countries will remain on our side throughout our struggle to lead the revolution to its historic goals."[131] Presumably this meant a continued Soviet-Cuban military presence along with economic aid.

Drawing in of East European Allies

To bolster its own positions and supplement its own efforts, Moscow has made full use of its allies and other clients to underscore the idea that ties with the USSR make Angola, Mozambique and Ethopia part of a much broader international system which can be a source of strength and psychic satisfaction presumably transcending local nationalism. Moscow has accordingly encouraged an interlocking series of high-level visits as well as political, military, ideological, economic and technical agreements especially between Eastern Europe

[129]Radio Havana, March 15, 1978.

[130]B. Asoyan, "Ethiopia: The Revolution's Arduous Path," *New Times,* No. 37, September 1979, p. 27.

[131]Mengistu Haile Mariam, "Thank You For Your Support," *New Times,* No. 38, September 1979, p. 14.

and these countries as well as between the countries themselves to formalize and solidify this process.

Two of Moscow's most faithful allies, East Germany and Bulgaria, have played a special role in solidifying bloc ties with Angola, Mozambique and Ethiopia. Their top leaders, Honecker and Zhivkov, are the only two to have made pilgrimages to Africa in obviously surrogate roles (Zhivkov in 1965 and 1978, Honecker twice in 1979). Romanian leader Ceausescu has made six journeys (in 1972, 1973, 1974, 1975, 1977 and 1979), but while Moscow may welcome aspects of these visits such as support for general Soviet foreign policy initiatives and the idea of bloc-LDC cooperation, Romania's primary focus on independence, both its own and that of the host countries, and as much of the USSR as from the West, is not the message that Moscow wants to get across.

Meanwhile, lesser leaders from the other bloc countries have visited Africa in recent years: President Jablonski of Poland to Nigeria in 1977, Angola in 1978; the Hungarian Foreign Minister to Angola and Mozambique in 1978; the Czechoslovak Foreign Minister to Tunisia, Ethiopia, Mozambique and Zambia in 1979. Angolan leader Neto, in turn, visited Bulgaria in October 1976, Poland in April 1977. Mengistu went to Bulgaria in May 1977 and made a grand tour of Eastern Europe at the end of 1978 which included the GDR, Poland, Hungary, Czechoslovakia, Romania and Yugoslavia. Mozambique President Machel visited Hungary in June 1978.

East Germany and Bulgaria have served both to supplement and to set the stage for Soviet actions especially in Ethiopia. As a warm-up for Mengistu's first visit to the USSR, he spent a few days in Bulgaria. Possibly helping to set the stage for a later delegation to the USSR, an Ethiopian delegation attended the 9th Congress of the East German ruling Socialist Unity Party (SED) in May 1976 and the East German Foreign Minister reciprocated with a visit to Ethiopia in December 1976. During 1977, SED Politburo member Werner Lamberz visited Ethiopia three times, where he evidently served as "the key man in the organization of foreign military and political support, in cooperation with the Soviet Union and Cuba, for Mengistu's regime."[132] Lamberz was also reported to have been especially active in Angola, Mozam-

---

[132]Martin McCauley, "Ethiopia Mourns in East Germany," *Soviet Analyst,* Vol 7, No. 12, 15 June 1978, p. 4.

bique and Libya until his death in a Libyan airplane crash in March 1978. In June 1977, he headed a formal party-government delegation to Ethiopia, Angola, the Congo, Nigeria and Zambia.

Climaxing these efforts, Bulgaria and the GDR have both signed treaties of friendship with Angola and Mozambique (during Zhivkov's trip in October 1978 and Honecker's in February 1979), while Honecker's visit to Ethiopia in November 1979 was capped by the signature of a comparable treaty between the GDR and Ethiopia. Romania, during Ceausescu's tour of Africa in April 1979, also signed friendship treaties not only with "socialist-oriented" Angola and Mozambique, but with Zambia and states much farther afield from bloc influence: Burundi, Gabon and the Sudan.

As in the Soviet case, the Bulgarian and East German treaties established a broad framework for closer relations in political, economic, cultural and ideological fields. The treaties with Angola and Mozambique proclaimed that the parties concerned were each guided by Marxism-Leninism and proletarian internationalism, a formula, it might be noted, which did not appear in the USSR's treaties with these countries. The treaties between Bulgaria and the GDR with Angola did not contain any provisions on military aid or regarding the establishment of contacts in case of a threat to peace, whereas both their treaties with Mozambique did. The GDR-Ethiopian treaty omitted any references to Marxism-Leninism, proletarian internationalism, military cooperation or possible action in case of a threat to the peace. Presumably the lack of a vanguard party explains the ideological omissions in the Ethiopian documents. The absence of military clauses in the treaties with Angola may have been considered unnecessary in view of the heavy Soviet-Cuban involvement, while their inclusion in the Mozambique treaty may have reflected that country's needs for continued bloc assurances in its ongoing conflict with Rhodesia.

The process leading up to signature of some of these treaties was roughly comparable to their Soviet counterparts. Thus, two years before the GDR-Angolan treaty, the two countries signed a declaration on general principles governing their relations. Similarly one year before signature of the GDR-Ethiopian treaty in November 1979, Mengistu concluded a general declaration in East Berlin. He also signed such declarations in Prague, Warsaw and Bucharest (but not in Budapest) though these have not been followed by friendship trips. A Bulgarian-

Ethiopian declaration was included in Zhivkov's trip to Ethiopia in October 1978 which, past patterns indicate, might eventually also culminate in a treaty.

In addition to the German and Bulgarian treaties, a third tier of treaties has also been concluded by Angola and Mozambique with other Soviet client states. In October 1977 Cuba and Mozambique signed such a treaty during Machel's visit to Havana. In September 1978, Angola and Mozambique concluded such a treaty with each other. Angola also signed a friendship treaty with Guinea-Bissau in September 1977.

Moscow's Eastern European allies, particularly East Germany, have had a significant role in providing military aid to Angola, Mozambique and Ethiopia. In May 1978, East German Defense Minister Hoffman went to Angola and the Congo, in May 1979 to Zambia, Mozambique and Ethiopia, where he obviously discussed military aid to the countries concerned as well as to liberation movements stationed in these countries. While the East Germans deny that they have troops in these countries, they loudly proclaim their military support for the countries and movements concerned. Thus, after his second trip, GDR Defense Minister Hoffman, told of seeing thousands of Ethiopians "practicing assaults with GDR machine guns and steel helmets." In general, he expressed confidence in prospects in the Horn and southern Africa because of the "aid and support granted by the Soviet Union, Cuba and the other socialist states, among them the GDR, in a political, economic, scientific-technical and also in a military respect, in the spirit of proletarian internationalism."[133] According to Western sources, since 1973 when the GDR signed its first military agreement with the Congo, it has sent up to 15,000 "advisers and experts" covering all spheres of security activities. Mozambique President Machel's elite guard and Ethiopian Chief Mengistu's police force were said to have been trained by the GDR.[134] A *New York Times* survey of East German activity in Africa reported the presence of 2,500 East German advisers in Angola and 1,500 in Mozambique to supervise the training of Rhodesian guer-

---

[133]*Horizont* (East Berlin), No. 28, 1979, p. 3.
[134]William F. Robinson, "Eastern Europe's Presence in Black Africa," *Radio Free Europe Research Report,* No. 142 (Eastern Europe), 21 June 1979, p. 7.

rillas. The East Germans were also said to have planned and supplied logistics for the Katangan incursion into Zaire from Angola in May 1978.[135]

The other bloc countries also appear involved to varying degrees. Czechoslovakia, as a major arms manufacturer, has been an important source of arms throughout the Third World. A special role appears to have been given Hungary in Mozambique. Thus in January 1978 the chief of the Hungarian general staff headed a military delegation to Mozambique in January 1978, reciprocated by a FRELIMO military delegation to Hungary in April. In November 1978 the Hungarian Defense Minister signed a formal military cooperation agreement with Mozambique in Maputo which he then visited three months later evidently to discuss implementation of the agreement.[136]

Moscow has also encouraged an interlocking series of economic, scientific and technical, cultural and other agreements between the Eastern European countries and African countries. Thus, in addition to the friendship treaties with Angola and Mozambique, Zhivkov's visit in October 1978 also brought the signature of agreements with Angola on party ties, economic, scientific and technological cooperation, radio and television program exchanges, press agency cooperation, and fishing cooperation. In Mozambique, agreements were signed on party cooperation, long-term economic cooperation (up to 1990), agriculture, air and sea transport. In Ethiopia, Zhivkov's visit involved not only the signature of an agreement on general principles but economic, scientific-technical, cultural and radio-television accords. Polish President Jablonski's visit to Angola concluded with a general agreement on cooperation and friendship (evidently in lieu of a treaty), as well as economic, cultural and radio-television protocols, and an agreement on party ties. Honecker's visit to Angola and Mozambique evoked a similar series of agreements, including a second block agreement with Mozambique on economic relations up to 1990.

Over and above all these and many other specific agreements, the USSR has brought Angola, Ethiopia and Mozambique into the bloc-wide Council for Economic Mutual Assistance (CEMA), for the time being with observer status. Angola made its first appearance at a

---

[135]*New York Times*, Section IV, November 18, 1979.

[136]Aurel Bereznai, "Hungary's Presence in Black Africa," *Radio Free Europe Research Report*, No. 75 (Hungary), 2 April 1979, p. 20.

CEMA meeting in 1976, Ethiopia in 1978 and Mozambique in 1979. Initially at least, these appearances are important more for their symbolism than for any practical consequences.

In addition to the government-to-government agreements, as important elements in this growing intercourse with Africa, has been a growing series of agreements between the ruling parties of Eastern Europe, Cuba and Moscow's African clients. The MPLA in Angola has concluded such agreements with the parties in East Germany, Bulgaria, Poland, Czechoslovakia, Hungary, Cuba and the Congo. Mozambique's FRELIMO has agreements with its counterparts, at least in East Germany, Hungary, Cuba and the Congo. The SED and Hungary also have party agreements with the Congo. These agreements provide for exchanges of delegations, ideological training in East Europe and attachment of East European advisers to key sectors of the ruling parties in Africa. In addition, delegations from the socialist-oriented states are an increasing feature of international communist party and front convocations both in the bloc and through massive communist attendance at meetings of the African parties.

CHAPTER EIGHT

The Struggle for Rhodesia

IN THE AFTERMATH OF ITS TRIUMPHS in both Angola and Ethiopia, Moscow set its sights on the ultimate three targets of southern Africa: Rhodesia, Namibia and the Republic of South Africa. A number of Soviet analyses made the point that the fall of the Portuguese empire and particularly the victory of "progressive" regimes in Angola and Mozambique had removed a buffer between these three and black Africa, thereby putting the struggle for their "liberation" on the immediate agenda.

Thus an important *Pravada* article on February 11, 1976 emphasized that the "consolidation of people's power" in Angola would not only remove it from Western influence but would "represent a powerful stimulus in mounting the liberation struggle of the peoples of Namibia, the Republic of South Africa and Zimbabwe against the racist regimes."[1] Although Brezhnev did not specifically mention these countries in his address to the 25th Soviet Communist Party that same month, he declared that "out Party supports and will continue to support peoples fighting for their freedom" and that in doing so "we act as we are bid by our revolutionary conscience, our communist convictions."[2]

[1]Observer, "Concerning the Situation in Angola," *Pravda,* February 11, 1976.
[2]*Pravda,* February 25, 1976.

Soviet Approach Toward Liberation Movements

From the Soviet point of view, a major problem in Rhodesia as it had been in Angola, was the existence of a number of national liberation movements and leaders, often at odds with each other. Evidently wanting to keep its options open to deal with all of them, Moscow gave few indications of the substantive difference dividing these groups. In one of its few discussions on Rhodesia in 1975, the Soviet foreign policy journal *New Times,* while praising the agreement at the time to form the African National Council, noted that the process proved to be difficult—"the ideological platforms differed and there was disagreement on tactics."[3] At a later stage a Soviet ethnographer attributed difficulties in maintaining the Patriotic Front together to colonialist efforts "to use intertribal disagreements" and to "incite tribalism in order to split the forces of the patriots and not permit their unification."[4] However, neither of these articles dicussed the intricacies of these disagreements, and other Soviet references simply mentioned them as a regrettable phenomenon which was hampering the struggle against the Smith regime.

Until 1978, Soviet commentaries included all the black leaders within the "liberation movement"—Nkomo, Muzorewa, Sithole and, after the formation of the Patriotic Front in 1976, Mugabe. Though always skeptical when one or another of them negotiated with the U.S., U.K. or even with Ian Smith, Moscow did not charge that engaging in such negotiations made a leader a "capitulationist" until Smith's "internal settlement" was implemented in 1978.

The usual Soviet approach—for example in early 1976 when Nkomo engaged in a three-month parley with Smith—was to combine complete silence about the talks with veiled warnings that evil forces were at work seeking to seduce Zimbabwean "patriots." A typical Soviet broadcast to Africa, without mentioning the Nkomo-Smith negotiations, warned that all talk of a constitutional settlement "is aimed at dulling the vigilance of the Zimbabwe people and compelling them to give up their armed struggle for freedom." The broadcast reviewed

---

[3]Arkady Butlitsky, "The Racists Manoevre," *New Times,* No. 35, August 1975, p. 22.

[4]V. P. Gorodnov, "The Crisis of the Racist Regimes in Southern Africa," in USSR Academy of Sciences, Institute of Ethnography, *Races and Peoples Annual,* No. 8 (Moscow:Nauka 1978), p. 87.

anti-guerrilla preparations by the Smith government which, it stated demonstrated that Smith had no intention of giving up power. Accordingly, it concluded, "among the patriots of Zimbabwe there is a growing understanding that only by an armed struggle is it possible to gain genuine independence."[5] When, obviously to Soviet relief, the talks failed to reach an agreement, Soviet media for the first time explicitly discussed them in order to dismiss them. *Pravda* on March 25 said the breakdown showed that the "racists" were unchanged,[6] on April 1 that "the white racist clique is thereby demonstrating its intention to stay in power by any means,"[7] on April 26 that "the question now at issue is that of the unconditional handing over of power in Rhodesia to the African majority."[8]

Beginning in 1977, however, Joshua Nkomo forged into the lead as Moscow's favorite Zimbabwe leader. According to Nkomo's own testimony to a Soviet journal, he first established contact with Soviet representatives in 1959 while visiting Egypt where "I heard the truth about the October Revolution."[9] Presumably there were further contacts following Nkomo's release (along with Sithole and Mugabe) after 10 years in prison, especially since Soviet arms began to be channeled to Nkomo's forces in Zambia.

Nkomo's political orientation, at least initially, was extremely murky. In a March 1976 interview, he told a Danish newspaper that apart from sympathy for Scandinavia, "I cannot say at the moment what my political philosophy is." He was said to consider himself a democrat but expressed dismay at Western refusal to back him while "Russians, Chinese, Czechoslovaks and East Germans came to our aid." According to the Danish correspondent, Nkomo at that time said that the issue in Rhodesia was the right vote.[10]

In 1977, however, Nkomo sharply increased his overt ties with the communist world and began to adjust his rhetoric. Soviet attention to Nkomo's pronouncements also increased. Nkomo made his first visit to the USSR in the second half of 1976. This visit, which was not

[5]Moscow Radio Peace and Progress in English to Africa, December 30, 1975.
[6]V. Korovikov, "Supporting the Zimbabwe People, *Pravda,* March 25, 1976.
[7]V. Tiurkin, "They Are Playing With Fire," *Pravda,* April 1, 1976.
[8]F. Tarasov, "Urgent Necessity," *Pravda,* April 26, 1976.
[9]Joshua Nkomo, "A Life of Struggle," *New Times,* No. 7, February 1979, p. 27.
[10]*Berlingske Tidende* (Copenhagen), March 2, 1976.

reported in the Soviet media, was part of a five month tour Nkomo made to a number of countries in East and West Europe as well as Africa, following the failure of his talks with Smith and before the onset of a new set of talks sponsored by the U.S. and U.K. in Geneva.[11] Subsequent developments suggest that mutually satisfactory arrangements were made between Moscow and Nkomo on this occasion.

After that, Nkomo visits to the USSR and Eastern Europe became increasingly frequent. From February 28 to March 7, 1977, Nkomo made his first public visit to the USSR at the invitation of the Soviet Afro-Asian Solidarity Committee. Not long afterward he met Soviet President Podgorny when the latter was in Tanzania. In November 1977 he was in Moscow again to help celebrate the 60th anniversary of the October Revolution and, according to Western press reports, once more unannounced in October 1978. Nkomo was reported by a Soviet journal to have addressed a seminar organized on January 27–28, 1979 by the Soviet Afro-Asian Solidarity Committee for Southern African Students in Moscow. In 1977, he formally visited Bulgaria, Hungary, and Romania; in 1978, all of Eastern Europe except Romania as well as Cuba; in January 1979, Prague once more. In January 1978, Nkomo attended the opening of a ZAPU (Zimbabwe African Peoples' Union) office in East Berlin.

Interviews with Nkomo have become frequent in Soviet and East European media as well as in the Soviet-sponsored international journal, *Problems of Peace and Socialism*. The Soviet press and radio especially in 1978 frequently cited Nkomo statements except for a hiatus during the summer when he engaged once more in talks with Smith. In 1979, a new twist appeared as several Radio Moscow broadcasts in February and March beamed Nkomo statements in the Shona and Matabele languages toward Rhodesia.

In his statements for Soviet media, Nkomo increasingly identified his struggle with the Soviet Union. In one of his first interviews, in March 1977, he told a Soviet journalist that "we in ZAPU are thinking about a socialist state."[12] Eight months later, at the October Revolution anniversary he was much more ardent. "We in Zimbabwe," he said, "are following the same path that was pioneered by the Soviet people under

---

[11]Paris, AFP, September 25, 1976; *Sunday Times* (London), September 26, 1976.
[12]Joshua Nkomo, "Freedom Is Close," *New Times,* No. 12, March 1977, p. 15.

the leadership of the greatest revolutionary of all time, Vladimir Ilich Lenin."[13] Furthermore, he went on, "the war of liberation in Zimbabwe is based on the Marxist-Leninist ideology which alone can bring genuine freedom to all peoples of the world."[14] Then, nailing his message down, he repeated that "we in Zimbabwe wish to assure you that we are on the same socialist path."[15] In a 1979 interview, he said he and his followers "are conscious of our common destinies and interests" with those of the Soviet Union.[16]

Not surprisingly, Nkomo's statements are replete with expressions of gratitude for the aid he has received from the Soviet Union and protestations that Moscow has no ulterior motives in its dealings with him. He told one Soviet interviewer, for example, that "our patriots are deeply grateful to the Soviet Union,"[17] and another that the armed struggle in Rhodesia "would have been impossible without the assistance and support given us by the Soviet Union, the other socialist countries and all the progressive forces of the world."[18] In an earlier interview, Nkomo emphasized that "no responsible Soviet official has ever tried to impose anything on me,"[19] while on several other occasions he described Soviet aid as "disinterested."

At least for Soviet and bloc interviewers, Nkomo's definitions of the aim of his struggle increasingly resembled those of his interlocutors. Generally interviewed when Western-sponsored settlement proposals were at an impasse, Nkomo's statements in 1977 and 1978 were expectedly critical of the West for not accepting his point of view. In 1979, however, his statements expressed more deep-dyed doubts about Western motivations. Thus while in Prague in January, he told the Czechoslovak party paper that southern African white leaders were "only agents for larger forces," particularly the United States which wanted to "protect the Western world's interests, their capital invest-

---

[13]Speech by Nkomo, *The 60th Anniversary of the Great October Socialist Revolution* (Moscow: Progress Publishers, 1977), p. 301.

[14]*Ibid.*, p. 302.

[15]*Ibid.*, p. 303.

[16]Nkomo, "A Life of Struggle," p. 27.

[17]*Ibid.*

[18]Joshua Nkomo, "Until Final Victory," *New Times*, No. 16, April 1979, p. 14.

[19]Nkomo, "Freedom Is Close," p. 12..

ments and permit them to exploit raw materials" of the region.[20] For Soviet benefit, he described Western settlement plans as designed "to preserve their dominant position in southern Africa with the help of their puppets and continue to plunder the wealth of Rhodesia and Namibia."[21] Elsewhere he declared: "In Zimbabwe, it is not a war between races, but a class struggle of the forces of progress against a colonialist, imperialist regime."[22]

In a Radio Moscow broadcast in Shona on March 1, 1979, Nkomo was quoted to the effect that the Soviet Union and other communist countries "enjoy total freedom" and that the aim of his struggle was "not only the destruction of racist regimes, but the entire system that favors the rule of the rich." Accordingly, he said, "our friendship with the Soviet Union is very close." In other broadcasts he denounced capitalism and Western anti-communist "dirt." In perhaps his most pro-Soviet statement, Nkomo is quoted by a Radio Moscow Shona-language broadcast on April 5, 1979 about the "great joy" he felt in talking about ZAPU friendship with the Soviet Communist Party and government. Nkomo described the USSR as "our greatest and most reliable ally" as well as "a great friend to all the liberation movements throughout the world." Noting Western descriptions of "freedom-fighters as communists," Nkomo said that he had turned to communists for help because "the freedom fighters of Zimbabwe know that there are no greater lessons than the teachings of Marx and Lenin."

The extent to which these statements are merely tailored to his audience must be a matter of conjecture. Thus when interviewed in Copenhagen in June 1978, Nkomo refused to comment on his own ideas about the nature of a future Zimbabwe. He also was reported to the effect that he did not feel bound by the military aid his forces received from the USSR, Cuba and other communist states.[23]

How far the USSR trusts or is committed to Nkomo is another question. *Literary Gazette* on November 1, 1978 flatly stated that "Nkomo is the only African leader capable of solving the Rhodesian problem." And, as noted, he receives far greater attention than is given

[20]Milos Krejci interview with Joshua Nkomo, "Zimbabwe Will Be Victorious," *Rude Pravo* (Prague), January 12, 1979.

[21]Nkomo, "Until Final Victory," p. 14.

[22]Joshua Nkomo, "Our Answer—Strengthening of the Struggle," *Asia and Africa Today*, No. 4, April 1979, p. 24.

[23]*Berlingske Tidende* (Copehagen), June 23, 1978.

any other black Rhodesian leader. Moreover, the bulk of Soviet military aid has evidently gone to his ZAPU group.

Nevertheless, Moscow has eschewed total commitment to Nkomo. In almost all instances, he is referred to as "one of the" leaders of the Patriotic Front, and Moscow has put considerable emphasis on the need for unity among the liberation movements. The Kremlin may also be uneasy about the fact that Nkomo's major African sponsor is Zambia with which the USSR has good but not outstanding close relations. Despite the *Literary Gazette* statement cited above, Moscow is aware that Nkomo is a member of the minority Matebele tribe. In its constant urging of unity efforts between Nkomo and Mugabe, Moscow may also want to keep on the good side of Mugabe's major African sponsor, Mozambique.[24] Moreover, Moscow's misgivings have been evident whenever Nkomo has engaged in negotiations with Smith or Western representatives.

At the same time, despite its call for unity between Nkomo and Mugabe, Moscow has been reluctant about its support for the latter. In January 1979, Mugabe told a Dutch paper that "we maintain friendly links and hope to obtain material support from the Soviet Union. At present it supports ZAPU with weapons and goods, but we hope to show that ours is the true progressive socialist party."[25] One month later, he told another Dutch paper that "we have received arms supplied from both China and the Soviet Union".[26] But in a later interview he stated that "our relationship with the Soviet Union started only last year" and "has not yet taken concrete shape,"[27] while in another he said that "we still do not receive direct arms shipments from the Russians, but our relations with them are improving."[28]

Exactly what role Moscow played in the squabble between Nkomo and Mugabe is difficult to determine. Moscow's constant emphasis that victory was possible only on the basis of armed struggle should logically put it more strongly on the side of Mugabe not only because his rhetoric on this issue was close to Moscow's, but because it is generally conceded that his forces accounted for the bulk of the guerrilla

[24]S. Kulik, "Rhodesia: Death Agony of a White Paradise," *Literary Gazette*, November 1, 1978.

[25]*De Volkskrant* (Amsterdam), January 10, 1979.

[26]*NRC Handelsblad* (Rotterdam), March 2, 1979.

[27]*Mainichi Shimbun* (Tokyo), May 4, 1979.

[28]*The Guardian* (London), May 16, 1979.

operations inside Rhodesia. Moreover, Moscow clearly was uneasy about Nkomo's willingness during 1976 and 1978 to explore possibilities for a peaceful settlement. During these periods, the Soviet press ceased quoting Nkomo and warned about sinister efforts to split anti-Smith forces. On the other hand, Mugabe's long ties with Peking obviously did not recommend him to Moscow, although Soviet relations with other originally pro-Peking leaders such as Machel of Mozambique suggest an ability to adjust to this unpropitious starting point.

Meanwhile, it might be argued that Moscow was looking beyond the current situation to a later showdown between Nkomo and Mugabe. According to Western sources, Nkomo "under apparent Soviet advice" has concentrated on building up a more conventional army and has operated with an eye to eventual control over the capital and other urban areas.[29] Moscow acknowledged in June 1978 that Cuban advisers were training his forces both in Africa and in Cuba itself. In July and again in November 1978, he made pilgrimages to Havana, and in February 1979 he expressed gratitude not only to the USSR but to Cuba as well for its support.[30]

In January 1978, reports began to appear that Cubans were training Mugabe's ZANU (Zimbabwe African National Union) guerrillas in Mozambique.[31] In the year that followed, the Cubans were said to have doubled the number of their troops assigned to ZANU camps in Mozambique,[32] while according to another Western report, 450 East Germans arrived in Mozambique in early 1978 to train Mugabe's forces.[33] In September, while in Ethiopia, Castro met separately with Nkomo and Mugabe.[34] In September 1979, Mugabe attended the non-aligned conference in Havana.

Whether Moscow and the Cubans will intervene in Rhodesia as they did in Angola and Ethiopia will be governed by a number of variables: the attitudes of the front-line states, their estimate of counteraction by the West and/or South Africa, their estimate of the situation on the

[29]*Washington Post,* May 22, 1979

[30]*World Marxist Review,* No. 2, February 1979, p. 108.

[31]*The Times* (London), January 19, 1978.

[32]*Washington Post,* January 21, 1979.

[33]Peter Janke, "Angola as Springboard for Moscow," *Soviet Analyst,* 17 August 1978, p. 2.

[34]Radio Havana, September 18, 1978.

ground. Both Moscow and Havana probably derive satisfaction that the very speculation about their possible intervention demonstrates their enhanced role in African affairs and can be used to persuade the Africans of the value of ties to the USSR and its allies.

Meanwhile, especially in the aftermath of their success in Angola, Cuban spokesmen sought to dispel the notion of imminent Cuban intervention in Rhodesia. In a May 1976 Tokyo press conference reprinted in detail by *Izvestiia*, Cuban Vice President Carlos Rafael Rodriquez declared that the situation in Rhodesia was "radically different" from that of Angola because the latter involved a request for aid by a government. Rodriquez said it was "Cuba's conviction" that liberation "cannot be achieved by the actions of force of other countries."[35] In an interview over the BBC on February 1, 1977 Rodriquez made much the same points. In a later London newspaper interview, however, Rodriquez was quoted to the effect that "we will give the Patriotic Front all the help they need, just as we helped the MPLA before it became the Government of Angola."[36]

Another option that the communists held in reserve was the proclamation of a rival Patriotic Front government which would then request aid. From time to time in 1978, when he and Mugabe were implying that the Patriotic Front had control of 70 to 90 percent of Rhodesia, Nkomo was cited in communist sources about the possibility of setting up formal liberation zones within Rhodesia. TASS on April 23, 1978 reported that Nkomo, speaking in London, said "that a popular government of Zimbabwe can be created in the future in the liberated lands." In a later Prague interview, after describing the purported scope of his forces' successes, especially in the countryside, Nkomo remarked that "we do not call them liberated areas yet, but operational zones."[37] A few weeks later he told a Soviet journal: "In fact, one can speak about the existence of liberated areas although we have not declared their creation. But the time will come for that too."[38]

This question, it should be noted, was one of many which divided Nkomo and Mugabe. As described by the latter, Nkomo favored immediate political unification of the two movements as a prelude to joint

[35]*Izvestiia,* May 23, 1976.
[36]*Observer* (London), February 26, 1978.
[37]*Rude Pravo* (Prague), January 12, 1979.
[38]Joshua Nkomo, "Our Answer," *Aziia i Afrika Segodnia,* No. 4, April 1979, p. 24.

military operations. Magabe, in turn, sought closer military ties including an increasing share of Soviet military aid, leaving overall political questions to a later time. He evidently envisaged formation of a ruling party after military victory, and he told an interviewer: "If we win on this battlefield, we intend to be that party."[39] Rendered unnecessary by the London accord this concept might surface again should that agreement break down.

Countering Western Efforts for a Solution

In setting its sights on Rhodesia and Namibia, and especially on the absolute necessity for an armed fight to the finish, Moscow not only sought to take advantage of its successes in Angola and Ethiopia but to price the West politically out of the competition for influence among liberation movements begun by Kissinger in 1976 and continued under the Carter Administration. Moscow with single-minded intensity has striven to discredit U.S. and other Western efforts to achieve compromise settlements on both Rhodesia and Namibia.

One notable feature was the harshness of the attacks on Kissinger. A Soviet broadcast to Africa by *Izvestiia* correspondent V. Kudriavtsev on April 28 declared that "Dr. Kissinger is going to Africa as a representative of American imperialism and neocolonialism and as a mouthpiece of racism." In an article shortly afterward, Kudriavtsev derided Kissinger's "hypocritical statements" and "unsupported promises."[40] Kudriavtsev spelled out a major theme then and thereafter of Soviet coverage of U.S. policy: that the U.S. was seeking to salvage a losing position in southern Africa through subterfuges designed to maintain the white regimes in Rhodesia and South Africa in power. According to his article in *Izvestiia:* "The aim of [Kissinger's] visit was to find ways to save the present regime in South Africa, where U.S. billions have been invested and which is a bulwark of multinational imperialism on the African continent. For this the U.S. ruling circles decided to resort to a maneuver, declaring themselves to be supporters of majority rule in Rhodesia in order to stem the tide of the national liberation move-

---

[39]*De Volkskrant* (Amsterdam), January 10, 1979.
[40]V. Kudriavtsev, "Southern Africa: The Struggle Grows," *Izvestiia,* May 6, 1976.

ment, and 'to become aligned' with the 'liquidation' of the racist order in Rhodesia.''

Kissinger's announcement in Boston on August 2, 1976 of a new U.S. policy toward Africa met the same Soviet response. *Pravda* on August 14 portrayed an all-out Western campaign by the West to save the resources of Southern Africa whose importance especially to the U.S. was spelled out in detail.[41] The ubiquitous Kudriavtsev charged that the series of trips to Africa by Kissinger and other high U.S. officials ''were all pursuing the same objective: to keep Africa a raw material reserve and market outlet for the monopolies and, with this end in view, to extend political domination in the continent, using neo-colonialist methods.'' Kudriavtsev said that U.S. ruling circles were ''posing as a friend to the African peoples'' and passing themselves off ''as supporters of African majority rule in Rhodesia but with one qualification: the privileges of the white minority must be preserved.'' U.S. ''maneuvers'' in Rhodesia and Namibia were said to ''have the single objective of saving South Africa as an imperialist bridgehead in Africa.''[42]

The top Soviet leadership, without naming the U.S. directly, gradually stepped up its show of irritation with Anglo-American peace efforts. Speaking to the U.N. General Assembly in September 1976, Foreign Minister Gromyko denounced ''political subterfuges and handouts of money to turn the national liberation movement away from genuine independence and freedom,''[43] the first epithet a reference to Anglo-American peace plans in general, the second to proposed postsettlement aid for both blacks and whites in Rhodesia. Within weeks, Brezhnev chimed in at a dinner in honor of visiting Angolan President Neto against unnamed persons ''attempting to substitute a fictitious liberation of southern Africa for a true one and in essence to preserve imperialism's positions in that region and to prop up the shaky stronghold of racism.''[44]

In his General Assembly speech, Gromyko set forth extreme positions on all southern African issues. ''We are in favor,'' he asserted, ''of

---

[41]L. Valentinin, ''Imperialism Is the Enemy of the African Peoples,'' *Pravda,* August 14, 1976.

[42]V. Kudriavtsev, ''Conspiracy Against Africa,'' *Izvestiia,* August 14, 1976.

[43]*Pravda,* September 29, 1976.

[44]*Pravda,* October 8, 1976.

the unconditional ending of the policy of apartheid and racism in the Republic of South Africa, its immediate withdrawal from Namibia, and the unconditional handing over of full power to the people of Zimbabwe.''[45] These uncompromising formulas were frequently reiterated and constituted a standard next to which all attempts at negotiation, anything short of surrender, obviously fell short. Indeed a *Pravda* article on October 12, 1976 made this explicit with respect to Rhodesia. Denying that Nkomo, Mugabe, and their African supporters had consented to the Anglo-American settlement plan except for the principle of majority rule, *Pravda* declared: ''Only a complete and unconditional capitulation by the racist regime or its removal can lead to the liberation of the Zimbabwe people.''[46]

Another feature of Gromyko's 1976 General Assembly speech was his rejection of any suggestion that the USSR might acquiesce in something less than total surrender by the existent regimes in Rhodesia and South Africa. Immediately after enunciating the extreme Soviet positions, Gromyko declared: ''No one will ever live to see the day when the Soviet Union will not oppose attempts to prolong colonial and racist oppression under whatever label.'' This sentence was presumably aimed directly at Kissinger who, according to the London *Times,* had just protested to the Soviet Union for encouraging African leaders to reject Kissinger's proposals on Rhodesia and Namibia.[47]

Summing up U.S. policy toward southern Africa in the final year of the Republican administration, the Soviet journal *USA* concluded ''It is quite likely that the United States has never before undertaken in such a comparatively brief period so many actions concerning the south of the dark continent both directly in Africa and beyond it.''[48] The article saw Kissinger seeking to repeat in Africa what he had done in the Near East. Spurred by events in Angola and a perception that ''the liberation movements have become such an impressive factor that it is simply dangerous to disregard them,'' the United States, according to the Soviet journal, sought ''more flexible forms for its policy toward

---

[45]*Pravda,* September 29, 1976.

[46] Yu Alimov, ''Zimbabwe's Liberation Approaches,'' *Pravda,* October 12, 1976.

[47]*Sunday Times* (London), September 26, 1976.

[48]N. D. Turkatenko, ''Washington's Calculations and Miscalculations in Southern Africa,'' *USA: Economics, Politics, Ideology,* No. 2, February 1977, p. 24.

southern Africa in order to safeguard long-term U.S. economic and military-strategic interests throughout Africa."

A rare discussion of these issues in the Soviet theoretical journal *Kommunist* attributed U.S. activity not only to the growth of "progressive" regimes and movements in Africa, but to a shifting balance in comparative influence between the USSR and the U.S. According to *Kommunist,* "the imperialists are particularly alarmed by the fact that, with every passing year, the prestige of the Soviet Union and the entire socialist community among the African nations is growing, while that of the Western countries continues to decline."[49] In a subsequent passage, the article declared that because of its ties to South Africa and Rhodesia, "the political prestige of the United States among the African nations is steadily continuing to decline."

Soviet commentaries acknowledged some changes in form but none in the substance of the Carter Administration policy toward southern African issues. Summing up this policy six months later, the Soviet journal *USA* concluded that the new administration had introduced "new features" into its African policy which, however, were nothing more than modifications in style and emphasis aimed at "preventing or postponing large-scale sociopolitical changes on the African continent."[50]

One year later, the same journal described Carter Administration policies as "mainly a repetition of previously declared ideas" adjusted "to correct the fundamental errors committed by its predecessors, who ignored the national liberation movement and the struggle of the African people for political and economic independence."[51] U.S. goals under both administrations were proclaimed to be the same: "struggle against the national liberation movement, against the prestige of forces for peace and socialism, and for the reinforcement of imperialist positions of strength on the continent."[52]

Moscow was careful in its handling of the negotiating efforts of U.S. U.N. representative Andrew Young and skittish about the willingness

[49]L. Tamarin, "Imperialist Calculations and Miscalculations in Africa," *Kommunist,* No. 18, December 1976, p. 97.

[50]M. L. Vishnevskii, "Washington's African Maneuvers," *USA: Economics, Politics, Ideology,* No. 8, August 1977.

[51]M. L. Vishnevskii, "The United States and the National Liberation Movement in Africa," *USA: Economics, Politics, Ideology,* No. 8, August 1978, p. 40.

[52]*Ibid.,* p. 43.

of Nkomo and Mugabe as well as frontline state leaders Kaunda and Nyerere to negotiate with U.S. and U.K. representatives. Soviet commentaries on the eve of these negotiations featured warnings about U.S. motives along with declarations that the Africans would not let themselves be misled by the U.S. and U.K. Thus the Soviet newspaper *Sovetskaia Rossiia* in early 1978 cautioned that "it would be dangerous to underrate" Anglo-American peace efforts but contended that "Zimbabwe patriots" and their African supporters "will not allow themselves to be bamboozled by fruitless talk, just as they will not allow themselves to be intimidated by threats."[53] Speaking in Maputo, Mozambique in March 1977, Soviet President Podgorny decried any illusion of reconciliation with racist regimes since "it is not in the labyrinth of capitulationist deals but only through the final elimination of colonial and racial oppression that the way to national liberation lies."[54] Speaking in Angola in December 1977, Soviet Politburo member Kirilenko declared that "the imperialists are maneuvering and feigning friendship with the African people" in an effort to fan fratricidal conflict "and to install puppet regimes."[55] After the failure of the Malta talks between the U.S., U.K., Nkomo and Mugabe in early 1978, *Izvestiia* crowed that the U.S. and U.K. had overestimated the disagreements within the national liberation movement" and the influence of those "prepared to meet the perfidious plans of the imperialists halfway."[56]

And in its most authoritative pronouncement on Africa in recent years, a Soviet government statement on June 23, 1978 once more charged that the West was seeking to establish puppet regimes in southern Africa and recapitulated Gromyko's extreme positions. The Soviet government, the statement said, favored "liquidation of the racist regime in Rhodesia and the handing over of full power to Zimbabwe in the person of the Patriotic Front, for the immediate and full withdrawal of the Republic of South Africa from Nambia and the handing over of power to SWAPO, the genuine representative of the

[53]V. Smirnov, "Rhodesia: What Is Keeping the Question From Being Solved," *Sovetskaia Rossiia*, January 28, 1977.

[54]*Pravda*, April 1, 1977.

[55]*Pravda*, December 6, 1977.

[56]V. Kudriavtsev, "Sentence Has Been Passed On Racism in Rhodesia," *Izvestiia*, March 3, 1978.

people of its country, for the liquidation of the system of apartheid in the Republic of South Africa."[57]

Moscow took cognizance of, but sought to belittle, Western pressures on Rhodesia and South Africa designed to generate concessions acceptable to the Patriotic Front and its supporters. After years in which they castigated the U.S. for the Byrd amendment permitting U.S. purchase of Rhodesian chrome despite U.N. sanctions, Soviet media barely noted Congressional action in March 1977 repealing the amendment.

Soviet commentaries sometimes took the line that both the U.S. and South Africa were willing to sacrifice the Ian Smith regime in Rhodesia as a device to ensure the salvation of the main prize in the region, the Union of South Africa. *USA,* summing up the policy of the Ford Administration, concluded that "the main thrust of Washington's 'new African policy' now primarily consists in striving to get the heat off Pretoria by 'sacrificing' the Smith regime" and the channel changes in southern Africa which would give more weight "primarily in Namibia and southern Rhodesia for forces which would be oriented toward the United States and other Western powers."[58]

Similarly, Soviet commentaries for a time suggested that South Africa also was in accord with this approach. To bolster its policy of dialogue with black Africa, "the South African authorities," according to *Izvestiia,* "were at one time even prepared to sacrifice their ally— the racist regime of Ian Smith in Rhodesia."[59] In this connection, Moscow contended that Angolan events had discouraged South Africa. According to *New Times:* "Smith's South African counterparts now have their own future to worry about, besides which the defeat of their Angolan expedition can hardly encourage Pretoria to plunge into another hopeless venture."[60] Smith, however, is said to have balked at this role, and Soviet propaganda has reverted to the line that the two regimes were operating more in tandem.

Meanwhile, the United States, in its support of a negotiated settlement involving the Patriotic Front was seen by Moscow as necessarily

[57]*Pravda,* June 23, 1978.

[58]Turkatenko, "Washington's Calculations," p. 34.

[59]Kudriavtsev, "Southern Africa."

[60]Dmitri Volsky, "Rhodesia: The Beginning of the End," *New Times,* No. 11, March 1976, p. 10.

continuing its efforts to keep some sort of distance from the white regimes in Rhodesia and South Africa. Anatoly Gromyko wrote at one point that "the West has come to realize that the growing odiousness of the Vorster and Smith regimes threatens to reduce the influence of capitalism on the continent and partly on the global level and to discredit its policy throughout the Third World."[61] Another Soviet journal speculated that in an effort "to rehabilitate itself in the eyes of the peoples of Africa," the West "must at least formally set itself off from the Rhodesian and Namibian racists and achieve the neocolonization of these countries in a purer form than the RSA would want it."[62] More specifically, according to Soviet commentator Kudriavtsev, the United States "cannot afford to disregard the anti-racialist sentiments not only in the progressive states of the continent, but even in those holding pro-colonialist positions."[63]

To sharpen the West's dilemmas and to maximize its own leverage, Moscow has consistently emphasized that the situation in Rhodesia can only be resolved by violence. This stance has gone hand in hand with the Soviet stress on the need for total capitulation of the Smith regime and insistence that the Patriotic Front is the only true representative of the people of Rhodesia. The point made from time to time that the Front had nothing against negotiations and a peaceful settlement is always balanced by the charge that Smith's negotiating position and his military actions can only be met by military actions on the part of the Front. Whenever negotiations of any sort were going on whether between Smith and African leaders or between the Western powers and the parties, Moscow strongly emphasized that only armed struggle could bring the desired ends.

Thus on the eve of Smith-Nkomo talks in early 1976, Radio Moscow reported that "among the patriots of Zimbabwe there is a growing understanding that only by an armed struggle is it possible to gain genuine independence."[64] On the eve of the meeting between Secretary of State Kissinger and South African Prime Minister Vorster in

[61]Anatoly Gromyko, "Neocolonialism's Maneuvers in Southern Africa," *International Affairs*, No. 12, December 1977, p. 96.

[62]A. Runov, "Plot against Namibia and Zimbabwe," *Aziia i Afrika Segodnia*, No. 8, August 1978, p. 18.

[63]V. Kudriavtsev, "Africa Fights for Its Future," *International Affairs*, No. 5, May 1978, p. 35.

[64]Moscow Radio Peace and Progress, December 30, 1975.

Zurich in September 1976, *Pravda* praised the OAU for having "acknowledged armed struggle as the only effective means leading to genuine freedom."[65] In 1977, *Pravda* rejected the "talks game" by the West as "aimed at extinguishing the flame of the liberation struggle."[66] A commentary in a Soviet foreign policy journal on Western efforts concluded that "developments in southern Africa are making it increasingly apparent that colonialism and racism recognize only force."[67]

Several Soviet commentaries state quite frankly that a violent solution will redound to the Soviet advantage both directly and through the increased prospect that armed struggles are more likely than negotiations to result in the emergence of radical regimes. Both these thoughts were expressed with particular clarity in an *Izvestiia* article by one of its most prestigious commentators Aleksandr Bovin. In a discussion of U.S. policy, Bovin wrote:

> Washington is perfectly aware, first, that the armed struggle being waged by the peoples of southern Africa promotes the authority of those who support this struggle and helps the rebels. And second, if southern Africa gains freedom as a result of armed struggle, it will adopt firm anti-imperialist positions.[68]

Many other commentators have focused even more tellingly on the second idea. Shortly after the Western-sponsored Geneva conference broke down, *New Times* speculated that the key reason was Western unwillingness "to see the emergence in southern Africa of another African regime which they consider radical and the formation of a belt of independent states opposed to the West's last bastion in the area— South Africa."[69] Putting the issue even more succinctly, *International Affairs* said that "what the imperialists fear most of all is a repetition in Zimbabwe and Namibia of what happened in Mozambique and Angola where power was taken by the progressive forces."[70]

[65]Valentinin, "Imperialism Is the Enemy."

[66]Yu. Tsaplin, "The Talks Game," *Pravda,* May 26, 1977.

[67]K. Uralov, "The Acute Problem of Southern Africa," *International Affairs,* No. 5, May 1977, p. 114.

[68]A. Bovin, "Washington and Pretoria," *Izvestiia,* July 13, 1976.

[69]V. Sidenko, "From Rhodesia to Zimbabwe," *New Times,* No. 4, January 1977, p. 12.

[70]Uralov, "The Acute Problem," p. 112.

Policy Toward Front-line States

Another major element in Moscow's strategy has been to encourage the "front-line" states neighboring Rhodesia both in their opposition to Western compromise proposals and in their readiness to support a military solution of the Rhodesian question. In so doing, Moscow has sought to make common cause with countries which had been apprehensive about or resistant to Soviet influence and which, as bases for Zimbabwe guerrilla actions, would seek Soviet aid. Three principal objects of the Soviet effort—Tanzania, Zambia, Mozambique—were particularly attractive targets for Moscow because of their previous ties with China.

The Angolan action provided Moscow's first opportunities to alter these countries' relationships with the USSR. Tanzania, for example, initially had supported naval movements in Angola. In 1973 Tanzanian President Nyerere had been instrumental in persuading the Chinese to supplement Zairian training of Holden Roberto's FNLA forces in Tanzanian camps. In April 1975 Nyerere and Botswana President Khama formally supported UNITA leader Savimbi as their candidate to lead a coalition government when Angola achieved independence and they arranged for Chinese arms aid to Savimbi. However, as a result of MPLA victories, thanks to massive Soviet arms shipments, Nyerere stopped delivery on Chinese armaments which had arrived in Dar es-Salaam and, following South African intervention in Angola, went all-out in defense of Soviet-Cuban intervention in Angola. According to British newsman Colin Legum, Nyerere's shift was the "strictly pragmatic" one of going with the winner "in order to avoid the greater risk of an embittering civil war and chaos."[71]

A much tougher nut for Moscow to crack was Zambia which was publicly apprehensive about Soviet-Cuban intervention and insisted well into 1976 that a government of national unity including all three liberation groups, be formed in Angola. At the OAU meeting in January 1976, Zambian President Kaunda countered Nigeria's justification of Soviet involvement on the basis of its past aid to liberation movements with the statement that such assistance "must not be an excuse for establishing hegemony in Africa."[72] His praise of China for

---

[71]Colin Legum, *After Angola* (New York: Africana Publishing House, 1976), p. 34.
[72]*Ibid.*, p. 31.

its lack of imperial ambitions and its hands-off policy toward Angola must also have enraged Moscow. Nevertheless, less than one month later, in February 1976, Kaunda acquiesced in an OAU decision recognizing the Neto regime in Angola, and in April he established relations with it. In September Angola became a full-fledged member of the "front-line" grouping.

The Angolan affair also greatly facilitated Soviet efforts to wean the previously strongly pro-Chinese regime of Samora Machel of Mozambique toward closer ties with the USSR. As late as November 1975, Mozambique Foreign Minister Chissano chided the Soviet Union for seeking to use its aid as a form of pressure.[73] Yet, within weeks the situation had changed, as Machel joined Moscow in support of the MPLA and a process of closer Soviet-Mozambique relations began.

The Rhodesian issue then became the catalyst for intensification of Soviet efforts to solidify its relations with Mozambique. On March 3, 1976 Machel announced the closure of Mozambique's border with Rhodesia despite the heavy cost of this move to the economy of Mozambique. While it is doubtful that the USSR played a direct role in Machel's decision, there can be little question that Soviet-Cuban actions in Angola and Soviet rhetoric pointing to the next targets in southern Africa encouraged Machel in making his move. Thus, when he announced his decision, Machel declared that he looked to his African friends and "to our natural allies—the socialist countries—to be with us."[74]

Soviet coverage of Machel's action was low in volume and restrained in tone, suggesting Soviet hesitation about being asked to make up Mozambique's economic losses. But Moscow was far from hesitant in the military and political fields about taking advantage of the heightened tension on the Rhodesian-Mozambique border. On April 22, Mozambique Defense Minister Chipande left Maputo on a visit to the USSR at the invitation of Soviet Defense Minister Grechko. Following his return eleven days later the Mozambique radio declared that

---

[73]Cited in Library of Congress, Congressional Research Service, *The Soviet Union and the Third World: A Watershed in Great Power Policy* (Washington, D.C.: U.S. Government Printing Office, 1977), p. 99.

[74]Radio Maputo, March 3, 1976.

the visit had "served to map out a joint strategy in the fight against imperialism."[75]

Shortly thereafter Machel himself went to Moscow, where joint action on the Rhodesian question was clearly a major subject of discussion. Speaking at a dinner in Moscow on May 17, 1976, then Soviet President Podgorny emphasized the need for "unity of action of the liberated peoples and their close collaboration with the countries of the socialist community and with all the progressive forces of the world." More specifically, he assured Machel that "where the fighting continues against the last bastions of colonialism and racism," this collaboration permits a combination of "all forms of struggle, including military and political forms."[76]

For his part, Machel made no bones about the role he envisaged for Mozambique: "The People's Republic of Mozambique is aware of its special responsibility in the matter of the liberation of Zimbabwe. We see this struggle as our struggle. Our country is the base for the national liberation of the Zimbabwe people."[77]

In this context Soviet agreement, announced in the joint statement signed upon conclusion of the visit, "to render assistance to Mozambique in consolidating its defense capability"[78] was clearly a pledge to support Mozambique's role as a guerrilla base against Rhodesia. Although Moscow also announced its support for Mozambique's March 3 action closing the border, the joint statement indicated no new Soviet economic aid. In fact, the statement mentioned such aid only with respect to fields in which Mozambique "has already been granted the appropriate credit" by the USSR.

The breakdown in early February of British attempts at Geneva to negotiate a settlement on Rhodesia was seized upon by Moscow to renew its year-long message to the area: instead of negotiations, armed struggle with Soviet aid would bring total, even quick victory. During March and early April 1977, Soviet President Podgorny and Fidel Castro made trips of varying lengths to four of the five front-line states facing Rhodesia and South Africa—both going to Tanzania, Zambia and Mozambique, Castro to Angola as well. According to *Izvestiia*

[75]Radio Maputo, May 3, 1976.
[76]*Pravda*, May 18, 1976.
[77]*Ibid*.
[78]*Pravda*, May 24, 1976.

midway during these trips, "the African peoples' national liberation movement has entered a decisive period of struggle for the continent's complete and definitive liberation from colonialist-racist regimes" in which "special responsibility" lay with the front-line states.[79] *Pravda* on the same day carried an article entitled "The Hour of Liberation Is Near," which reported Podgorny as having "expressed the Soviet people's confidence that the day is not far distant when freedom and equality will cross the River Zambezi and bring independence and justice to the peoples of Rhodesia, Namibia and the Republic of South Africa."[80]

Throughout his trip, Podgorny not only sought to allay suspicions of Soviet motives, but beyond that to establish a community of interest between the USSR and the front-line states on southern African issues. In one of his first speeches after arrival at his initial stop in Tanzania, Podgorny strongly assailed attempts "to foster distrust in Soviet foreign policy" which was exacerbated at the time by the first Katangan incursion into Zaire from Angola. And in an extra sally against the Chinese, he attacked "the notorious concept of the two superpowers."[81] At several points of his tour, Podgorny cited Brezhnev about the USSR's lack of "special interests" in Africa.

Focusing on the major issue uniting the USSR and his hosts, Podgorny in all three countries emphasized Soviet support for insurgencies in Rhodesia, Namibia and South Africa. In his most succinct statement of his principal message, he stressed "that the Soviet Union and the imperialist powers hold polarized positions in regard to the national liberation movement."[82] In Lusaka, moveover, Podgorny on March 28 formally received Nkomo, Sam Nujoma of SWAPO, and Oliver Tambo of the African National Congress.

A major theme in joint statements signed in all three countries was the alleged armed provocations and "aggressions" against the front-line states by Rhodesia and South Africa, charges presumably justifying both Soviet military aid and armed incursions into Rhodesia, Namibia and South Africa from their neighbors. In this connection, one of the

---

[79]V. Kudriavtsev, "Zaire: Interference Continues," *Izvestiia,* March 31, 1977.

[80]P. Demchenko, V. Korovikov, "The Hour of Liberation Is Near," *Pravda,* March 31, 1977.

[81]TASS, March 24, 1977.

[82]*Ibid.*

main purposes of the Podgorny and Castro trips would appear to have been the strengthening of military ties with the countries concerned.

From the Soviet point of view, one of the most successful aspects of Podgorny's trip was its generation of strong expressions of gratitude for Soviet aid to liberation movements from Tanzanian and Zambian Presidents Nyerere and Kaunda. In a banquet honoring Podgorny, Nyerere proclaimed his support for armed struggle in the south of Africa, expressed "enormous satisfaction" for the USSR's "great contribution to Africa's struggle for independence" and declared that "we in Tanzania value highly the aid which the Soviet Union gives liberation struggles."[83]

Kaunda was even more lavish:

> Your fruitful talks with us and with the leaders of the southern African national liberation movements are an important landmark on the way to victory and a specific manifestation of the determination to continue to support the just cause of the oppressed peoples of the south of our continent. The Soviet Union has consistently played and continues to play its historic role of reliable ally of the liberation movements. When we leaders of the movement for Zambia's independence became disappointed in the West's two-faced policy, we also turned to the traditional allies of freedom fighters—the Soviet Union and the other socialist countries.[84]

Capping his visits, Podgorny signed joint statements in all three countries proclaiming, in the words of Radio Moscow on April 4, "the solidarity of the Soviet Union with the oppressed peoples of the south of Africa and the USSR's readiness to provide all possible aid to the national liberation struggles." Perhaps Podgorny's outstanding success was the final statement with Zambia which said that "the Soviet Union and the Republic of Zambia solemnly declare their determination to further render all-round support for the just struggle of the oppressed peoples of Zimbabwe, Namibia, and South Africa."[85]

A similar statement appeared in the document concluded by Podgorny in Mozambique with which he also signed a friendship treaty on March 31, 1977. The treaty, like its counterpart signed with Angola on October 8, 1976, and reaffirming the Soviet pledge during Machel's

[83]*Pravda,* March 24, 1977.
[84]*Pravda,* March 30, 1977.
[85]*Ibid.*

1976 visit to Moscow, provided that the two sides "will continue developing cooperation in the military sphere."[86]

It was not too long after Podgorny's departure that evidence began to appear of new preparations by the front-line states for action against Rhodesia. TASS on April 4, 1977 reported from Mozambique that a meeting had just taken place in the town of Quelimano "devoted to the strengthening of the Patriotic Front and the intensification of the struggle in Rhodesia." Taking part were Machel and Kaunda, the Defense Ministers of Tanzania and Angola, as well as Nkomo and Mugabe.

Meanwhile, there were hints that not everything had gone smoothly during Podgorny's visit. The Tanzanians had agreed to their joint statement with Podgorny that "all progressive forces" should help liberation movements but had evidently balked at suggesting this as a joint Soviet-Tanzanian undertaking, as Zanbia and Mozambique later did. Radio Dar-es-Salaam on April 1 said that Podgorny had called off a sightseeing trip in order to engage in substantive talks with Nyerere on Rhodesia.

In Mozanbique, a Podgorny statement on March 31 that "we do not have excessive means" hinted that the scope of Soviet economic aid remained an issue in Soviet relations with Machel. Podgorny's warning in the same speech against "the illusion that it is possible now to speak of any reconciliation with the racist regimes" may have been aimed at his hosts who, in Soviet eyes, may have been too willing to acquiesce in Western-sponsored negotiations. Podgorny's printed statement noting Mozambique's sacrifices "in order to support actively the fighters for the freedom of their oppressed brothers in the south" implied more expectation than praise.[87] Moscow continued to count on the festering Rhodesian question as a means for maintaining its leverage on the front-line states and through them to radicalize the Patriotic Front and other southern African movements. Podgorny expressed the thought at a dinner in Mozambique on March 29, 1977 when he said:

> The People's Republic of Mozambique and the People's Republic of Angola are not simply two new progressive states in the south of Africa. They are today as it were the crest of a mighty anti-colonial, anti-racist wave. Is it not symbolic that your borders with Rhodesia and the RSA have become not only inter-state but class borders? The wind of free-

[86]TASS, April 3, 1977.
[87]*Pravda*, April 1, 1977.

dom blows from Mozambique and Angola, inspiring the patriots of all southern Africa.[88]

Attitude Toward an Internal Settlement

Similarly, Moscow has defined the domestic situation with Rhodesia in class rather than racial terms. While far from loath to take advantage of racial aspects of the conflict, it has been the revolutionary role of the black struggle against a dominant class which has engaged most Soviet attention. At the same time, Moscow is aware that the racial aspects compound the problems of any compromise settlement and has played on this factor first in encouraging opposition to Anglo-American peace proposals and then to the internal settlement engineered by Ian Smith in 1978–79. Hence the constant charge in Soviet commentaries that these efforts leave power in the hands of "white racists" or a "racist minority."

Only rarely, therefore, has Moscow even mentioned the concerns of the white population about its fate under black majority rule. Increasing expressions in the West during 1976 of the possibility of a race war were dismissed by Moscow. "It is not the Africans fighting for their inalienable rights, or their friends," wrote one Soviet journal, "who are to blame for the danger of a race war which the racists' Western patrons are hypocritically warning against. In doing so these gentry are by no means concerned for the fate of the white settlers whom they themselves have placed in jeopardy, but for their own selfish economic and strategic interests in the south of Africa."[89] Soviet analyses nevertheless often pointed to the exodus of white Rhodesians as evidence that the Smith regime was collapsing or that guerrilla activities were making progress.

However, from time to time, presumably to show that it was reasonable, Moscow did address the issue of what would happen to whites who remained in Rhodesia. In one of the few top level statements, Podgorny said in Lusaka at a dinner in his honor in March 1977:

The best guarantee of security for the white population is dissociation from the racists, unconditional and speedy renunciation of the racist or-

[88]*Pravda*, March 31, 1977.
[89]Volsky, "Rhodesia: The Beginning of the End," p. 11.

der. The program statements of the Zimbabwe, Namibian and South African freedom fighters about the fact that the democratic rights of the white citizens in these countries will be insured in conditions of majority rule are endorsed in the Soviet Union.[90]

Anatoly Gromyko, son of the Soviet Foreign Minister and head of the Soviet Institute of Africa, has touched on the subject in his articles over the years, though generally only in passing. In his only treatment of any length, Gromyko contended that the Patriotic Front was simply seeking equality:

> The Patriotic Front is by no means setting itself the goal of "driving the Europeans from the country." Majority rule does not mean the exclusion of Europeans from the life of the country but only the granting of equal rights and opportunities to all of its inhabitants.[91]

Perhaps the only discussion of any length bearing on the subject came in an *Izvestiia* article in May 1979 by V. Kudriavtsev, one of Moscow's most prolific writers of African subjects. Kudriavtsev, in an unusual twist, suggested that past Soviet yardsticks "when colonialism was on one side of the barricades of the national liberation struggle and the peoples it oppressed were on the other, could not be applied." Whereas previously, he wrote, the metropolitan countries, such as the U.K., could leave their colonies and continue to exist, "no such prospect lies before the ruling circles of the Republic of South Africa and Rhodesia." Accordingly, he concluded, "a solution must also be found to the question of the white minority, which unlike the white population of the 'classic' colonies cannot evacuate to the mother country."[92] Kudriavtsev, however, hazarded no solution to this problem, merely saying that it "complicates" matters and "explains the sophistication of the maneuvers the racists and imperialists" to preserve "racist states camouflaged as 'independent,' 'African' and even 'democratic.' "

Kudriavtsev's suggestion that the situation was complicated came against the background of the formation of a black-led Rhodesian government under Bishop Muzorewa and seemed a grudging admission that this approach might cause special difficulties. Thus, *New Times* in

[90]*Pravda*, March 30, 1977.
[91]Gromyko, "Neocolonialism's Maneuvers," p. 100.
[92]V. Kudriavtsev, "The Southern African Whirlpool," *Izvestiia*, May 4, 1979.

May 1979 declared: "It has long been plain to see that the racist regimes in southern Africa are in the throes of their death agony. The process, however, has proved to be a protracted one."[93]

Moscow roundly denounced Ian Smith's moves toward an "internal settlement" involving black leaders as they unfolded in 1978 and 1979. Soviet propaganda sought to discredit these moves on both racial and political grounds by denying that any significant power was being surrendered by the white minority or that the procedure followed constituted a true expression of the will of the majority in Rhodesia. Moscow's major concern was that the internal settlement might garner sufficient support from black Rhodesians either to isolate the Patriotic Front or to draw it into negotiations with Smith or the Western powers. Thus, one of Moscow's first commentaries in 1978 on negotiations between Smith and black leaders Muzorewa, Sithole and Chirau saw these talks as a "show staged with the purpose of softening the position of the genuine patriots and making them more pliable."[94] As later Soviet commentaries also were to do, this one claimed that these African leaders "represent an insignificant stratum of the indigenous population." As the process unfolded, Moscow increasingly used epithets such as "puppet" and "traitor" to describe the African leaders involved, particularly Muzorewa.

Soviet media denounced the agreements on February 15 and March 3, 1978 between Smith and the three black leaders as a "shameful deal" designed to cover the Smith regime with a "thin layer of Africanization"[95] and to induce an end to the guerrilla struggle which was threatening white rule in Rhodesia. According to *New Times,* these agreements along with Angolo-American peace efforts contained "the basic deficiency" of providing "for legalization of the Smith racist regime, retention of all the privileges of the white minority, and an end to the armed guerrilla struggle."[96]

Repeated Soviet emphasis on unabated Patriotic Front determination to continue armed struggle suggested that the Kremlin was in fact worried that war-weary black Rhodesians and front-line states

---

[93]D. Volsky, "Protracted Convulsions," *New Times,* No. 22, May 1979, p. 7.

[94]V. Sidenko, "Zimbabwe Patriots Stand Firm," *New Times,* No. 1, February 1978, p. 16.

[95]Radio Moscow, March 3, 1978.

[96]Stanislav Vasilyev, "Racist Manoeuvre," *New Times,* No. 14, April 1978, p. 10.

might be tempted to see either in the Smith or Anglo-American proposals a way out of the fighting. Discussing the March 3 agreement, a Radio Moscow roundtable participant five months later on August 14, 1978 noted:

> Evidently one of the aims was to quell, somehow, the partisan wave, the wave of the liberation movement. They calculated that a few concessions, combined with the influence and former prestige of Muzorewa and Sithole, would lead to a split in the ranks of the liberation movement, and above all in the ranks of the fighters for national independence.

According to another participant "perhaps there was a certain number of deserters or some vacillators who took this bait." However, he went on, "the bulk of the guerrilla army, the main forces, remained firm." Nevertheless, coming at a time when Nkomo was once more negotiating with Ian Smith in Lusaka, this reference to "vacillators" undoubtedly reflected Soviet nervousness about the turn of events. A *New Times* article at this time, without mentioning the Nkomo-Smith talks, warned against "sterile bargaining" with Smith who was said to be seeking to "isolate the true patriots" thereby "compelling them to enter into compromises tantamount to capitulation."[97] The article also decried efforts "to brainwash leaders of African states that support the liberation struggle waged by Zimbabwe patriots" presumably meaning Kaunda for helping arrange the Smith-Nkomo talks.

It was with an almost palpable sigh of relief that Moscow greeted the failure of these talks and renewed emphasis on continued guerrilla warfare by Nkomo and his African supporters. *Izvestiia* welcomed the meeting in Lusaka after a six-month lapse of the presidents of the front-line states and their confirmation of the "stillborn nature" of the internal settlement. Moreover, wrote *Izvestiia*, the settlement "has not only failed to halt the armed partisan movement but, on the contrary, has been its catalyst. Fresh fighters are constantly enlisting under the banners of the Zimbabwe Patriotic Front. Its operations have acquired the scale of a nationwide uprising."[98]

Breaking Soviet silence on the Nkomo-Smith talks after they were over, a Soviet commentary noted in mid-September 1978 that Nkomo

[97]Ye. Tarabrin, "The Neo-Colonialist Strategem in Africa," *New Times,* No. 35, August 1978, p. 18.
[98]B. Pilatskin, "Just Cause of Zimbabwe," *Izvestiia,* September 5, 1978.

had "reemphasized" in these talks with Smith that the issue was transfer of power to the Patriotic Front, including "the establishment of a new army under Patriotic Front control." The very fact of Smith's talking to Nkomo was said to indicate lack of confidence in an internal settlement and desire "to split the Zimbabwe Patriotic Front and weaken the guerrilla ranks."[99]

Well before the April 1979 Rhodesian elections, Moscow appeared relatively confident that the turnout would be small and the elections discredited. *New Times* in November 1978 explained the failure to hold elections as originally planned because "it is beyond Smith's power to hold the election in the countryside, where the guerrillas are very active."[100] In March, the same journal speculated that "intensified guerrilla actions could torpedo the holding of the April elections."[101] Numerous commentaries condemned the elections out of hand as a "farce." Throughout its coverage, Moscow stressed that the Patriotic Front was the "genuine" representative of the entire black population and that its boycott meant the elections had no legitimacy. Indeed, reflecting its own system of government, Moscow clearly did not believe that any kind of free elections were suitable for Rhodesia.

In an unusual pair of articles, Soviet analyst Kudriavtsev argued that Western-style democracy was unsuited to the Rhodesians and indeed to the entire African scene. In the first, he stated that events since 1960 had demonstrated to Africans "that the constitutions imposed on them by the imperialist metropolitan states, like 'general' elections on the basis of the principles of bourgeois democracy, serve mainly to delay their independent development and promote a policy of neocolonialism."[102] Two months later, he supplemented this argument with two others: "In Africa, Western pluralism has turned into the creation of tribal or even 'personal' parties. And it means military agreements which have permitted the West to continue having military bases and even garrisons on foreign territory."[103] The model Moscow has in mind is a replica of its own revolution with the Patriotic Front

[99]V. Kirsanov, "Racists in Trouble," *New Times,* No. 38, September 1978, p.11.

[100]V. Sidenko, "For Whom the Bell Tolls," *New Times,* No. 47, November 1978, p. 13.

[101]Ye. Tyunkov, "Zimbabwe's Firm Resolve," *New Times,* No. 11, March 1979, p. 15.

[102]V. Kudriavtsev, "The Rhodesian Merry-Go-Round," *Izvestiia,* January 26, 1978.

[103]Kudriavtsev, "Sentence Has Been Passed."

assuming the role of vanguard and Soviet-style elections following, not preceding the assumption of power. Kudriavtsev makes this explicit in his first article. A solution in Rhodesia, he wrote, consists "in Britain of removing the racists from power and transferring that power to the African majority represented by the Patriotic Front which will itself organize general elections, elaborate a constitution, organize the maintenance of internal order, and insure that security of all citizens."

In this context, therefore, the facts of the elections were irrelevant and Moscow duly condemned the dispatch of U.S. Congressional observers as another form of connivance. Not surprisingly, the Soviet media condemned the results as a prearranged scenario and explained the large turnout as the result of coercion. *Pravda* on April 23, just after the elections, carried a commentary pointedly entitled "At Gunpoint" which charged that "even the very procedure of the elections clearly revealed their fraudulent and coercive nature." Rather than the extent of the turnout, Soviet sources emphasized that a third of the Africans did not take part. A *New Times* analysis declared that the results were determined by the relative strength of the private armies of the candidates with Muzorewa winning because his army of Mashona tribesmen "was the largest in numbers and the most ruthless in actions."[104] Anatoly Gromyko several months later charged that "the only freedom at these elections was for the bayonets of Smith's racist thugs with which they drove the Africans, literally drove them, to the polling booths."[105]

While aware of Western misgivings, the bulk of Soviet commentaries sought to identify the West one way or another with Smith's internal settlement efforts. While conceding that these efforts cut across those of the U.S. and the U.K., some Soviet commentaries charged that by negotiating with Smith, the West gave him the respectability which made possible his own initiatives. Further, by setting in motion these negotiating efforts, the West "gave a respite" to Smith, who then decided to "seize the initiative himself."[106] Thus, it was agreed, there was in fact a "precise distribution of functions"[107] and even "conniv-

---

[104]V. Sidenko, "The 'Internal Settlement' Farce," *New Times,* No. 20, May 1979, p. 10.

[105]Radio Moscow, July 10, 1979.

[106]Kudriavtsev, "The Rhodesian Merry-Go-Round."

[107]Kudriavtsev, "Sentence Has Been Passed."

ance"[108] in a plot to defuse the guerrilla actions in Rhodesia and the position of the Patriotic Front. Basically, many Soviet spokesmen claimed, there was no difference between the Anglo-American proposals and the internal settlement.

Moscow pounced on Ian Smith's visit to the United States in October 1978 to suggest that Washington was setting the stage for ultimate recognition of the internal settlement. *Izvestiia* on October 26 said that U.S. authorities "pretended" to oppose granting a visa to Smith but then proceeded to do so.[109] *New Times* added: "What is more, he was not only afforded ample opportunity to make public appearances, but given a cordial official welcome."[110] *Pravda* then summed it all up: "By all appearances a 'scenario' was elaborated there [in Washington] in accordance with which the 'internal settlement' plan being implemented by Smith is to receive the formal blessing of Western states."[111] In a further effort to discredit the U.S., Soviet propagandists charged Rhodesian raids into Zambia which were mounted concurrently with Smith's visit were part of the U.S.-approved plan.

The high point of the whole scenario, according to Soviet predictions, would be the lifting of sanctions against Rhodesia by the U.S. and the U.K. In addition to taking the heat out of guerrilla operations, this has been adduced by Moscow as Smith's major objective. Thus wrote *New Times* in connection with Smith's U.S. visit: "It was clearly with a view to persuading the West openly to back his policy and, in particular, to lift economic sanctions that Smith staged the internal settlement farce."[112] Following the April 1979 elections, further statements along these lines appeared, reinforced by the vote in the U.S. Senate in May recommending an end to sanctions and the election in May of Mrs. Thatcher in the U.K. who was avowedly sympathetic to such action.

At the same time, Moscow saw certain constraints on the West which caused it to hesitate either in accepting the Muzorewa government or in lifting sanctions. First, Soviet commentaries indicated the Carter Administration in the U.S. and the Labor Government in the U.K. have been dubious about a settlement which would exclude the

[108]TASS, Otober 24, 1978.

[109]V. Kudriavtsev, "A Lie To The Rescue of Racism," *Izvestiia*, October 26, 1978.

[110]Sidenko, "For Whom The Bell Tolls, " p. 12.

[111]M. Zenovich, "Rhodesia's Camp David," *Pravda*, November 5, 1978.

[112]Sidenko, "For Whom the Bell Tolls," p. 13.

Patriotic Front and mean continued guerrilla warfare. Thus, conceded *New Times* after the April elections, the internal settlement approach "was not at first received with much enthusiasm" in the West because "the imperialist strategy planners would prefer a more subtle neo-colonialist version envisaging an 'all-party' conference or, in other words, bring the Patriotic Front leaders and the racist puppets to the negotiating table with a view to securing their agreement to U.N.-supervised elections in Rhodesia" which would "in the final analysis" lead to a regime "subordinate to the West."[113]

Secondly, according to Moscow, the West was fearful of the impact that recognition of Muzorewa and lifting sanctions would have on its relations with the rest of Africa and the Third World. *Pravda* on May 28 said such moves were "fraught with the threat of a serious deterioration in British and U.S. relations with the dozens of African states which support the Patriotic Front's struggle for real independence and freedom for Zimbabwe."[114] Anatoly Gromyko in July noted the possibility that Nigeria might stop oil deliveries to the U.S. and the U.K. Accordingly, he declared, the West intended "to bide its time as far as the recognition of Muzorewa is concerned in order not to have the privileges of its monopolies threatened over a wide area of Africa."[115]

Although there were fewer predictions of imminent victories in mid-1979, Soviet analyses still considered that the tide of events was going in favor of the Patriotic Front. Kudriavtsev claimed that "Rhodesia's economy has been heading steadily toward disaster,"[116] *New Times* that 80 percent of the territory is controlled by guerrillas and "the emigration of Europeans has assumed the character of a mass flight from the country."[117] Radio Moscow in June praised renewed efforts by Nkomo and Mugabe "toward further cohesion of the country's liberation forces in the new stage of the struggle against the racist regime and its screen of puppets."[118] Finally, Moscow greeted with satisfaction actions in the U.N. Security Council rejecting the internal settlement and in the OAU reaffirming support for the Patriotic Front.

---

[113]Sidenko, "The 'Internal Settlement' Farce," p. 11.
[114]V. Korovikov, "Gambling on Puppets," *Pravda,* May 28, 1979.
[115]Radio Moscow, July 10, 1979.
[116]Kudriavtsev, "The Southern African Whirlpool."
[117]Sidenko, "The "Internal Settlement' Farce," p. 11.
[118]Radio Moscow, June 3, 1979.

What Moscow appeared to envisage was a relatively prolonged war of attrition in which the situation would polarize with the USSR and black Africa on one side, the West, South Africa and the Muzorewa regime on the other.

This expectation was presumably altered once more by the British-sponsored talks beginning in London on September 10, 1979 which culminated in the signature on December 21 of a full-scale agreement on a ceasefire, new constitution, an interim arrangement to be followed by new elections in 1980. Soviet coverage ranged from hostile to skeptical at every stage of the process which led to the agreement.

On the eve of the Commonwealth conference in Lusaka in August 1979 at which U.K. Prime Minister Margaret Thatcher set the wheels in motion, TASS predicted that the U.K. wanted to get the meeting to put the Commonwealth on record behind the Muzorewa regime.[119] When the British instead put forward proposals for a settlement which would replace the Muzorewa government, Soviet media were skeptical. Radio Moscow on August 11 acknowledged that the U.K. had indeed changed its position but suggested that it had done so "under pressure" from African countries and with the aim of getting the Patriotic Front to cease guerrilla operations and of securing a respite for the Muzorewa government. One Radio Moscow commentator on August 12 claimed that "most African states opposed the British proposals," while another on August 14 said the Patriotic Front rejected them as a scheme "to maintain the rule of the white minority." Moscow remained critical even after agreement was reached. In the one major written commentary, *New Times* contended: "Britain wants to protect neocolonialist interests by slightly brushing up the present Muzorewa-Smith regime in order to legalize the *de facto* dominion of the racists and their servitors in Rhodesia."[120]

This and other commentaries indicated a continued Soviet insistence that the Front maintain its maximum positions which, it may be assumed, were also communicated to Front leaders privately. *New Times* pointed out that the "realistic approach" it had in mind was the transfer of the "full plenitude of power to the Zimbabwe people in the person of the Patriotic Front as its sole representative." Radio Mos-

[119]TASS, July 31, 1979.
[120]Veniamin Midtsev, "Behind the Lusaka Agreement," *New Times*, No. 35, August 1979, p. 13.

cow on August 17 asked "can a compromise be achieved in such an important matter as the liberation of a people from the colonialist and racist yoke? Never." And a Soviet journal, while reporting that the Patriotic Front had agreed to take part in the London conference, approvingly noted the Front's refusal to agree to a ceasefire until a full settlement was reached.[121]

Throughout the course of the Lancaster House conference, Soviet dispatches cast doubt on U.K. motives and tactics as well as prospects for the negotiations. Radio Moscow on September 11, 1979, for example, charged that the U.K. had invited the Patriotic Front to London as a show of fairplay but that the U.K. and the U.S. "have no intention of taking account of the Front's just demands." Conceding that the U.K. had, however, taken the Front's views on a constitution into account, Radio Moscow on September 17 declared, "One gets the impression that London does not intend to honestly play the role of a totally unbiased judge." U.K. Foreign Secretary Lord Carrington's ultimatums at key points of the negotiations were denounced as unwarranted arm-twisting directed at the Patriotic Front and the U.K. portrayed to the end as against the Front. In December, *New Times* charged that U.K. proposals were "redolent of colonialism" because of a strong pro-Salisbury lobby in London. It concluded that "it is indeed very difficult for the London 'mediators' to be impartial when their class and property interests are so directly involved."[122]

In the latter stages of negotiations, Soviet commentaries sought to give the impression that whatever progress had been made was attributable to the Patriotic Front, especially to the extent that it remained firm. *New Times* in September said that the Lancaster conference itself was "the direct result of the successful armed struggle waged by the patriots of Zimbabwe."[123] Radio Moscow on November 17 declared that "this conference was not a game of concessions, it was a tenacious struggle" in which the Front forced the British to recognize its legitimacy and to repudiate "the force that led Muzorewa to the office of prime minister." Several commentaries suggested that the

---

[121]V. Shubin, "Zimbabwe or Rhodesia," *Aziia i Afrika Segodnia*, No. 10, October 1979, p. 27.

[122]A. Butlitsky, "Salisbury Lobby," *New Times*, No. 49, December 1979, p. 25.

[123]V. Pavlov, "The Lancaster House Conference," *New Times*, No. 39, September 1979, p. 9.

Front had foiled U.S. and U.K. efforts to show that it was intransigent or to bar it from taking part in a Rhodesian settlement. *Pravda* on December 23, 1979, in the first Soviet comment of any consequence on the total agreement, declared that "the position of the front, which advocates a peaceful solution to the Rhodesian problem based on regard for the real situation in the country and for the role and influence of the national liberation movement, has objectively received recognition."[124]

Nevertheless, the main thrust of the December 23 *Pravda* commentary and other Soviet writings was one of skepticism about the durability of the London agreement. *Pravda* noted that "many commentators are predicting not without grounds that the development of events in the country will encounter many difficulties." *Pravda* saw a "fierce political struggle" in the offing, especially since the British would seek to insure a victory for Muzorewa and "Smith's white colonialists" so that "just as it did during the conference, the Patriotic Front will again have to deal with the enemy's combined forces—with London and Salisbury."

In another expression of Soviet skepticism, the USSR abstained on December 21 when the Security Council voted to lift sanctions against Rhodesia. As noted by *Pravda,* the Soviet representative took the position "that under present conditions the lifting of sanctions against Rhodesia is premature and could play into the colonialists' and racists' hands."

Soviet commentators at year's end in 1979 appeared to be establishing the framework for a charge that the U.K. and the West generally would seek to use the elections called for by the London agreements to rob the Patriotic Front of the victory it had gained through military action. TASS on September 29 had contended that "no one doubts that free elections will be won by the Patriotic Front," but later commentaries claimed that the U.K. was seeking to rig the elections in Muzorewa's favor.

On the eve of final signature, Radio Moscow on December 18 even expressed doubts about statements by Nkomo and Mugabe that the agreement could provide the basis for a truly democratic Zimbabwe. According to the Soviet commentator, "Political observers in many

[124]Yu. Yakhontov, "International Week," *Pravda,* December 23, 1979.

countries wonder whether this agreement will really become a basis for resolving the Rhodesian problem or whether London and the puppet will not attempt to use it for gaining unilateral advantages." Because the U.K. was said to be seeking "to insure the success of the puppet officials" and Muzorewa to have built-in advantages for the forthcoming elections, the commentator said, "the basis for giving power in Rhodesia to a regime obedient to the West and to Pretoria is already being laid." *Pravda's* December 23 article implied the same when it stated: "Certain Western powers and monopolies have put down too deep roots here. They have a great interest in preserving an obedient neocolonial regime in the south of the continent." Speaking to a Radio Moscow forum on December 23, 1979 the influential Soviet political analyst Aleksandr Bovin declared that he found it difficult "to draw the conclusion that the way has altogether been paved for a peaceful development and a peaceful transformation of Rhodesia into, as it were, the democratic republic of Zimbabwe."

During the visit of new Angolan President dos Santos to Moscow in December 1979, Soviet Foreign Minister Gromyko obviously had Rhodesia (and Namibia) in mind when he warned on December 21 that "the Western patrons of the racialists seek to replace genuine liberation of peoples with a false one, to impose formulae for settlement of burning problems of the south of Africa that are advantageous to themselves," adding that "they are trying to split the fighters of the freedom of Africa from their reliable friends—the socialist countries."[125] The final communique of that visit, ignoring the London talks, proclaimed that both sides opposed "maneuvers aimed at debarring the Zimbabwe Patriotic Front from the process of gaining independence by imposing inequitable terms" and reaffirmed "support for the Patriotic Front as the true representative of the Zimbabwe people."[126]

Moscow's lack of enthusiasm for the Lancaster House agreements not only implied criticism of the Patriotic Front and front-line states for acceding to it, but suggested concern that Soviet leverage would be reduced if the agreements were effectively implemented. Continued Soviet insistence that only a complete transfer of power to the Patriotic Front would represent a legitimate outcome of a Rhodesian settlement suggested both an estimate that the Front would in fact have to share

[125]*Pravda*, December 22, 1979.
[126]*Pravda*, December 23, 1979.

power and an effort to persuade Front leaders that such a sharing was not acceptable. Soviet predictions that the agreements would be difficult to implement thus represented a hope as much as they did an analysis. Even at worst, however, Moscow probably expected that it would retain considerable leverage by cashing in on its previous ties to the Patriotic Front, and particularly to the Nkomo faction.

CHAPTER NINE

New Pressure on Namibia

As in the case of Rhodesia, the fall of the Portuguese empire and Soviet-Cuban intervention in Angola brought Namibia increasingly to the fore as a target of Soviet interest and efforts. Before that, Moscow had viewed Namibia mainly as a convenient issue to demonstrate its support for black Africa and to berate the West for unwillingness to support extreme U.N. actions to force South Africa to withdraw from its "illegal occupation" of Namibia. The emergence in Angola of a militant anti-South Africa regime flooded with Soviet advisers and Cuban troops obviously transformed the situation and Moscow's views of the opportunities which were opening up. Instead of a small point of entry in the northeast corner of Namibia, South Africa now had a long border to be concerned about, the Soviet-favored Southwest Africa People's Organization, a new and willing sanctuary, vastly increased possibilities for training by Soviet and Cuban advisers and acquisition of arms—in general, much more scope in which to operate.

However, as duly noted by Moscow, the circumstances increasing Soviet opportunities also increased Western alarm which found its expression in the diplomacy of Henry Kissinger continued and modified by the Carter Administration. On Namibia, as on Rhodesia, Moscow sought to sharpen the dilemmas facing the West in seeking to bridge the gap between South Africa and SWAPO, and in reconciling Western interests in Namibia with an effort to avoid identification with South Africa.

Opposition to Western Plans

Moscow's main objective clearly was to push both protagonists into extreme positions which would jeopardize the position of Western mediators. With the same intensity it displayed on Rhodesia, Moscow insisted that the issue in Namibia came down to a simple choice between a total transfer of power to SWAPO (which, as Moscow incessantly noted, had been anointed by the OAU and U.N. as the only genuine representative of the Namibian people) and a military fight to the finish in which moderate and pro-Western elements would be swept out of the picture and the prime need would be for Soviet arms and presumably, therefore, Soviet guidance.

Moscow consistently belittled Western efforts to negotiate a settlement in which SWAPO would have to share power or in which Western and South African interests would be taken into account. Soviet media denigrated Western motivation, warned that the final results could not be satisfactory, ignored or cast doubt on moments of agreement, and barely concealed its satisfaction at moments of apparent breakdown.

As portrayed by Moscow, the U.S., after years of neglect or unwillingness to back up its claims of support for Namibian independence, sought to apply the same step-by-step approach to the problems of southern Africa that Kissinger had devised for the Middle East. The main feature of this phase, according to Soviet commentaries, was an effort to work with and cajole the South African government of Prime Minister Vorster toward a compromise settlement in Namibia. Thus, just after Kissinger met Vorster in Zurich in 1976, *Izvestiia's* political observer Kudriavtsev excoriated "the behind-the-scenes maneuverings of U.S. diplomacy, conducted jointly with the South African racists and directed toward preserving—under the guise of all sorts of constitutional procedures—South African control over Namibia's affairs."[1] *Pravda* on September 19 declared that, "worried by the growth of the liberation struggles" in Rhodesia and Namibia, Kissinger "unbidden" had offered his good offices for a peaceful solution. "To save" the white regimes "by inducing them to make certain concessions to the African population—this is the aim of Kissinger's mission."[2]

[1] Radio Moscow, September 12, 1976.
[2] O. Orestov, "The International Week," *Pravda,* September 19, 1976.

A major element of this approach, according to several Soviet analyses, was to draw SWAPO into talks with South Africa on the latter's terms. According to the journal *USA,* the United States was seeking "to nudge SWAPO into talks with Pretoria and exert pressure on the organization to make it agree to the creation in Namibia of a coalition government with the participation of henchmen of the Vorster regime and to sound out SWAPO from the standpoint of the opportunity of splitting the organization into quarreling groups."[3]

With the advent of the Carter Administration, Moscow saw a significant change in the U.S. approach to the Namibian question involving stepped-up pressure on South Africa and a more determined effort to involve SWAPO in peace talks. "Taught by bitter experience," *New Times* wrote in July 1977, "the Western powers displayed a greater understanding of the seriousness of the situation in Namibia than their South African partners"[4]—hence Western insistence on South African concessions in talks held at Cape Town between Vorster and representatives of the five Western members of the U.N. Security Council.

The journal *USA* one month later put it more bluntly: "Washington found it necessary to exert overt diplomatic pressure on the Republic of South Africa in regard to the question of Namibia." *USA* explained this "definite departure" from Kissinger's policy as a response to pressure in the U.N. Moreover, the journal acknowledged as a concession that South Africa had agreed to elections under U.N. supervision in which SWAPO could participate. At the same time, *USA* reported with relish that U.S. pressure was not without cost: "The South African monopolies have been there [in Namibia] for a long time, their position is strong and they are hardly likely to accept the one-sided American approach without putting up a fight."[5]

Thus, Moscow has sought to have it both ways: to play on differences between the West and South Africa on Namibia in order to isolate South Africa, and at the same time to identify the West with South Africa in order to exacerbate relations between the West and the rest of Africa as well as to discourage SWAPO from negotiating with

[3]V.D. Turkatenko, "Washington's Calculations and Miscalculations in Southern Africa," *USA: Economics, Politics, Ideology,* No. 2, February 1977.

[4]Yuri Tsaplin, "Independence—Real or Sham?" *New Times,* No. 27, July 1977, p. 9.

[5]M. L. Vishnevskii, "Washington's African Maneuvers," *USA: Economics, Politics, Ideology,* No. 8, August 1977, p. 84.

the West. For example, on the eve of a visit by U.S. Secretary of State Vance and British Foreign Secretary David Owen to Pretoria in April 1978, a TASS commentary saw "difference only in details" between the West and South Africa on Namibia, with the former wanting to include SWAPO, the latter seeking to bar it. However, TASS concluded:

> Really there is no substantial discrepancy between the goals of the diplomacy of the USA and Britain on the one hand and the Republic of South Africa on the other, in spite of the verbal wrangle. All three states seek first of all to insure Western control over Namibia, just as over Rhodesia, with the help of black puppets so as subsequently to connect the territories with the Republic of South Africa economically and politically, and create a strong bastion of imperialism in the African continent's south.[6]

Throughout the process, Moscow has glossed over South African concessions and focused more on still outstanding issues. Signs of flexibility are always outweighed in Soviet accounts by charges of intransigence. Thus, in January 1977, *Pravda* first conceded that even the tribal leaders whom Moscow regularly denounced as puppets recognized the need for SWAPO participation in a Namibian settlement, and called it "indicative that Pretoria has made a number of curtsies in the direction of SWAPO," including an invitation for it to attend the South African sponsored Turnhalle talks in Windhoek, designed to set the stage for an independent Namibia. However, *Pravda* then noted that SWAPO refused to attend unless certain obviously unacceptable conditions were met, and concluded that "the refusal of the racists to enter into negotiations with SWAPO leaves the patriots no other alternative but to intensify the liberation."[7]

Similarly, after the Vance-Owen talks in Pretoria in early 1978, *Pravda* declared that they "confirm yet again that the racists are only prepared to make minor concessions, while continuing to ignore the main demands of the patriots and of U.N. resolutions."[8] Radio Moscow described South African agreement to U.N.-sponsored elections

[6]Sergei Kulik, "Double-Faced Policy," TASS, April 14, 1978.
[7]V. Tyurkin, "Namibia: The Difficult Path to Freedom," *Pravda,* January 19, 1977.
[8]Moscow Radio Peace and Progress, April 26, 1978.

as "seemingly smooth and sugar-coated promises [which] contain many underwater reefs and outright traps."[9]

When a breakthrough appeared to have been reached in July 1978, with the signature of an agreement between SWAPO and Western negotiators concurred in by South Africa, it was completely ignored by the Soviet press at the time. Radio Moscow on July 15 admitted that South Africa "appears to have agreed" on key points at issue but added that "there is reason to believe this is not sincere." A second broadcast on July 27 focused on still unresolved issues to show that assertions that the Namibian problem was solved "are false and harmful." Moreover, the broadcast said, "the West still closes its eyes to all the trickery and dodging of the racists."

Similarly it was only Radio Moscow, not the Soviet press, which noted two South African messages to U.N. Secretary General Waldheim on December 22, 1978 informing him that South Africa and the Democratic Turnhalle Alliance (DTA) in Southwest Africa both agreed to accept U.N. plans for the independence of Namibia. Radio Moscow on December 26 charged, however, that these messages constituted "an attempt to achieve international recognition" for South African-sponsored elections in Namibia in September 1978 in which the DTA had won 41 to 50 seats. Radio Moscow further charged that "the real leaders of the Namibian people, the leaders and members of SWAPO, are being put in prison, tortured, eliminated or discredited as terrorists." The barring of SWAPO, it said, "is the essence, not only of the two messages, but in the final analysis of the whole political games being played by Pretoria and the West in Namibia."

Nevertheless, Moscow scarcely hid its uneasiness about SWAPO's willingness to participate in Western-led negotiations under U.N. auspices. Soviet representatives made clear when they abstained in Security Council votes on July 27 and September 29, 1978 that they did so only because they were "taking into account SWAPO's position and the position of other African States" accepting proposals by the West and the Secretary General on how to achieve Namibian independence. However, Soviet U.N. delegate Oleg Troyanovsky in July reaffirmed "the negative view which the USSR had expressed on many occasions concerning the Namibian settlement plan as proposed by the five

[9]Valery Volkov, "The Just Cause of Namibia," *Pravda,* April 24, 1978.

Western members of the Security Council," and attacked the West in general as bearing "major responsibility for the continued occupation of Namibia by South Africa."[10] His deputy, Mikhail Kharlamov, in September 1978 criticized the resolution passed there for its failure to condemn South Africa and warned that the whole course of the consideration of the Namibian question in the Council increased doubts and fears regarding future developments in Namibia and the possible role to be played by the United Nations in that connection."[11]

Moscow only sporadically and grudgingly saw any utility in SWAPO's negotiations with the West and South Africa on a settlement. Radio Moscow on July 15, 1978 quoted the SWAPO leader's characterization of his agreement with the five Western members of the Security Council and SWAPO as a "dramatic victory," and a broadcast on July 27 pointed out that SWAPO's willingness to meet with the West demonstrated that it did "not rule out the possibility of solving the [Namibian] problem by peaceful means." A Radio Moscow discussant on November 12, 1978 contended that despite South African attempts to provoke SWAPO rejection, "the SWAPO leadership nevertheless decided to approve the proposals of the Western countries on the basis of their view that in general despite all its negative points the plan would allow some sort of peaceful solution of the problem." In a later analysis Anatoly Gromyko acknowledged that "in the end, pressure from independent Africa and other factors, have forced the Five to modify their plan for Namibia so as to take into account SWAPO's positions and demands," an outcome he described as an "unquestionable success for the Namibian patriots and the forces supporting them."[12]

Another Soviet discussion saw SWAPO's negotiations with the West as a "second front of struggle" to be pursued "without ceasing activities on the fields of battle,"[13] a stance also enunciated by Nujoma

[10]United Nations, *Monthly Chronicle,* Vol. XV, No. 8, August-September 1978, p. 12.

[11]*Ibid.,* Vol. XV, No. 9, October 1978, p. 13.

[12]Anatoly Gromyko, "Western Diplomacy vs. Southern Africa," *International Affairs,* No. 3, March 1979, p. 25.

[13]I. A. Ulanovskaia, "Calculations and Miscalculations of the Imperialists in Namibia," *The Working Class and the Contemporary World,* No. 5, September-October 1978, p. 127.

when he addressed the Security Council in September 1978.[14] The same Soviet discussion said that SWAPO had conditionally accepted Western proposals in July 1978 in order to "spare the Namibian people superfluous sacrifices."[15]

However, these relatively positive assessments were few in number and usually balanced by cautionary notes and expressions of doubt about South African and Western sincerity. The July 27 broadcast by Radio Moscow warned that "the African public should not allow itself to lose vigilance in the face of the short and long-term plans of the West and South Africa concerning Namibia."

Most significantly, between these two broadcasts Nujoma journeyed to Moscow presumably to explain to Soviet leaders why he had concluded the agreement with the Western Five. A statement following his meeting with Boris Ponomarev, candidate Politburo member and Central Committee Secretary, on July 17 reported that "Nujoma told of the struggle being waged by the people of Namibia under the leadership of SWAPO to liberate the country from South African occupation, and for the genuine independence of their homeland."[16] Nujoma's reported expressions of gratitude for Soviet aid were less effusive than when he talked to Ponomarev in August 1976 and October 1977.[17] Presumably more to Moscow's liking, Nujoma in a Luanda interview with a Soviet correspondent in August reemphasized the theme of armed struggle after noting that SWAPO "has held talks which have been wrecked every time by the Pretoria authorities and the West."[18]

Sporadic claims in Soviet discussions that the West was seeking to generate splits within the ranks of SWAPO suggested a certain amount of Soviet concern about SWAPO cohesion and the susceptibility of some of its members to the blandishments of the West. In one of the few Soviet commentaries to devote attention of any length to this theme, the Soviet journal *Asia and Africa Today* noted several cleavages, which the "imperialists" were said to be trying to exploit: between SWAPO members operating legally within Namibia and those engaged in guerrilla operations; between those in the country and

---

[14]United Nations, *Monthly Chronicle*, Vol. XV, No. 9, October 1978, p. 11.
[15]Ulanovskaia, "Calculations and Miscalculations, " p. 128.
[16]*Pravda*, July 18, 1978.
[17]*Pravda*, August 12, 1976 and October 8, 1977.
[18]*Pravda*, August 26, 1978.

Namibian emigres; between SWAPO groups in Angola and those in Zambia. This article reaffirmed the timeliness of a SWAPO Congress resolution in May 1976 to the effect that the "struggle for unity and purity of the ranks of the organization remains one of the most important tasks of the organization."[19]

To bolster African opposition to Western peace efforts, Moscow also has been quick to seize on punitive raids by South Africa against SWAPO camps in Zambia and Angola as evidence of South African insincerity and the fruitlessness of negotiations with it. Moscow, however, passed over without comment the involvement as reported in the Western press of these states, notably Angola, in the Western search for a compromise settlement in Namibia.

SWAPO irritation over the attitude of its African allies was unmistakeable in an interview given the Italian communist newspaper *L'Unita* in September 1977 by SWAPO's Organizational Secretary Homatemi Kaluenja. When asked by the correspondent about "pressure from some front-line countries to persuade SWAPO" to accept Western proposals, Kaluenja replied that "it is nothing new for us to undergo pressure" and that "of course, there were tensions" about negotiating with South Africa. In a remark evidently aimed at Angola, he stated that "if anyone is tired of fighting against imperialism he has only to say so, but he must realize that if he abandons the struggle he will be attacked and invaded by South Africa."[20]

Opposition to the Electoral Process

An evident cause of Soviet concern is the apprehension that SWAPO might be "cheated" of its victory if not by Western efforts, then by those of South Africa to work out its own settlement. Citing Western sources, Soviet commentaries often contend that SWAPO would get 70 percent of the votes in a free election, providing such an election were held under U.N. supervision and took place following withdrawal of South African military forces. However, Soviet predictions are de-

---

[19]V. Shubin, "Maneuvers of the Racists Doomed to Failure," *Aziia i Afrika Segodnia,* No. 6, June 1977, p. 17.

[20]*L'Unita* (Rome), September 30, 1977.

signed to bolster claims that SWAPO is the "genuine" representative of the entire Namibian people rather than an indication of Soviet preferences about how to achieve power.

Moreover, these predictions were meant to bolster explanations of why any elections sponsored by South Africa or the West will necessarily be faulty. Thus in mid-1979, when questions about South African and SWAPO military dispositions were holding up implementation of U.N. settlement plans for Namibia, a Soviet journal complained that the "Western powers are stubbornly trying to prolong the myth about the possibility of attaining a just political solution of the Namibian question with the aid of the RSA racists."[21]

In view of this SWAPO strength, according to Moscow, what South Africa really wants is a Namibian warrant of Ian Smith's internal settlement. According to *New Times* in December 1976, the Constitutional Conference convened at Turnhalle in Windhoek in September 1975 was "an attempt by Pretoria to create a semblance of the racist regime's acquiescence to granting Namibia independence in the hope thereby of taking the heat out of the liberation struggle." Initial deadlocks over seating apportionments were explained in *New Times* by the contention that "the delegates, though hand-picked by the racist regime, plainly realized that Pretoria actually sought to establish in Namibia a system of Bantustans."[22]

The only full scale discussion of Namibia to appear in the Soviet foreign policy magazine *International Affairs* took the interesting position that South Africa was misreading underlying developments in Namibia. According to the journal, the Turnhalle Declaration of September 1975, sought a solution which took into account tribal sensibilities, although "Pretoria is aware that the chiefs in Namibia no longer wield their traditional power and that there is no traditional African society but a conglomerate of separate tribes and tribal groups living on their homelands. This structure has been destroyed by the colonialists and racists." SWAPO was said to be proceeding "from a deep understanding of this important circumstance" and proposing

---

[21]Yu. Borisoglebskii, "Liquidation of the Strongholds of Colonialism and Racism—Demand of the Times," *Mezhdunarodnaia Zhizn'*, No. 7, July 1979, p. 27.

[22]Yu. Tyunkov, "Racist Strategem Stalled," *New Times,* No. 49, December 1976, p. 16.

instead a single indivisible Namibia transcending "long outdated tribal communities" and seeking as well to eliminate racial discrimination.[23]

Subsequent South African actions, such as encouragement of the Turnhalle Democratic Alliance and the holding of elections in December 1978, were denounced by Moscow as "dirty tricks" by Pretoria designed to lead to the establishment of a "puppet" regime under South African control. Foreshadowing Moscow's response to the Rhodesian elections four months later, TASS on December 9, 1978 said the outcome of the Namibian election was "predetermined" and the turnout obtained through the use of force. Soviet commentaries stressed SWAPO's opposition to the elections and charged that its supporters were being persecuted by South African authorities. Moscow approvingly reported U.N. rejection of the elections as invalid.

While conceding from time to time that the U.S. and U.K. sought to dissuade South Africa from going ahead with its own plans for Namibia, Moscow generally sought to blame the West for these plans and to use them to discredit Western proposals which, in fact, were designed as alternatives. Whatever the West's pressures, they were never enough to suit Moscow's position that the basic issue was total transfer of power to SWAPO. And despite the pressures, Moscow continuously identified the West as South Africa's "patrons."

An early Soviet analysis of the Carter Administration's first moves in Namibia saw them as "counter to Pretoria's plans worked out in January 1977" at Windhoek and designed by the United States "to strengthen its influence in Africa and to win the future African leaders of Namibia over to its own side."[24] Vorster, according to the same article, had hoped the U.S. would remain neutral on his actions.

Similarly, in 1978 Moscow noted Western efforts to get South Africa not to hold unilateral elections in Namibia when snags arose in Western negotiating efforts. *New Times* pointed out that the West "did not venture openly to approve of the racists' decision."[25] *Asia and Africa Today* went further: "Western diplomacy, understanding the inevitability of political changes in Namibia and striving to put them under its

---

[23]A. Galybin, "Namibia's Fight for Freedom," *International Affairs*, No. 12, December 1976, p. 62.

[24]Vishnevskii, "Washington's African Maneuvers," p. 85.

[25]Yu. Tyunkov, "Pretoria Reckless of Risk," *New Times*, No. 47, November 1978, p. 16.

control, was also forced to reject the 'Turnhalle plan" and begin steps
to draw SWAPO into negotiations.''[26] During Secretary of State
Vance's visit in October to Pretoria in order to persuade South Africa
to agree to U.N.-sponsored elections, Radio Moscow on October 18
went so far as to report that South Africa was "being coaxed and even
intimidated" by the West. Reviewing this sequence of events later,
Anatoly Gromyko remarked that Pretoria's unilateral actions "put the
Five [Western negotiators] in a rather awkward position. It was not
merely because they saw their plan threatened (such a threat they
could tolerate). The actual challenge in this case was to whatever cred-
ibility Western policy might still have in southern Africa.''[27]

However, the major thrust of Soviet comment was designed to use
Turnhalle to discredit Western negotiating efforts and the West in general. A number of statements charged that the West was only paying lip
service to criticism of South Africa and that by negotiating with it, the
West gave it respectability and made it possible for South Africa to
proceed with its own efforts at settlement. On the eve of the Pretoria-
sponsored elections in December 1978, for example, *Izvestiia* declared
that in talking with RSA Prime Minister Botha, Western representatives were only "pretending to try and persuade the RSA to consent to
holding elections in Namibia under U.N. auspices. In reality, all these
hypocritical arguments serve just one purpose—to create a smoke-
screen under whose cover Pretoria is completing preparations for the
farce involving the elections set for 4–8 December.''[28] A statement on
December 5 by the semi-official Soviet Afro-Asian Solidarity Committee stated that "the Namibian elections, held under the muzzles of
South African rifles, were arranged by the racists under the cover of
diplomatic initiatives by imperialist circles.''[29]

South Africa's ability and determination to go ahead with the elections was possible, according to Moscow, because the West in reality
stands behind Pretoria and is not willing to apply the level of pressure
which would really be necessary to get South Africa to desist. Thus
the Solidarity Committee said, "the South African racists would not
have been able to pursue their criminal policy without the active politi-

[26]Ulanovskaia, "Calculations and Miscalculations," p. 126.
[27]Gromyko, "Western Diplomacy," p. 26.
[28]S. Nikonov, "Conspiracy Over Namibia," *Izvestiia,* December 3, 1978.
[29]TASS, December 5, 1978.

cal, military and economic support of the United States and the other Western countries." Soviet commentaries in this and other connections often blame the lack of resolution of the Namibian question of Western opposition to the application of sanctions against South Africa.

Evidently responding to Western reports that Western plans for a Namibian settlement were back on track, an *Izvestiia* article in January 1979 sought to stiffen SWAPO and African opposition to such a settlement. The "maneuvers of the racists and their patrons," wrote *Izvestiia*, "cause a sharp need for the adoption of real measures for a consistent defense by the world public of the interests of the Namibian people, a need for actively supporting the well-recognized role of SWAPO in achieving the independence of its homeland." For this purpose, *Izvestiia* stressed the need for sanctions against South Africa.[30] As for SWAPO, *Izvestiia* quoted with obvious approval, a declaration of the organization's Central Committee to the effect that "armed struggle is the only real path for Namibia's liberation" and that the aims of the organization included "destruction of all forms of exploitation of man by man."[31]

The Soviet media studiously ignored statements by SWAPO representatives in early January that they would be willing to participate in U.N.-sponsored elections in accordance with ideas put forth by the five Western members of the Security Council (the U.S., U.K., France, FRG and Canada). *Izvestiia* on January 12, 1979 charged that the five countries "whose ties to the RSA are wellknown, have tried to create the illusion in the Security Council of a 'settlement' of the Namibian problem but on a different basis suiting Pretoria more than those contained in previous U.N. resolutions." *Izvestiia* cited in particular the fact that South African forces would remain alongside U.N. personnel in an interim period. *Izvestiia* derided South African acceptance of the U.N. proposal for the holding of new elections in Namibia because of attendant conditions attached to this acceptance.

The impasse during the first half of 1979 in Western negotiations increasingly led to Soviet predictions that in the end the West would, in

---

[30]S. Novikov, "The Patriots of Namibia Activate the Struggle for Liberation of the Motherland," *Izvestiia,* January 12, 1979.

[31]V. Lashkul, "A SWAPO Declaration," *Izvestiia,* January 12, 1979.

Namibia as in Rhodesia, accept the internal settlements worked out by the white regimes. A Radio Moscow broadcast beamed to Africa on April 16, 1979 said that "the Western powers are acting in unison with the South African racists since the West supports the United Nations' plan on Namibia only in words. Due to this they appear to be most inert and helpless when it comes to talks with Pretoria." Accordingly, the broadcast suggested, Western mediation efforts were "operating in anticipation of a variant being enforced for internal settlement that would be acceptable to them." A unilateral declaration of independence by the DTA, it went on, "should undoubtedly be viewed in this context."

It should be noted, moreover, that even the Western-sponsored plans which involve a role for SWAPO were dismissed by Moscow as a "Namibian variant" of the Rhodesian internal settlement. Thus *New Times* in April 1979 described Western plans as providing only for "sham independence," and a passage covering both Western and South African proposals declared:

> What they want is to replace the present South African occupation set-up by a neo-colonialist puppet regime completely dependent on Pretoria and the West. This would mean preservation of the status quo, with the facade slightly adapted to the demands of the present time, when broad sections of world opinion are challenging the racist regimes in southern Africa.[32]

Encouragement of a SWAPO Military Solution

Rejecting both Western and South African moves toward a settlement, the total upshot of the Soviet position is that the Namibian question is soluble by a trial of military strength. Despite frequent statements that SWAPO is well on the way to success, Soviet sources as of August 1979 have never asserted, as they have in the case of Rhodesia, any claims as to the percentage of the territory under SWAPO control. The Soviet media most often report SWAPO military operations in the northern part of Namibia and from time to time in other areas as well. *International Affairs* in December 1976 praised

[32]Yu. Tyunkov, "The Namibian Variant," *New Times,* No. 19, May 1979, p. 10.

SWAPO fighters as "well-trained,"[33] while a SWAPO official interviewed by a Soviet journal pointedly noted that Namibian forces "using heavy armament"[34] had conducted a successful operation in June
1977. In addition to military operations, Soviet sources also cited
strikes and allegedly successful SWAPO political agitation as evidence
that a favorable trend existed in Namibia.

Soviet sources occasionally suggested the existence of "liberated
areas" which would imply firm SWAPO control or, more ominously, a
preliminary step toward proclamation of SWAPO government, possibly setting the stage for requests for aid. A Soviet interviewer in
November 1977 asked Nujoma about "social measures in the liberated
regions."[35] In reply Nujoma described medical, educational and
"political mobilization" activities but then went on at length about
South African repressive measures. A leading Soviet international affairs journal in February 1979 declared:

> Over the years of the liberation struggle, which has been especially
> strengthened in recent times, the patriots have cleared the occupiers out
> of significant territory in the north of Namibia, where organs of peoples'
> power are already being created, a program of socio-economic measures
> being realized, a system of education and health care begun.[36]

Although Nujoma, as cited by Prague in March 1979, predicted that
"within two years the National Liberation People's Army will succeed
in completely defeating the occupiers," a later interview in Hungary (in
July 1979) suggested a somewhat longer-range perspective. According
to Nujoma, "we have liberated several larger areas far away from the
cities, mainly in the northern and northwestern parts of the country."
Current strategy, he explained, called for attacks in the countryside to
force white settlers to go to the cities or leave the country. "Later," he
said, "when our successes proliferate and our strength increases, we
will surround the cities as well and force the white oppressors to flee
the country." He claimed the process is "quite advanced already" but

[33]A. Galybin, "Namibia's Fight for Freedom," *International Affairs*, No. 12, December 1976, p. 62.

[34]John Ya. Otto, "New Stage of the Struggle of the People of Namibia," *Aziia i Afrika
Segodnia*, No. 1, January 1978, p. 18.

[35]"Namibia's Resolve," *New Times*, No. 45, November 1977, p. 20.

[36]Ye. Tarabrin, "Africa At a New Twist of the Liberation Struggle." *Mirovaia
Ekonomika i Mezhdunarodnye Otnosheniia*, No. 2, February 1979, p. 46.

made no final predictions. Nujoma did not rule out a negotiated settlement or U.N. mediation but explained that SWAPO pursued armed struggle "to force our enemies to the negotiating table from a position of strength . . . to force them to hand over power to us."[37]

Soviet emphasis on armed struggle went hand in hand with increasing demonstrations of strengthened ties between SWAPO and the USSR, which has featured training and weapons supply to SWAPO guerrillas by the Soviet bloc and Cuba. A SWAPO delegation attended the 25th Soviet Communist Party Congress in February–March 1976. SWAPO President Sam Nujoma visited the Soviet Union in August 1976, October and November 1977, July 1978, November 1979 and has made numerous visits to Eastern Europe during the same period. Nujoma also visited Cuba in October 1976, June 1977, August 1978. When Soviet President Podgorny and Fidel Castro made their criss-crossing journey to Africa, they both ostentatiously received African national liberation leaders, including Nujoma and Podgorny in Lusaka, Castro in Luanda. In the latter case, Nujoma and his colleagues made a special flight from Lusaka on March 29, 1977 in order to have an audience with Castro.[38] Interviews in the Soviet and other communist media with Nujoma and other SWAPO officials have become increasingly frequent since 1976.

Apart from November 1977, when Nujoma headed a SWAPO delegation attending the 60th anniversary of the October Revolution, Nujoma's visits have obviously been business trips. Soviet announcements on each of the other occasions have stated that he was received by Boris Ponomarev, candidate member of the Soviet Politburo and Secretary of the Central Committee, accompanied by R. A. Ulianovskii, deputy chief of the CPSU Central Committee International Department and a leading Soviet expert on liberation movements. Generally, SWAPO delegations are billed as having come at the invitation of the Soviet Afro-Asian Solidarity Committee, the major overt Soviet vehicle for contacts with liberation movements.

Numerous generalized statements by Moscow emphasized its willingness to render all kinds of support, including military aid, to liberation movements though Soviet sources never discussed directly the

---

[37] *Magyar Hirlap* (Budapest), July 5, 1979.
[38] Paris, AFP, April 1, 1977.

military relationship between the USSR and SWAPO. However, SWAPO spokesmen were much less reticent. Shortly after his meeting with Ponomarev in August 1976, Nujoma told Western correspondents that the main purpose of his trip had been to seek military aid. In virtually all interviews with Soviet correspondents, Nujoma and his lieutenants are enthusiastic about the USSR's response to these requests.[39] In his speech on the October Revolution anniversary in 1977, after praising Soviet military might and past aid to Third World countries and movements, Nujoma went on: "This increase in material assistance enables the people of Namibia . . . to continue and intensify the liberation struggle in Namibia, which in our view is the only effective way to dislodge racist South Africa from Namibia and lead our people to genuine freedom and national independence."[40] Not only has Nujoma expressed his "heartfelt gratitude" for Soviet aid but he has stressed that without this aid "we would not be capable of opposing the forces which oppress our people"[41] or "we would have been unable to achieve the results which we have today."[42]

At the time of Nujoma's visit to the USSR in August 1976, SWAPO sources indicated that he was hoping for Cuban military aid as well, in the form of training and military supplies. At the same time Nujoma's trip to Cuba in October 1976 was billed by SWAPO sources as a shopping trip for arms.[43] Castro, in turn, was reported to have pledged when he met southern African liberation movement leaders in Luanda that Cuba would meet their military aid requests.[44] Nujoma's statements, while in Cuba in June 1977,[45] about SWAPO military successes and about SWAPO's "firepower" and military "effectiveness" could be read either as a plea for more aid or as an expression of satisfaction with the amount already received. At the same time, he was quoted to the effect that "we do not necessarily need assistance from other countries in the fight."[46] And unlike his statements in Moscow, those in Havana did not include expressions of gratitude for direct Cuban aid.

---

[39]London, Reuters, August 22, 1976.
[40]*Pravda,* November 5, 1977.
[41]Radio Moscow, September 15, 1976.
[42]Radio Moscow, August 30, 1978.
[43]Paris, AFP, October 22, 1976.
[44]Paris, AFP, April 1, 1979.
[45]Havana, Prensa Latina, June 28, 1979.
[46]London, Reuters, August 22, 1977.

The admission of SWAPO as a full member of the nonaligned movement announced by Radio Havana on October 3, 1978 may, in addition to its obvious political purposes, also have been designed to provide another vehicle for justifying outside military aid to the organization. In an interview with the Yugoslav newspaper *Borba* shortly afterward, Nujoma asserted that "now, when we have become full members of the nonaligned movement, . . . we expect from the nonaligned countries that they increase their material assistance, particularly in the field of modern armament, anti-tank weapons and rockets."[47]

Little of the speculation about Cuban interventionism in Africa has included Namibia as a possible object of Cuban action. With Angola not fully digested and U.N.-sponsored negotiations in process, the communist powers may have wanted to avoid even hinting at such a possibility especially since they frequently claimed that SWAPO was on the verge of victory through a combination of its own efforts and bloc military aid. Both Moscow and Havana may calculate that intervention into Namibia would involve a confrontation with South Africa far exceeding the one in Angola and a level of involvement they did not seek.

At the same time, it can be presumed that SWAPO in particular was not loath to keep alive the concept of possible Cuban intervention as a pressure point especially on the West to elicit concessions from South Africa. Thus trips by Nujoma to Cuba and statements there in praise of Cuban intervention in Angola may have been designed as hints that Angola could be a precedent for Namibia.

In seeking a total victory for SWAPO, Soviet sources indicate that the gains will be more than worthwhile. Soviet commentaries show an acute consciousness of Namibia's mineral wealth and its potential importance to the West. For propagandistic purposes, Moscow frequently cites this wealth as the prime reason for Western interest in Namibia, but by implication the victory of a radical regime would mean the loss of investments already made and future availability of Namibian resources. Thus, *New Times* wrote in August 1976:

> Namibia, it may be recalled, is rich in natural resources. It has deposits of high-grade diamonds of which it is the world's second biggest producer. There are also uranium, copper, zinc, lead and tin. The country exports

[47]*Borba* (Belgrade), November 8, 1978.

large amounts of vanadium, beryllium, lithium, manganese, tantalite and other rare metals. The mining industry is chiefly in the hands of British and U.S. monopolies. Associated with Namibia are the bosses of giant international concerns—Oppenheimer, Getty and other multi-millionaires who had made fortunes exploiting the labor of the Namibian people. Neither the Pretoria authorities nor the imperialist monopolies, which in fact connive at the continuing unlawful occupation of the country, want to part with this treasure-trove.[48]

According to Soviet writing, South Africa's open door to Western investment is a determining factor in basic Western support for South Africa on the Namibian issue. Another *New Times* article pointedly entitled "Imperialist Stake in Namibia" cited a report by the U.N. Committee on Decolonization as concluding that "the Western monopolies' dominant position in that country [Namibia] is the main obstacle to the achievement of political and economic independence by its people. To retain the source of its immense profits the West is strengthening its ties with the racists and looking for ways of consolidating its positions in Namibia."[49] Or as prominent Soviet political correspondent Yuri Zhukov put it after going over the same data: "After this it is not hard to understand why people in both London and Washington regard the racist South African regime with such favor."[50]

By implication, therefore, a complete SWAPO victory would strike a direct blow at Western interests. Indeed, Soviet spokesmen have been explicit about this. A Soviet pamphlet on Africa issued for mass circulation in the Soviet Union, in its section on Namibia, noted that "of course, the rise of a new progressive state, moreover one bordering on the Republic of South Africa, is completely undesirable to the imperialists." Specifically, it went on: "The imperialist monopolies are afraid that in case SWAPO comes to power in Namibia, they will have to bid farewell to their capital in this country." Moreover, the same author noted that a SWAPO victory would affect the South African stock exchange: "With receipt of independence by Namibia, the shares of companies operating in the RSA will fall even lower."[51]

[48]Yu. Tyunkov, "The Struggle of Namibia," *New Times*, No. 35, August 1976, p. 8.

[49]Sergei Petukhov, "Imperialist Stake in Namibia," *New Times*, No. 34, August 1977, p. 26.

[50]Yuri Zhukov, "Dangerous Plans," *Pravda*, March 3, 1977.

[51]L.A. Alekseyev, *Africa: The Struggle for Political and Economic Independence* (Moscow: Znanie, 1978), pp. 51-52.

In another typical statement, *New Times* in August 1977 declared: "No one doubts any longer that sooner or later Namibia will gain independence. This endangers the West's position in a country in which it has a great vested interest."[52] The same point also emerged from an interview by two Soviet correspondents with a top SWAPO official in Conakry in which the latter attributed South African and Western opposition to SWAPO to their realization "that SWAPO's advent to power would threaten" what he described as their "economic and stategic interests" in Namibia.[53]

In pursuit of these objectives, Moscow attributed special importance to a July 1976 meeting in Lusaka of the SWAPO Central Committee at which a moderate faction was purged and the winning group proclaimed as their objective the establishment of a Soviet-style state in Namibia. Thus, Soviet sources approvingly quote a new SWAPO Central Committee program stating that the organization's objective was the unification of the Namibian people "especially the working class, peasants and progressive intellectuals, in a vanguard party capable of defending national independence and building a classless society free of exploitation based on the ideals and principles of scientific socialism."[54] In another passage, the statutes proclaim SWAPO to be the "embodiment of the national unity of the entire people" and its immediate aim victory and the "establishment of a people's democratic government."[55] To Soviet readers, the concept "vanguard," "scientific socialism," "classless society," "people's democratic" necessarily mean the establishment of a Soviet-type regime.

In a number of statements in communist and leftist papers and journals Nujoma and his colleagues reaffirmed these aims. Speaking at a press conference in Havana in August 1978, Nujoma said that "after Namibia's liberation, the country's exploitation system will be destroyed and the colonial institutions will be converted into new organizations which will permit the people to benefit from their natural re-

---

[52]Petukhov, "Imperialist Stake," p. 26.

[53]V. Tyurkin, N. Sologubovskii, "Namibia: Grapes of Wrath are Ripening," *Pravda,* December 11, 1978.

[54]Alekseyev, *Africa: The Struggle,* pp. 19–50.

[55]Shubin, "The Maneuvers of the Racists Doomed to Failure," *Aziia i Afrika Segodnia,* No. 6, June 1977, p. 18.

218

sources."[56] In a meeting with East German leader Honecker in Angola in February 1979, Nujoma delcared that "SWAPO's aim in Namibia is to eliminate the system based on racist oppression and plunder and to build a free and nonracist society that will be free from exploitation."[57] In a interview with a Soviet journal, SWAPO official John Ya. Otto reaffirmed that its objective was a "classless society based on the ideals and principles of scientific socialism."[58]

At the very least, it is clear, SWAPO has in mind the nationalization of all Western enterprises in Namibia. When asked in 1977 what a government under his leadership would do about multinational corporations, Nujoma replied that they "all lost legal status in 1966" when South Africa's mandate over Namibia was cancelled and with the establishment of the U.N. Commission for Namibia." The exploitation and commercialization of Namibian natural resources have been acts of pure and simple piracy."[59]

Eighteen months later, when asked by the same journal if a SWAPO government would cut off mineral supply to the West, Nujoma replied:

> What we want is to end the unrestrained exploitation of our resources and our workers. We will insure that our mines are controlled by the Namibian state and not by the South African racists or private companies. Of course, we will maintain commercial relations with all countries whether in the west, east or north.[60]

Soviet analyses also put considerable stress on Namibia's importance as a "springboard for further aggression against neighboring countries."[61] During the conflict in Angola, Soviet propaganda often noted that it was only South African "illegal occupation" of Namibia that made possible South Africa's incursion into Angola. The Soviet media sporadically report either plans for renewed activities by South Africa or the use by the anti-MPLA Angolan forces of UNITA of Namibia as a sanctuary for operations into Angola. South Africa's bombing of SWAPO camps in Angola and occasional hot pursuit of

[56]Havana, Prensa Latina, August 5, 1978.
[57]East Berlin, ADN, February 18, 1979.
[58]Otto, "New Stage," p. 18.
[59]*Afrique-Asie* (Paris), 19 September–2 October 1977, p. 16.
[60]*Ibid.*, 19 February–4 March 1979, p. 27.
[61]Sergei Petukhov, "The Racists Go All Out," *New Times,* No. 41, October 1978, p. 23; see also Petukhov, "Imperialist Stake," p. 27.

SWAPO guerillas into Zambia are pointed out by Moscow to demonstrate the danger posed by a South African-controlled Namibia to its neighbors. Apart from the general propaganda, utility of theme of South African aggressiveness, the South African "threat" is obviously useful as justification for the retention of Cuban troops in Angola and for Soviet military aid to front-line states. This would also explain the tenacity with which Moscow has opposed any settlement in Namibia short of a complete SWAPO victory even though the withdrawal of South African forces from the Angolan border and presumably by the reduction of outside help for UNITA would ease the situation for the regime in Angola. But, from Moscow's point of view, the optimum solution for this set of problems would come if SWAPO acceded to power.

And most important, a total SWAPO victory especially one achieved by armed force, would constitute an important step forward toward the last major target in the region, the Republic of South Africa. The concept of Namibia as a stepping stone to the RSA was implied in a statement by a leading Soviet African specialist to the effect that the West favors maintenance of the status quo in Namibia as "the defense of the RSA from further broadening of its frontiers with independent Africa." Therefore, the writer went on, "as never before, the colonial-racist regime in Namibia predetermines the political stability in the RSA itself as the bulwark and outpost of imperialist influence in Africa."[62]

The notion that Namibia will serve as a base for the "liberation" of South Africa is implied by the frequent linkage of the struggles in Rhodesia, Namibia and South Africa. Nujoma, however, was explicit on this score, telling a Cuban journal that "we will truly be committed, after the liberation of our country, to supporting our brothers and sisters in South Africa in their liberation."[63]

Put another way, the issue for Moscow is whether Namibia and Rhodesia will be added to the list of frontline states against South Africa or whether they will, in effect, remain buffers between the RSA and the rest of Africa or, together with it, become the base for reversing radical trends in southern Africa. Should SWAPO and Namibia's

[62]Ulanovskaia, "Calculations and Miscalculations," p. 119.
[63]*Prisma del Meridiano 80* (Havana), 1–15 January 1978.

neighbors accept a compromise solution, despite all Soviet efforts to discourage them from doing so, Moscow can be expected nevertheless to claim that its support will have made possible concessions extracted from South Africa and the West and to pursue its standard worldwide practice of seeking to radicalize and enhance Soviet influence in a successor state.

CHAPTER TEN

The Supreme Target: The Republic of South Africa

ALL RECENT DEVELOPMENTS IN AFRICA have been interpreted by Moscow as preliminary rounds to an onslaught on the final target, the Republic of South Africa, which is often identified as the key to success on the entire continent. Moreover, in Moscow's view, the fate of South Africa has become an increasingly important part of the outcome of the East-West struggle central to Moscow's image of the world. All these themes were pulled together in an article by Vladimir Kudriavtsev on "Africa Liberation Day" in May 1977 when he wrote: "History has ordained that the struggle between the forces of progress and reaction on the continent is concentrated at present in its south. However, everything that happens there has repercussions elsewhere in Africa and is reflected in growing confrontation between the forces of progress and reaction throughout the continent. More, the events in the south not only affect the whole of Africa and its future, but also the future of the entire capitalist world."[1]

Soviet Perspective on South Africa

Moscow has indicated full awareness of the importance of South Africa as a source of minerals, as a market and source of investment

---

[1]Vladimir Kudriavtsev, "Africa in Struggle," *New Times,* No. 21, May 1977, p. 4.

and as a vitally strategic location. In a typical commentary, *New Times* wrote:

> The "loss" of South Africa would deprive the multinational monopolies and their global strategy-makers of an important military and political outpost at the junction of the Indian and Atlantic Oceans. The West's control over rich natural resources—South Africa occupies first place in the capitalist world in the extraction of gold, platinum, chromites, manganese and antimony, second place for diamonds and third for uranium oxide—would be placed in serious jeopardy. The implications of this are obvious, especially in the light of the continuing raw materials crisis. As for the political, social and ideological consequences of the extirpation of the seats of racism, these are easy to foresee. The result would be a further weakening of the positions of all the forces of reaction, war and national and social oppression.[2]

Soviet analysts indeed appear to give far more attention to South Africa's strategic importance than do Western observers. One Soviet pamphlet, for example, stressed that the Republic of South Africa occupies "key positions at the junction of the Indian and Atlantic Oceans, controlling the sea routes around the southern extremity of Africa. Along these routes cross 75 percent of the oil of the Arab East and 44 percent of the freight trade of the NATO countries. The strategic role of RSA has grown especially after the fall of Portugal's colonial empire in Africa which deprived the Western powers of very important bases on the African continent."[3]

In this connection, Soviet media for the past several years have frequently contended that the U.S. is sponsoring a South Atlantic Treaty Organization which would include South Africa and countries in the southern half of Latin America, both to supplement NATO and to strengthen Western interest in both Africa and Latin America. Visits by U.S. military officials to South Africa or their counterparts to the United States are linked to these purported plans. Reviewing one such round of visits, the Soviet army newspaper *Red Star* in 1977 noted that "commentators link the military contacts between the United States and the Republic of South Africa to the idea nurtured by the West's

[2]Dmitri Volsky, "Southern Version of NATO," *New Times,* No. 36, September 1976.
[3]I. A. Ulanovskaia, *South Africa: Racism Doomed* (Moscow: Znanie, 1978), p. 20.

imperialist circles of setting up a new military bloc in the south Atlantic."[4]

The key development in Moscow's perspective on South Africa has been the emergence of radical states on South Africa's borders which, because of the USSR's relationship to them, has given it a direct policy role in affairs of the region. The signatures in 1976 and 1977 of Soviet friendship treaties with Angola and Mozambique, the growing Soviet military ties with those two countries and the stationing of Cuban expeditionary forces in Angola have not only given the USSR an unprecedented stake in South African domestic trends and external relationships, but drastically transformed the context of Soviet declaratory policy. Since the fall of the Portuguese empire, Soviet calls for international isolation of South Africa and the overthrow of the South African government are more than the propaganda exercises they were before to demonstrate Soviet solidarity with black Africa and to embarrass the West for its ties with South Africa. Because of the USSR's influence among South Africa's neighbors, and the increased Soviet capacity through these neighbors and directly to provide aid and training to insurgents inside South Africa, the same Soviet calls have more ominous policy consequences. In seeking to strengthen the dependence of the front-line states upon the USSR, Moscow is also increasing its commitment to these states and the prospect that regional issues will become enmeshed in the East-West conflict. Similarly the militancy of Soviet pronouncements comes against a background of stepped up Western attempts to achieve peaceful changes in South Africa and constitutes a conscious effort to disrupt these attempts.

Whereas in earlier years, Rhodesia and Namibia were designated as the principal targets, with South Africa defined as a distant future objective, one of the most striking aspects of recent Soviet propaganda and analyses has been the increasing frequency with which South Africa has been put on a par with the other two territories as immediate objectives of "national liberation" and "armed struggle." Crucial to this upgrading of the struggle in South Africa has been the Soweto riots of June 1976 and their aftermath. Shortly after Soweto and the spread of unrest to other parts of the country, *New Times* asserted: "The

[4]Capt. 1st Rank B. Rodinov, Maj. Yu. Gavrilov, "Alliance Against Africa,"*Krasnaia Zvezda*, March 6, 1977.

224

conflict that has been maturing for years has broken out. The country has become a battlefield."⁵ On August 28, a *Pravda* article by A. Davidson (of the Institute of General History of the USSR Academy of Sciences) quoted South African communists to the effect that "the era of the South African revolution has come."⁶ A Radio Moscow commentator said on September 28 that the elimination of all racist regimes in southern Africa "has been put on the agenda as an immediate task," and "that the flame of revolutionary actions has now embraced the main citadel of racism and colonialism, the Republic of South Africa."

Moscow saw a direct relationship between the events in Soweto and the emergence of radical regimes in Angola and Mozambique, and especially the setback suffered by South African forces in Angola. *New Times* in July 1976 declared that the events in Soweto "came in the wake of the major successes scored by the national liberation movement in Africa as a result of the collapse of the Portuguese colonial empire."⁷ Citing Soweto among other significant developments, a leading *Pravda* correspondent at about the same time declared that "the South African Republic's policy has found itself in a state of profound crisis since the victory of the national liberation movement in the Portuguese colonies and particularly since the ignominious failure of South African intervention and rout of the reactionaries and mercenaries in Angola. Lines of tension surround the bastion of racism in southern Africa."⁸ Indeed, wrote a leading Soviet journalist on Africa much later, "it is hard to overestimate the psychological effect of the failure of South African intervention in Angola, which inflicted a terrible blow to the prestige of Vorster's regime."⁹

Statements by South African Communist Party (SACP) chairman Yusuf Dadoo and African National Congress (ANC) President Oliver Tambo in the Prague-based international communist journal *World Marxist Review* spelled out these themes even more precisely. Discussing in one article the precondition for Soweto, Dadoo asserted that "the battles of Angola have forever shattered the myth of the superior-

⁵Editorial, "The Echo of the Gunfire in Soweto," *New Times*, No. 26, June 1976, p. 1.
⁶A. Davidson, "Southern Africa: Liberation Draws Near," *Pravda*, August 28, 1976.
⁷Yuri Tyunkov, "Battle for Human Dignity," *New Times*, No. 27, July 1976, p. 15.
⁸G. Ratiani, "Pretoria's Gamble," *Pravda*, July 21, 1976.
⁹I. Yastrebova, "New Aspects of South African Reality," *Aziia i Afrika Segodnia*, No. 6, June 1978, p. 26.

ity of the colonialists and the invincibility of the armed forces of the South African imperialists." He stressed in addition that guerrilla actions in Namibia and Rhodesia had "greatly contributed to the growing ferment of resistence in South Africa."[10] These same developments, according to Tambo, "had a tremendous mobilizing impact on the masses in South Africa."[11]

While for propaganda purposes, Moscow and its supporters devote a great deal of attention to the evils of apartheid, they make clear that their aims go beyond the racial issue and consist in the total reordering of society in South Africa. Moscow is avowedly seeking to transform opposition to apartheid into a class struggle which must and will be resolved by force of arms.

Thus *Pravda* in August 1976 criticized as "one sided" the view that "all the evil in southern Africa lies exclusively in the racial conflict." Smith and Vorster, it went on, find it convenient to explain conflicts in their countries as exclusively racial as a way to rally the white population and in case of South Africa the "coloreds" and Indians behind them. The racial issue exists and is important, *Pravda* went on, "but the contradictions tearing southern Africa apart have assumed a social nature."[12]

Soweto therefore was interpreted as a new stage in the onslaught of South African society as a whole. Thus the SACP plenum concluded: "There is no doubt that, taken as a whole, the Soweto events have opened a new chapter in the history of the revolutionary struggle." They have "demolished the myth that the government's security forces are able to destroy the people's revolutionary spirit" and have "raised the level of the people's preparedness and willingness to sacrifice to a higher level enhancing enormously the striking power of the liberation movement."[13]

In this regard, it should be stressed, Soviet and non-Soviet communist sources emphasize that "armed struggle" has since the early sixties been the main path that the SACP and ANC must follow in their

---

[10]Yusuf Dadoo, "Crisis in the Citadel of Racism and Apartheid," *World Marxist Review,* April 1977, p. 71.

[11]Oliver Tambo, "South Africa After Soweto," *World Marxist Review,* February 1978, p. 102.

[12]Davidson, "Southern Africa."

[13]*The African Communist,* No. 70, Third Quarter, 1977, pp. 30–31.

search for power. Ulanovskaia's 1978 pamphlet on South Africa credits the SACP and ANC with joint formation of a military arm in 1961, labeled the Spear of the Nation, to prepare for military operations against the South African government. After several SACP and ANC leaders were arrested, the two organizations regrouped and began training their military contingents. In 1967, the ANC was said to have signed an agreement with ZAPU and engaged in joint operations with it against the Smith regime in Rhodesia.

Following Soweto in 1976, the pamphlet goes on, "the liberation struggle entered its decisive stage" and the South African communists "adopted a decision about the need for the gradual preparation of the popular masses for armed struggle." For the time being, this preparatory stage is to feature "political education and mobilization of the people to rebuff the discriminatory policy of the authorities" and formation of a "united anti-imperialist front" under SACP and ANC leadership.[14]

The April 1977 SACP plenum confirmed that current actions have as their ultimate aim an attempt by force of arms to overthrow the government of the RSA. According to the political report "Soweto closed the debate about the legitimacy of resorting to armed struggle." The report claimed the existence of "public evidence" that units of Spear of the Nation "have begun to act against the enemy."[15] However, it was emphasized, Soweto was only a precursor "in the absence of prior preparation of organized liberation-military structures within the country," a precursor which "has brought closer than ever the possibility of an effective beginning to the armed struggles."[16]

Statements by ANC and SACP officials between 1976 and 1978 still continued to describe the situation as one of preparations. ANP President Oliver Tambo told Le Monde in October 1976 that black South Africans had no arms and Nouvel Observateur in July 1977 that they had no choice but to resort to arms.[17] In interviews with the Soviet media in early 1978, ANC General Secretary Alfred Nzo stressed his organization's "great" and "particular" attention to preparations for armed struggle "for it is clear to us that the racialists will not yield

[14]Ulanovskaia, *South Africa,* p. 41.
[15]*The African Communist,* No. 70, Third Quarter, 1977, p. 34.
[16]*Ibid.,* pp. 31–32.
[17]*Le Monde* (Paris), October 6, 1976; *Nouvel Observateur* (Paris), 4–10 July 1977.

power voluntarily."[18] Tambo, in an article carried in the international communist journal *World Marxist Review* in February 1978, claimed that 1977 had brought "actions by the military formations of the African National Congress,"[19] while South African CP Chairman Yusuf Dadoo, writing a few months later in the same journal, hearkened back to the SACP political report on initial actions, but gave more emphasis to the need for measures "to insure that armed activities have a firm basis" in the future.[20]

A June 1979 article by Nzo made the most optimistic statement up to that time claiming that "government troops are meeting with growing armed resistance from units of the Umkonto Ve Sizwe (military wing of the ANC)," the Spear of the Nation. According to Nzo, government troops had suffered severe losses in an August 1978 clash which he said "was but a forerunner of things to come."[21]

As in the case of Rhodesia and Namibia, the Soviet leadership has kept in constant touch with African National Congress and SACP leaders. In the last several years, the Soviet media report that Soviet Party Secretary Ponomarev has met ANC Chairman Tambo, Secretary General Nzo and SACP Chairman Dadoo. According to the head of the Soviet Afro-Asian Solidarity Committee (SAASC), Mirza Ibragimov, "contacts with the leaders of the national liberation movements are also maintained during the trips to Africa by delegations of the SAASC and in the course of various international undertakings" of the Afro-Asian Peoples' Solidarity Organization. In addition, he disclosed, hundreds of activists from the ANC, SWAPO and ZAPU have studied in the USSR, which has also provided recreational facilities and medical treatment for "prominent figures of the liberation movements as well as for wounded fighters from the liberation troops."[22]

Moscow has also clearly been seeking to get the OAU to designate the ANC as the sole legitimate liberation movement in South Africa, a status given SWAPO in Namibia and the Patriotic Front in Rhodesia.

[18]*Komsomol'skaia Pravda*, March 14, 1978; *New Times*, No. 15, April 1978, p. 25.

[19]Tambo, "South Africa After Soweto," p. 102.

[20]Yusuf Dadoo, "South Africa: Revolution on an Upgrade," *World Marxist Review*, No. 7, July 1978, p. 30.

[21]Alfred Nzo, "Powerless to Stop the Storm," *World Marxist Review*, No. 6, June 1979, p. 51.

[22]Mirza Ibragimov, "Resolute Support" *Asia and Africa Today*, No. 2, March–April 1979, P. 3.

As often as possible, it links the three groups together. When then Soviet President Podgorny visited Zambia in March 1977, he met Tambo, Nkomo and Nujoma together. However, a comparison of the communiques following Podgorny's visits suggested he may have met some resistance regarding the ANC. Whereas the communiques with Tanzania, Zambia and Mozambique all acknowledged the status of SWAPO and the Patriotic Front, only the communique with Mozambique supported the ANC.

For their part, ANC leaders have expressed due gratitude to the Soviet Union. In an interview with the Soviet youth newspaper *Komsomol'skaia Pravda,* Alfred Nzo said that Africans knew the USSR was "their true ally" and that "it is clearer today than ever before that the successful development of the national liberation movement would be impossible without the assistance and support of the Soviet Union and the other socialist countries."[23] Similar statements are frequently made by the SACP which Moscow can also count on for complete support in international communist quarrels as well.

From Moscow's ideological perspective, the level of South Africa's economic development, and in particular the existence of a large working class, means that the struggle goes beyond the aim of national liberation characteristic of the rest of Africa and constitutes a struggle for a communist society. At the same time, the racial question—or what Soviet theoreticians, in a curious echo of official South African views, define as the national question is recognized as an important component of the situation in South Africa. In accommodating both, Moscow has worked out the unique formula that the struggle in South Africa is led by the South African Communist Party and the African National Congress. This formula, it should be noted, is used primarily in internal Soviet analyses, while for outside consumption, especially in Africa, Moscow focuses on the role of the ANC.

In accordance with this perspective, Moscow has attached great importance to the growing number of strikes following Soweto and what it sees as increased evidence of white involvement in the "liberation" movement. To some degree, Moscow sees the semi-legal South African Congress of Trade Unions (SACTU), a leftist-supported rival

[23]*Komsomol'skaia Pravda,* March 14, 1978.

of the Trade Union Council of South Africa, as a stand-in for the South African Communist Party. Once more, Ulanovskaia:

> The South African Congress of Trade Unions is becoming a recognized force in the RSA with whom the racist authorities and big capital cannot fail to reckon. Insofar as the SACP finds itself underground, the activity has an especially important significance for the South African proletariat and in the first place for African workers. In these conditions SACTU is becoming a support of the SACP in the masses. The Communist Party has often emphasized the important role of SACTU and the trade unions in it for the unification and transformation of the proletariat of the country into a class conscious force, capable of playing a decisive role in the definition of the future RSA.[24]

Soviet sources frequently note that the RSA has the largest "industrial proletariat" on the African continent. In addition, as cited by one Soviet source, the "specific weight" of African workers in the total proletariat grew from 72 to 80 percent between 1960 and 1970 of whom African workers in the industrial sector comprised 52.7 percent.[25] Moreover, during this period, the same author noted, there was a "certain increase" in the share of Africans among skilled workers and "somewhat higher" increases in average wages.

In reply to a British reader, *New Times* acknowledged that "the wages of some categories of black workers are higher in South Africa than in a number of independent countries." However, the journal's correspondent explained this as "understandable since South Africa is an economically highly developed state" and in line with a vast amount of Soviet literature on the subject emphasized the disparities between white and black salaries, the large number of blacks unemployed and the deficiencies in conditions of life, especially under the restrictions of apartheid.[26]

Over the long run, Soviet analysts cite a growing contradiction between the apartheid system and the increasing manpower needs of the South African economy. Until recently, wrote I. A. Ulanovskaia, South Africa was able to meet its needs for skilled manpower from

[24]I. A. Ulanovskaia, "Trade Unions in the RSA," *The Working Class and the Contemporary World*, No. 3, May–June 1976, p. 134.

[25]V. M. Sharinova, "The Economic Situation in the RSA in the Second Half of the Seventies," *Narody Azii i Afriki*, No. 2, March–April 1978, p. 25.

[26]Sergei Petukhov, "Taking Up A Point," *New Times*, No. 3, January 1979, p. 31.

white immigrants. By 1980, she pointed out, the economy would need 4 million trained workers of which the whites could supply only 175,000. Thus, "in closing to Africans admittance to skilled labor, the racists have artificially created a deficit of trained labor cadres which holds back the development of the economy of the RSA, undermines its financial base." Moreover, a number of entrepreneurs were said to feel the need for raising income levels of black South Africans in order to increase their purchasing power. Accordingly many businessmen, she said, were in fact bypassing the formal rules of apartheid and the government itself was easing some of these rules. However, she concluded, partial changes will not be enough. "Today apartheid is the main obstacle to the growth of the economy" and the only way out is "the complete destruction of the whole system of apartheid."[27]

Moscow evidently considers that because of the racial issue South Africa offers a better opportunity than other developed countries for fulfillment of the primeval Marxist expectation that industrialization under capitalism increases the chances for a communist revolution. Thus after noting that between 1967 and 1970 South African economic progress brought an increase of 370,000 in the number of the working class, of which only 34,000 were whites, one Soviet article explained: "This meant that new masses of Africans were drawn into the system of production relations and potentially also in the class struggle."[28]

In South African conditions, according to Soviet observers, strikes constitute both economic and political manifestations. For example, Ulanovskaia asserted that the "impossibility any longer to endure the very hard conditions in which indigenous Africans found themselves as a result of the restrictions of the 'color barrier' caused a powerful upsurge of the workers' movement."[29]

In a later article, she was even clearer on the political implications of South African strikes. "During the course of the strike movement of the seventies," she wrote, "the workers put forward traditional economic demands. But in the RSA they have a clearly expressed political

[27]I. A. Ulanovskaia, "RSA: Two Sides of the Color Barrier," *Aziia i Afrika Segodnia,* No. 12, December 1977, p. 19.

[28]Yu. Shvetsov, "RSA: The African Working Class Strengthens The Struggle," *Aziia i Afrika Segodnia,* No. 1, January 1977, p. 11.

[29]Ulanovskaia, "RSA: Two Sides," p. 18.

character constituting a challenge to the system of apartheid."[30] Accordingly, Ulanovskaia concluded: "The African proletariat is now a great social force, a mass base and the most active participant of the anti-imperialist and anti-racist struggle. Its growing revolutionary potential predetermines the contribution of the labor movement and the ripening of a crisis in the ruling circles of the RSA, i.e., in the rise of a very important component of a revolutionary situation in the country."[31]

Even more than strikes, Moscow has noted with growing hope the disturbances in South African urban centers where the vast majority of the black population lives. A *Pravda* observer speaking in a Radio Moscow forum of September 28, 1976 remarked that "popular action has embraced the entire Republic of South Africa's largest industrial centers" with the "most significant point" being that "the role in this movement is increasingly actively being taken by the hands of the working class, the most populous in Africa." The growing wave of strikes, the *Pravda* reporter said, thus has "already given birth to a new phenomenon for Africa—urban partisan war" which he saw as eventually leading to a "general uprising."

With their sights set on class struggle and a total revolution, the USSR and the South African Communist Party seek to use the racial issue toward the larger goal of a multiracial communist society. Within this context, both seek to exploit but are critical of black nationalism or black consciousness movements. "One of the greatest services of the South African revolutionary movement," wrote A. B. Davidson, "consists in its ability to come out with a program of internationalism in a state where everything is subordinated to inciting of race discord."[32] Davidson added that it was not surprising that the ideas of "black chauvinism" should appear in South Africa as "in some other African countries."

The South African Communist Party in its April 1977 plenary session took a dual line on the issue of "black consciousness." It praised the idea "as a general assertion of national identity, pride and confidence,

---

[30]I. A. Ulanovskaia, "The Labor Movement in The RSA," *Narody Azii i Afriki,*No. 2, March–April 1978, p. 26.

[31]*Ibid.*, p. 27.

[32]A. B. Davidson, "Where Is South Africa Going?" *Narody Azii i Afriki,* No. 2, 1978, p. 17.

as a healthy response to the insulting arrogance of the white suprema-
cists." In general terms, the SACP claimed, this "expresses an approach which was pioneered by the African National Congress and our
Party." The idea "contributed to the revitalized surge of national feeling, especially among the youth."

However, the party report emphasized, "as a substitute for scientific
social analysis [i.e., Marxism-Leninism], and as an alternative to
ideology of our liberation front, it becomes a harmful demagogic
cliche. . . . Used in place of genuine revolutionary doctrine, Black
Consciousness is a misleading doctrine and weakens the cause which it
purports to serve—the cause of national liberation." Why this is so is
explained in one sentence: "An ideology which proclaims colour as its
sole foundation can more easily obscure the real issues because of its
highly charged emotional content."[33] In other words, the communists
fear that focus on racial issues might divert those whom it is trying to
draw into communist ranks on a class struggle basis.

At the same time, because of the "emotional content" of the race
question, Moscow and the SACP have evolved a doctrine for South
Africa which, they hope, will enable the SACP and ANC both to
champion a multiracial revolution and broaden its appeal to the black
majority. According to this doctrine, there are two societies in South
Africa, a well-developed, white-dominated society which must be
overthrown by a classic communist revolution led by the working
class, i.e., the communist party, and a second underdeveloped black
society which requires a national liberation revolution in which not
only black workers but virtually all strata of black society are eligible to
participate.

The exact relationship between the two struggles and the two organizations does not emerge too clearly from communist documents. One
Soviet source who writes often on the Third World, starting from the
premise that in South Africa "the national liberation struggle bears a
complicated and contradictory character," declared that this struggle
is headed by the SACP—the oldest Marxist-Leninist Party on the African continent—and the African National Congress (ANC)—the mass
political organization of the African people of the country." While the
two are thus put on a par, the same source seemed to imply Communist

[33]*The African Communist,* No. 70, Third Quarter, 1977, pp. 36–37.

Party priority in a statement praising the party's "keen work to rally the oppressed and democratically inclined people of all strata and classes for realization of the national-democratic revolution dedicated to liquidate the role of the racist minority."[34]

The SACP, on the other hand, in its February 1977 political report seemed to want to give the impression that it was only a subordinate part of a struggle headed by the ANC. While stating that the SACP is the vanguard party of the working class, the report states that in the South African situation "the main immediate instrument for the achievement of the arms of our national democratic revolution is a mass movement capable of galvanizing all classes in an assault on racist power." The ANC, it went on, "is such an instrument and our loyal participation in the liberation front which it heads is in the best interests of the class whose vanguard we claim to be."[35]

As reflected in the above quotation, the SACP and ANC are seeking to use the national liberation slogan in order to rally as wide a spectrum as possible among the black population around their banner. While denouncing the existence of black "collaborationists" who cooperate with the South African government, the SACP said it gives a "positive answer" to the question of "whether the arms of our national movement continue to represent the aspirations of all the main classes within the ranks of the oppressed—working peasants and petty bourgeoisie."[36] Writing in the *World Marxist Review,* SACP Chairman Dadoo explained that "the African middle strata, such as they are, have very limited scope for development since they are as much the victim of racist laws and racial discrimination as all other sections of the Black population."[37] Dadoo also noted the need to intensify opposition to the government on the part of South Africa's Indian and "colored" population as well.

In a special twist in this effort, the ANC proclaimed 1979 "the Year of the Spear" commemorating the 100th anniversary of the battle of Isandlwana when Zulu forces inflicted heavy casualties on British troops. Sizekele Sigkashe told a Soviet correspondent during a visit to

[34]Ye. Tarabrin, "Africa in a New Turn of the Liberation Struggle," *Mirovaia Ekonomika i Mezhdunarodynye Otnosheniia,* No. 2, February 1979, p. 46.
[35]*The African Communist,* No. 70, Third Quarter, 1977, p. 44.
[36]*Ibid.,* p. 41.
[37]Dadoo, "South Africa," p. 37.

Moscow evidently sometime around July 1979 that the ANC was using the anniversary "for the mobilization of broad masses of the population, of all its strata, with the aim of activization of the struggle against the existing order in the RSA."[38] Sigkashe reiterated ANC's intention to carry out armed actions in South Africa.

Soviet sources purport to be especially heartened by evidences they see of changes in the South African white community. They see this as at least the first stages in the fulfillment of Lenin's dictum that revolutions come not only when the lower classes become dissatisfied, but when the upper classes are "unable to rule and govern in the old way." Within this context and also as part of their multiracial approach, Moscow and the SACP have avidly seized on all instances of white participation in South African disturbances since Soweto. Despite all contrary efforts by the government, *Pravda* claimed, "a democratic nucleus which opposes racist orders is growing among the white population."[39] Alfred Nzo told *New Times* in April 1978 that a "noteworthy feature" of the liberation movement was "the active fight against apartheid by young white radicals"[40] who are refusing to serve in the army and police. Even limited criticism of proposed constitutional changes in 1978 were interpreted by Moscow as demonstrating "undoubtedly that part of the white population of the RSA—certain strata of the intelligentsia, teachers, clergy, businessmen—are beginning to recognize the need for changes especially in conditions of the country's growing international isolation."[41]

The prolific Vladimir Kudriavtsev also saw "signs of a growing polarization among the white population of South Africa, with some people siding with the national liberation movement." According to Kudriavtsev, white workers are being transferred to jobs previously held by blacks and at lower wages. As a result, "the white workers are beginning to voice their discontent and resort to strike action, which inevitably brings their struggle closer to that of workers from among

[38]Yu. Tyunkov, ". . . And They Raised the Spear of Freedom," *Novoye Vremia,* No. 32, August 1979, p. 14.
[39]A. Davidson, "Southern Africa."
[40]Interview with Alfred Nzo, "We Fight On," *New Times,* No. 15, April 1978, p. 24.
[41]Yastrebova, "New Aspects," p. 26.

the African population."[42] Such statements are very few in number, however, suggesting that these manifestations are seen by Moscow more as possibly hopeful signs for the future than important realities at present.

Meanwhile, Soviet commentaries seem to attach particular significance to evidence they adduce that South Africa's white ruling class has lost its self-confidence and is rent with quarrels on how to deal with growing problems. Moscow's main expert on the subject appears to be one Arkady Butlitsky who has dealt with it in several articles in the past few years. In January 1977 he cited with satisfaction a New Year's message by South African President Diederichs who is quoted as having said that "the white population . . . was losing confidence in the country's future."[43] Another article more than one year later stressed white emigration from South Africa which "has reached proportions that have prompted some commentators to speak of a veritable flight of the white population."[44] The same article also emphasized the flight of capital which was said to reflect a "fear complex" fostered by the Nationalists themselves.

In the January 1977 article he wrote: "Sharp debates are going on between the Afrikaners and the English-speaking South Africans or Britishers as they are called in local political jargon. The ruling Nationalist Party and the racialists' secret society, the Broederbond, are torn by differences."[45]

And in a subsequent article, he said "the whites are divided as never before" on "knotty issues" which he posited as: "What should be done to weather the storms threatening to sweep away the anachronistic regime of racial oppression? What should be done to preserve in one form or another the dominant, or at least privileged, status of the white man?"[46]

Butlitsky also saw forces both uniting and further dividing Afrikaners and Britishers. Looking at the history of this relationship since

---

[42]V. Kudriavtsev, "Africa Fights for Its Future," *International Affairs*, No. 5, May 1978, p. 37.

[43]Arkady Butlitsky, "Twilight of the Apartheid Empire," *New Times*, No. 2, January 1977, p. 12.

[44]Butlitsky, "Fear Reflex," *New Times*, No. 17, April 1978, p. 24.

[45]Butlitsky, "Twilight of the Apartheid Empire," p. 12

[46]Butlitsky, "Time Is Running Out," *New Times*, No. 32, August 1977, p. 27.

1910, he concluded in one article that growing Afrikaner urbanization, together with the rise of an Afrikaner capitalist class has brought the two communities closer together or at least mitigated previous differences between them. The "ever greater interweaving" of Afrikaner and Britisher capital, he suggested, was leading to the formation of a single economic establishment with a common interest in apartheid "as a system of joint exploitation of African laborers."[47] More specifically, Butlitsky interpreted the November 30, 1977 elections as evidence that "the 'fear reflex' is impelling a good many Britishers" to join the Afrikaner camp. Noting that the more than 70 percent of the electorate had supported the Nationalists, whereas the Afrikaners make up 60 percent of the white population, Butlitsky concluded: "It is clear that the Nationalists were supported by a good many South Africans of British origin who previously usually voted for the opposition United or Progressive Reform parties."[48]

While generally dismissing these opposition parties as timid or ineffectual, Butlitsky has several times focused on the Progressive Reform party as evidence that pressure for change in the apartheid system exists in the Britisher business community, deemed to be the main backer of that party. Thus, in a typical remark about the views of "gold and diamond king" Harry P. Oppenheimer, Butlitsky wrote:

> One of the paradoxes of South African political life is that among the most readily responsive to calls to modernize apartheid are South African Big Businessmen, long irked by the existing system which, at this juncture, sometimes inhibits their activities. Thus, many businessmen want the so-called color bar relaxed if not completely lifted, as it deprives industry of much needed skilled Black manpower.[49]

Moscow has been even more impressed by signs it sees of divisions within the Afrikaner community and the Nationalist Party. According to Butlitsky: "What is new for South African reality is that 'reformers' of apartheid have appeared in the ruling party. The monolithic nature which once characterized it does not exist today."[50] In several other articles, Butlitsky emphasized the differences between *verkramte*

---

[47]Butlitsky, "RSA: Crisis of the Racist Regime," *Aziia i Afrika Segodnia,* No. 9, September 1977, p. 20.

[48]Butlitsky, "Fear Reflex," p. 24.

[49]Butlitsky, "Time Is Running Out," p. 26.

[50]Butlitsky,"RSA: Crisis,' p. 20.

(diehards) and *verligte* (enlightened) within Nationalist ranks. He suggested in one of them that because of pressures for change, "in each successive generation of its leaders, leaders continually appear who eclipse their predecessors by their reactionary nature."[51] The splitting off of the Reconstructed Nationalist Party under Albert Hertzog is seen as reflecting growing strains within Nationalist ranks.

Events in Soweto beginning in 1976 were said to have deepened the fissures within the Nationalist Party, generating a "Young Turk" group which wants reforms going beyond those advocated by *verligte*. This group is described as including "Afrikaner big businessmen, highly placed government functionaries, many well-known journalists from publications in the Afrikaans language."[52] In still another article, Butlitsky called it "another political paradox . . . that the Afrikaner Big Businessmen in the Nationalist Party reveal a much closer affinity of views with their Britisher opposite numbers than with the rank and file of their own party."[53]

Butlitsky saw in the September 1978 resignation of Prime Minister Vorster new evidence of malaise in South African government ranks. The succession process which led to the accession of Pieter Botha as Prime Minister was described as unprecedentedly difficult. The departure from South Africa not only of Britishers but of Afrikaners "gives grounds to speak of a 'crisis of power.'"[54] The "Muldergate" scandal which led to Vorster's resignation as President in June 1979, according to *New Times,* "has shaken the political system of the country to its foundation," especially "the myth that the Afrikaner leaders were 'strong, straightforward, unselfish and incorruptible.'"[55]

To keep up the pressure on South Africa, the USSR has fanned to the utmost African and world opposition to apartheid in which it has seen endless opportunities to proclaim Soviet solidarity with black Africa and the Third World and to berate the U.S. and the West for the inadequacy of their opposition to South Africa. The USSR annually marks Africa Liberation Day (May 25), holds a Week of Solidarity with the Struggle of the Peoples of Southern Africa (May 21–31), celebrates

[51]*Ibid.,* p. 21.
[52]*Ibid.*
[53]Butlitsky, "Time Is Running Out," p. 27.
[54]Butlitsky, "New Premier, Old Policy," *New Times,* No. 45, November 1978, p. 26.
[55]Irina Stepanova, "The 'Muldergate' Affair," *New Times,* No. 25, June 1979, p. 29.

the International Day for the Elimination of Racial Discrimination (March 21), the International Solidarity Day with the Struggling People of South Africa (June 16), South Africa Freedom Day (July 16), Namibia Day (August 26), Days of Solidarity With South African Political Prisoners, Heroes Day of South Africa and others.[56] Among other motives, all this commemoration work enables Moscow to parade itself as a champion of human rights of concern to the Third World thereby taking the heat off any criticism from that quarter about human rights in the Soviet Union.

The USSR attends, sponsors or supports innumerable conferences especially through the Soviet Afro-Asian Solidarity Committee. According to Mirza Ibragimov, the Chairman of the Committee, it not only attends U.N. conferences but "takes an active part in preparing international conferences on southern Africa and helps finance them. In particular, it bears the travelling expenses when representatives of the liberation movements attend various conferences." During September 1978, he noted, the committee "and other democratic organizations" had sponsored conferences in Addis Ababa, New Delhi and Baku. The organization also was said to maintain contact with more than 30 "anti-racists and anti-colonial organizations in the West." In addition, it annually donates $20,000 to the OAU for propaganda broadcasts to southern Africa.[57] It can safely be assumed that considerably more actions and funds are dispensed covertly by the USSR.

Soviet View of Western Policy

Moscow sees the West caught in a difficult dilemma in South Africa: possessing important interests in the Republic but wanting to avoid identification with the apartheid regime. The Kremlin has sought to take advantage of both parts of this dilemma. For the benefit of its policy in the rest of Africa and beyond, it has portrayed the West as a defender of South Africa, including its racial policies. At the same time, it has sought to isolate South Africa from the West through constant campaigns in the United Nations and elsewhere with the object of

---

[56]Ibragimov, "Resolute Support," p. 3.
[57]Ibid., pp. 3–4.

forcing the West to join in actions against South Africa. But when the West has brought pressure on the RSA, it has been derided by Moscow and the rest of Africa as insufficient and looked on with satisfaction as a source of tension between the West and South Africa.

As in the case of Rhodesia and Namibia, Soviet commentaries emphasize the importance of the fall of the Portuguese empire in spurring the West, and particularly the United States, into a new activist policy designed to induce South Africa to modify its domestic apartheid policies. The prestigious Soviet political analyst Aleksandr Bovin, commenting on Kissinger's talks with South African Prime Minister Vorster, noted the risks they involved for U.S. relations with the rest of Africa but said that the meeting went ahead because the U.S. felt it thereby could "avoid a race war which would inevitably have tragic consequences for all who it might involve," could prevent "foreign interference" (i.e., Soviet or Cuban involvement in Africa) and "prevent the radicalization of Africa." To accomplish these ends, Kissinger was said to be seeking "to persuade Vorster to implement a series of reforms, to abandon the most odious manifestations of apartheid" and adopt "palliative constitutional reforms" which if accepted would preserve South Africa "as a bastion of the Western world and receptive to American capital."[58]

As it said about U.S. policy in Namibia (see above), Moscow emphasized that the Carter Administration brought a shift in U.S. tactics toward South Africa. "The Carter Administration is changing its line," wrote the journal *USA,* "and is attempting to exert political pressure on Pretoria for the first time since 1963."[59] *USA* cited in this regard declared U.S. intentions to recall its military attaché in South Africa, sever relations with South African intelligence agencies, reduce Pretoria's line of credit with the Export-Import Bank and institute stricter visa requirements for South African visitors. All these measures were dismissed as "of a secondary nature" which could not have "any significant influence on the South African regime." *USA* also noted that during talks between Vice President Mondale and Prime Minister Vorster in May 1977, "for the first time in the history of the relations

[58]A. Bovin, "Washington and Pretoria," *Izvestiia,* July 13, 1976.

[59]M. L. Vishnevskii, "Washington's African Maneuvers," *USA: Economics, Politics, Ideology,* No. 8, August 1977, p. 83.

between the two countries, a top level representative of the United States publicly announced that the rapid elimination of the unjust system of apartheid would serve the interests of the 'free world' and would reinforce the 'stability' and defense potential of South Africa.''

As in the case of Kissinger's ventures, Moscow considered the new Administration's efforts as an attempt to save South Africa from itself. Thus Arkady Butlisky wrote in *New Times:*

> In inducing the supporters of apartheid to grant concessions to the Black majority, the West is prompted by the desire to prevent the long overdue revolutionary changes, indeed supplant them with an evolution of the existing order which, while erasing the more repugnant forms of racial oppression and inequality in the countries of the region, including South Africa, would retain the mainstays of the system of neo-colonialist exploitation of the Black population. The white minority is told that the only alternative to reform from above is a total racial war, which would eventually spell the end of the white presence in South Africa.[60]

Despite incessant propaganda charges that the West, and especially Western business concerns, benefitted from the cheap labor provided by apartheid, Soviet analysts sometimes indicated that Western businessmen, like similar groups in South Africa, favored modification of apartheid for economic reasons. Thus, the more propagandistic *Asia and Africa Today* said that "apartheid gives foreign and local capital the opportunity to get colossal profits through the utilization of the exceptionally cheap labor of Africans."[61] Ulanovskaia, in her pamphlet on South Africa, insisted that RSA "reality" refuted arguments by "apologists of racism" that investments in South Africa improved the lot of African workers.[62]

However, an Institute of Africa economist rejected these approaches as simplistic: "In our scientific literature, one can sometimes encounter the following reasoning: . . . foreign investors get large profits in the RSA; insofar as these profits are received in the conditions of apartheid, consequently they are received thanks to apartheid. Meanwhile conditions created by the system of apartheid for capitalist

---

[60]Butlitsky, "Time is Running Out," p. 20.
[61]V. Us, "The South of Africa: The Struggle Continues," *Aziia i Afrika Segodnia,* No. 5, May 1977, p. 24.
[62]I. Ulanovskaia, *South Africa,* p. 23.

exploitation are far from being as favorable as proponents of the above-noted point of view imply."

In this regard, the author cited the shortage of skilled labor because of the color barrier and of unskilled labor which has led to use of migrant labor from neighboring countries over paid white laborers, barriers to free movement of black workers, all of which resulted in low productivity. Accordingly, he concluded: "The capitalist would prefer to have the possibility to train the African worker, raise the productivity of his labor and prepare him for skilled labor (where there are so many vacancies) because precisely in that case he would be able, even in conditions of higher wages for that worker, to exploit him more effectively."[63]

Moscow has deplored Western negotiations with South Africa as enabling it to break out of international isolation, especially in Africa. Following the first meeting between Kissinger and Vorster in June 1976, *Izvestiia* declared that "the Bavaria meeting was an undoubtedly diplomatic success for Vorster" because he could "demonstrate that he has not yet entirely become a pariah cursed and abused by all."[64] A later Soviet commentary said that this and subsequent Kissinger-Vorster meetings were "intended to give Pretoria greater respectability in African eyes."[65]

Along the same lines Moscow has expressed concern that what the Carter Administration had in mind was a revival of South Africa's policy of dialogue with black Africa which the Kremlin considered had been overwhelmed in recent years. *New Times* in May 1977 described the main tactic of U.S. policy as one of "'adjusting' the regimes of Rhodesia, Namibia and South Africa to those African states of pro-Western orientation which, fearing the growth of the progressive forces, are willing to establish contact with the racists in the south provided the latter abandon the more scandalous and ruthless of their methods."[66] More than one year later, two Soviet commentaries said the West was seeking to liberalize "the regime of apartheid to a level

[63]V. M. Sharinova, "The Economic Situation in the RSA," p. 21.

[64]Bovin, "Washington and Pretoria."

[65]N. D. Turkatenko, "Washington's Calculations and Miscalculations in Southern Africa," *USA: Economics, Politics, Ideology,* No. 2, February 1977, p. 24.

[66]Kudriavtsev, "Africa in Struggle," p. 5.

which would permit 'moderate' African states to engage in open cooperation with it,"[67]

A new factor which has appeared in Soviet explanations of U.S. policy toward South Africa has been the influence of the U.S. black community on the formation of that policy. Discussing Kissinger's apprehensions about a possible explosive situation in South Africa, *Pravda* declared:

> It is understood perfectly well in Washington that such an explosion would put U.S. politicians in an extremely difficult situation. All the states of Africa would oppose the United States in its defense of the white's power. In the United States itself, this would arouse indignation over the administration's actions among the 25 million Negroes.[68]

Similarly a discussion of Carter Administration policies asserted that "Washington cannot fail to reckon with the presence in the United States of around 25 million black-skinned citizens whose political self-consciousness in recent decades has grown immeasurably and follow with special attention the White House's approach to problems of the struggle of African peoples for their liberation."[69]

Soviet commentaries frequently compared U.S. policy in southern Africa, especially under Kissinger, to its role in the Near East with the U.S. seeking to portray itself as an honest broker sympathetic to and seeking to reconcile the interests of both sides. The U.S. relationship with South Africa is often compared to that with Israel, with the implication of affinities which rule out honest broker aspirations but which also make possible the application of some pressure. Foreign policy considerations also figured strongly, according to Moscow, in U.S. efforts to distance itself somewhat from South Africa and cater to black Africa and the Third World. The U.S., wrote one, has been "forced to take into account the role which the African countries play in the international arena. It surely realizes that the open support now of racist regimes in the south of Africa is pregnant with the serious undermining of Washington's positions on a global scale and above all in the developing countries."[70]

[67]A. Kislov, V. Vasilkov, "The Current Stage of U.S. Policy in Africa," *Aziia i Afrika Segodnia*, No. 9, September 1978, pp. 4–5.

[68]Ratiani, "Pretoria's Gamble."

[69]Kislov, Vasilkov, "The Current Stage," p. 3.

[70]*Ibid.*, p. 3.

For both domestic and foreign policy reasons, therefore, the United States sought to portray itself in the position of championing black causes in southern Africa. The appointment of Andrew Young as U.S. Ambassador to the United Nations and his subsequent negotiating efforts were seen in this context by Moscow which sought to undercut them by sniping at his activities as "propaganda maneuvers" and playing back the statements of radical Africans who rejected Young's use of the U.S. civil rights campaign as a model for Africa.[71] At the same time, the Soviet media were careful in their treatment of Young to avoid all-out attacks and quick to seize on his statements on the Cuban role in Africa and on U.S. political prisoners which had generated controversy in the U.S.

While portraying U.S. pressures on South Africa as too little and too late, Moscow also emphasized that they were the source of mounting tensions between the U.S. and South Africa. Commenting on the Mondale-Vorster meeting in 1977, *USA* noted that "apparently the U.S. Government's determination to institute actual measures of pressure on South Africa, even though they are secondary measures, greatly annoyed South Africa and created a tense atmosphere during the talks."[72] And in a later passage: "The Vienna meeting was marked by the obvious intensification of American-South African conflicts and differences in the views of government circles in the two states on the major aspects of political settlement in South Africa."[73] Anatoly Gromyko explained differences between the U.S. and South Africa as stemming from a realization "that the growing odiousness of the Vorster and Smith regimes threatens to reduce the influence of capitalism on this regional and partly on the global scale and to discredit its policy in Africa and throughout the Third World."[74]

In addition, Soviet commentaries often suggest that it is no easy matter for the United States to bring pressure to bear upon South Africa. The authoritative Vladimir Kudriavtsev told *Izvestiia* readers that "it must not be thought that the Republic of South Africa's racist

---

[71]Vishnevskii, "Washington's African Maneuvers," p. 84; see also B. Piliatskin, "The South African Knot and U.S. Strategy," *Izvestiia*, August 11, 1977.

[72]Vishnevskii, "Washington's African Maneuvers," p. 83.

[73]*Ibid.*

[74]Anatoly Gromyko, "Neo-Colonialism's Manoeuvres in Southern Africa," *International Affairs*, No. 12, December 1977, p. 96.

government meekly carries out the imperialists' wishes."[75] In an item sarcastically entitled "Love's Not Complete Without a Quarrel," a TASS commentary on mutual expulsion of American and South African embassy officials in April 1979, said that the RSA, "spoiled" in the past by U.S. support, had decided to teach the U.S. a lesson by expelling the U.S. attachés.[76]

What Soviet commentaries often emphasize is that South Africa retains considerable leverage in its dealings with the West. Kudriavtsev pointed to "how badly the United States needs southern Africa's industrial raw materials,"[77] and TASS noted the "Western countries' tremendous economic and strategic interests." Several Soviet articles pointed out that South Africa has considerable support among influential U.S. forces. A Soviet article on U.K. relations with South Africa cited former British Foreign Secretary David Owen to the effect that its "volume of bilateral trade and investments in South Africa is so great that Britain cannot afford to take part in any sanctions against South Africa."[78] Other commentaries similarly cited French, German and other Western ties to South Africa. Because of these ties, Anatoly Gromyko wrote in December 1978, influential American forces were seeking "to persuade the American public that the U.S.A. is more dependent on South Africa than South Africa on the U.S.A."[79] Numerous Soviet articles used these ties to explain Western unwillingness to levy extreme sanctions against South Africa or expel it from international organizations.

Another source of South African leverage, occasionally noted by Soviet sources, but as a matter of some concern, has been South African economic ties, both current and potential, with the rest of Africa and particularly with its neighbors. According to one Soviet journal, "the South African monopolists consider Africans the main sphere of their activity." Through participation in multinational corporations, South Africa was "penetrating into African countries." Beyond that,

---

[75]V. Kudriavtsev, "The South African Whirlpool," *Izvestiia,* May 4, 1979.

[76]TASS, April 14, 1979.

[77]Kudriavtsev, "The South African Whirlpool."

[78]Z. Matyreshina, "British Monopolies and the Apartheid Regime," *Asia and Africa Today,* No. 1, January 1979, p. 31.

[79]Anatoly Gromyko, "African Realities and the Conflict Strategy Myth," *New Times,* No. 51, December 1978, p. 5.

"the RSA regime is striving to establish direct contacts with independent African countries."[80]

Several Soviet commentaries during 1979 noted a statement by South African Prime Minister Botha that the RSA was studying the question of creating an economic and military association of states in southern Africa. Most specified Rhodesia and Namibia as potential members, but one suggested an RSA intent "to attract certain sovereign African states which find themselves in economic dependence on the RSA."[81] Presumably, Moscow has in mind such countries as Lesotho and Botswana although their differences with South Africa on foreign policy issues has drawn Soviet praise in recent years.

Liberation Struggle: A Long Process

In addition to these international factors, there is considerable evidence that, while hopeful about ultimate prospects in South Africa, Moscow sees a long struggle ahead. In one of the few Soviet discussions that made any pretense of a scholarly analysis, a roundtable published in the spring 1978 issue of the journal *Narody Azii i Afriki* (Peoples of Asia and Africa), A. B. Davidson admitted that the situation was considerably more complicated than generally described in propagandistic tracts. He said that "nowhere in the world has there been implanted such ethnic segregation and division as in the south of Africa."[82] Stressing that the "current problems of the RSA are extremely complicated," Davidson pointed out that "it is difficult in Moscow to judge South African reality because the people of our country are deprived of the possibility of seeing it with their own eyes."[83] According to Davidson, the last Russian group to have traveled "unhindered" and to any degree in South Africa was one which went to the Transvaal during the Boer War at the beginning of the 20th century.

---

[80]I. Yastrebova, "RSA—Place D'Armes of Imperialism in Africa," *Aziia i Afrika Segodnia,* No. 6, June 1976, p. 29.

[81]Yu. Borisoglebskii, "Liquidation of the Strongholds of Colonialism and Racism—Demand of the Times," *Mezhdunarodnaia Zhizn',* No. 7, July 1979, p. 29.

[82]Davidson, "Where Is South Africa Going?" p. 16.

[83]*Ibid.,* p. 17.

Moreover, Davidson revealed, Soviet scholars "for long" have had disputes about a variety of questions about which Soviet propaganda has shown more certitude:

> How long can the current apartheid regime be preserved and along what paths will the RSA ruling circles go—will they really begin to carry out the liberalization of the existng order or continue turning the screws? How will revolutionary events develop—will they spill out into a "race skirmish" as many Western observers calculate or manifest themselves in other forms altogether? What will the correlation of national-liberation and social tasks of the struggle be? How will this be influenced by the specifics of the socio-economic structure of the RSA, the peculiarities of its ethnic and political history? What social and ethnic motives will force people to stand on one or the other side of the barricades?

Disputes over these questions, Davidson said, have "blazed up especially warmly" after events in Angola, Mozambique, Rhodesia, Namibia and Soweto. And, he concluded, a variety of interpretations is only natural since "the South African Republic is a country with many individuals, its reality is complicated, multifaceted and contradictory."[84]

Two complexes of factors figure in Soviet caution: one, dealing with weaknesses of the "liberation" movement and divisions within the groups on which it is concentrating, notably the trade union movement and the black communities of South Africa; the second is the continued capacity and will of the South African "ruling class" to suppress extremist opposition and maintain itself in power. Using various circumlocutions, Moscow and the South African Communist Party lament the lack of inroads made by the latter. Thus Ulanovskaia's pamphlet balances praise for the SACP and ANC with the following passage:

> At the same time, the liberation struggle of the African people is hampered by both objective and subjective difficulties created by the racist regime: the low level of class and political consciousness of the basic mass of the African population, the lack of experiences by the patriots in revolutionary actions, the absence of legal leadership on the part of the political vanguard of the South African people—the SACP and ANC, racial discord implanted by Pretoria, the spontaneous character of many actions, their scattered nature, etc. A serious obstacle to the liberation

[84]*Ibid.*, pp.15–16.

struggle is the powerful military-repressive regime of the racists and the many-sided aid rendered them by the West.[85]

Despite their emphasis on Soweto, Soviet and South African communists do not even claim that the SACP or ANC were directly responsible for the original incidents. What they have said in effect is that Soweto set forces in motion of which both could take advantage. Moscow's first full-scale description of the Soweto riots focused—as in Western accounts—on the language issue and described the subsequent "mass actions" of protest as "a spontaneous expression of the refusal of the vast majority of the country's population to reconcile themselves to the inhuman policy of racial discrimination."[86]

ANC President Tambo specifically rejected South African government charges that his organization was behind the Soweto events. "Since the ANC was banned" in 1960, he told Le Monde, "there has been no political structure in South Africa capable of organizing a mass mobilization." The ANC, he explained, operated underground and through smuggled pamphlets and radio broadcasts from outside the country, but "it lacks the means to reach the population in the way the high school pupils and the students do at their meetings."[87]

The South African Communist Party discussed the question at some length at a plenary session in April 1977. In its Political Report on the session, the Party sought to strike a balance between admissions that it and the ANC had not been directly involved at Soweto with attempts to identify with and ride on the coattails of events there. "The revolt," according to the report, "showed the marks of all popular upsurges which usually combine organized actions with others which are spontaneous and semi-spontaneous."

Insofar as it was organized, however, the Party gave major credit to the South African Student Movement (SASM), identified as a noncommunist organization interested mainly in the issue of Bantu education. The report stated "there is evidence that some of SASM's leaders turned to known activists of the ANC for advice and coordination" and that subsequently "many more have joined the ranks of the liberation movement and its armed wing, Umkhonto we Sizwe," but in general

[85]Ulanovskaia, South Africa, p. 41.
[86]Tyunkov, "Battle for Human Dignity," p. 14
[87]Le Monde (Paris), October 6, 1976.

248

concluded that the ANC had neither organized nor led the upsurge. And looking ahead, it predicted that the ANC "leadership in the immediate future will be the key factor in consolidating and advancing the revolutionary energies which have emerged."[88]

Meanwhile, however, the plenum stressed the communists' inability to get a serious armed uprising in motion. It attributed this inability both to the weaknesses of their forces and "the extremely difficult and unfavorable internal and external conditions in which we have been forced to operate."[89] It cited "the absence of prior preparation of organized liberation-military structures within the country" in the first regard, and the fact that "the enemy backed by imperialism still possesses considerable strength and resources" in the second. The lack of strength or "ferment of revolt" in rural areas was also cited in the plenum report and a later article by SACP Chairman Dadoo.[90]

One of the most telling admissions of the difficulty involved in any attempt at guerrilla warfare in South Africa appeared in a statement to *New Times* by ANC official Sizekele Sigkashe. Though claiming that "Spear of the Nation" units were "inflicting blows on military and economic objectives," Sigkashe went on: "Of course, the conditions of our country in which there are no dense forests or other places where it would be possible to take cover or create partisan bases to a definite degree holds back the unfolding of an armed struggle. We must seek out other methods, acting underground, hiding in the cities."[91]

The divisions within South Africa society loom large in Soviet perceptions about the difficulties facing opponents of the South African government. As Davidson noted in *Pravda:* "In southern Africa racist policy has erected walls of mutual lack of understanding, distrust and enmity not only between people belonging to different racial groups but even within the confines of one and the same group." A particular source of Soviet regret is the division of the working class and trade union movement in South Africa along racial lines. "The formation of the proletariat in conditions of racism, national colonial oppression and the undermining activity of the authorities," wrote one author, "has led

[88]See *The African Communist,* No. 70, Third Quarter, 1977, pp. 34–36.
[89]*Ibid.,* p. 33.
[90]Dadoo, "South Africa," p. 29.
[91]Tyunkov, " . . . And They Raised," p. 32.

to the factual split of the working class along racial lines."[92] Another cited a previous Soviet book to the effect that the African proletariat has been "forced to build its strategy and tactics" proceeding from the premise that "a significant substratum of a white labor aristocracy" exists, that is, a group which benefits from and is satisfied by the benefits it derives from South African society.[93] According to Ulanovskaia, the authorities allot "no small role to trade unions of white workers in the arsenal of means" for stabilizing the existing system. By giving white workers superior status, "the regime strives to use the majority of trade unions of white workers as an integral part of the state machine for the oppression of non-European workers."[94] Ulanovskaia noted that the majority of white trade unions discriminate against blacks but denounced a decision in 1974 by the Trade Union Council of South Africa to admit African trade unions as a trick designed among other things to bring them under white control.

In an interview with a Hungarian paper, SACP Chairman Dadoo was said to have "stressed very strongly" that "the white working class is completely prepared to defend the racist regime, thus protecting primarily its own status as privileged workers. In many respects, the distorted conditions between races have also distorted the class attitude of the white workers." For this reason, he also noted, the Communist Party is "almost exclusively a party of the black and colored people" which is also why it "places national liberation above all else."[95]

Nor has Moscow been prone to exaggerate the significance of the strike movement in general thus far. Despite its potential, Ulanovskaia cautioned, the "strike movement to a great extent still has a spontaneous character"[96] which, in Soviet parlance, means the failure or inability of the Communist Party to control the movement. Moreover, she deplored the "weakness of the political consciousness of the basic mass of African proletariat," another bit of communist verbiage signifying communist weakness in South Africa.

[92]Tarabrin, "Africa in a New Turn," p. 46.
[93]Yu. Shvetsov, "RSA: The African Working Class," p. 10 citing Lebadi, *The Great October and the Liberation Movement in South Africa,* p. 42.
[94]I. A. Ulanovskaia, "Trade Unions," p. 125.
[95]*Nepszabadzag* (Budapest), May 29, 1979.
[96]I. A. Ulanovskaia, "The Labor Movement," p. 27.

Indeed, Moscow has deplored government-fostered divisions within the black population. In speaking of "national liberation," Soviet and communist sources proceed from the concept of a single black nation and accordingly bitterly attack both the theory and practice of the South African government's homelands policy or Bantustanization as it is generally labeled by Moscow. "The main aim of Bantustanization," wrote Ulanovskaia, "is to prevent the historic process of the growth of a single African nation, representing a threat to the dictatorship of the white minority." By denying the existence of an African majority, "the racists on this basis reject the idea of transfer of power to it."[97]

Among other motivations attributed by Soviet analysts to the homelands policy is a desire by the white regime to foster the growth of a black bourgeoisie and middle class which will have a vested interest in the current system, be willing to cooperate with it, and act as a brake on calls for radical change. "The Bantustans," wrote one, "in the opinion of their creators should be not simply satellites of the apartheid regime, but in their own way the nourishers of an African 'mini-capitalism' in the economy, anti-democratic and anti-communist advance posts of the racists among the African population."[98] In fostering this development, the same article said, the authors of apartheid hoped that the "state interests of the Bantustans, reformism, and petty bourgeois nationalism, . . . might become a barrier on the path of penetration of revolutionary ideology among the masses of Africans, hinder the forming of their national and class self-consciousness."[99]

Moreover, according to Moscow, the homelands did not fulfill the aims they were ostensibly designed to serve because of their lack of territorial integrity and insufficient economic viability. Soviet commentaries attacked them further as schemes to deprive blacks working in white areas of their civil and political rights, to provide a source of cheap manpower for South African industry, to keep black workers docile because of their need to move frequently from job to job, and to

[97]Ulanovskaia, *South Africa*, p. 9.
[98]Yu. Shvetsov, "Bantustans—Pretoria's 'Black Line of Defense,'" *Aziia i Afrika Segodnia*, No. 6, June 1979, p. 30.
[99]*Ibid.*, p. 29.

serve as a dumping ground for unemployed and unemployable blacks.[100]

The failure of any other country to recognize the Transkei and Bophuthatswana homelands announced in October 1976 and December 1977, respectively, was of course welcomed by Moscow, which felt it reflected Pretoria's failure to achieve the international respectability their formation was designed to obtain. However, Moscow appeared perturbed and sought to discredit all evidences of independence by tribal or other leaders. Conceding that their criticism of apartheid was sometimes "sharp in form" and "objectively reflects the moods of the broad African masses," a Soviet commentator argued that this criticism was "dictated by anxiety about their own popularity and prestige" and constituted an attempt "to seize this historical initiative from the national liberation movement, to give it a negatively-nationalist character, to deflect from the real struggle, to emasculate its revolutionary and even more notably its class content."[101] The unwillingness of President Matanzima of Transkei to legitimize the Communist Party and the ANC was given as the main evidence that his anti-apartheid statements were not genuine.

Soweto has come to symbolize for Moscow not only the starting point for anti-apartheid actions but South African government efforts to counter forces which might transcend tribalism. Soviet historian V. P. Gorodnov, who appears to devote special attention to Soweto, argues that whereas the process of urbanization had been leading to "gradual detribalization," the government has been pursuing policies designed to preserve and strengthen tribal loyalties. Instead of allowing the spontaneous growth of towns in which different tribes lived together, South African authorities are now said to encourage townships along tribal lines. Thus, he wrote, apartheid foresees not only separate development but "tribal fractionalization"[102] which "has a definite aim—to split the developing common front of the struggle against apartheid, to counter the progressive, politically literate and conscious

---

[100]See especially I. A. Ulanovskaia, "Bantustans in the RSA—Production of Racism," *The Working Class and the Contemporary World,* No. 3, May–June 1977.

[101]*Ibid.,* p. 32.

[102]V. P. Gorodnov, "The Phenomenon of Soweto," *Narody Azii i Afriki,* No. 2, March–April 1978, p. 30.

forces of the African urban proletariat with the most backward and reactionary elements."[103]

Finally, despite the dire predictions about the ultimate course of events in South Africa mainly as a result of domestic factors, Soviet analysts also indicated considerable respect for its ability to withstand external pressures and its potential to exert influence regionally. In the words of a Soviet article on South Africa's military and economic potential,

> The ultrareactionary domestic policies of the racist regime of South Africa and the neocolonialist thrust of its foreign policy are made all the more dangerous because they have a considerable material basis. The country has the continent's major economy accounting, as it does for 22 percent of Africa's gross domestic product, 75 percent of steel output, 60 percent of electric energy and 40 percent of minerals.[104]

This same article also carefully analyzed South Africa's military strength, putting particular emphasis on the drive to establish an indigenous armaments industry. South Africa's war industry, it said, "does not yet have an adequate scientific and technological base," and still depends on foreign suppliers for heavy armaments. However, "allocations for military R&D are growing rapidly," and South Africa has "turned from importing to exporting some types of military goods," such as napalm. The article estimated that South Africa's armed forces of 51,300 as of 1975 could be brought to 400,000 men in case of total mobilization. Accordingly, despite South Africa's setback in Angola, "South Africa's war machine poses a real threat for the African national liberation movements inside the country, in Namibia and Zimbabwe and for the neighboring independent states."

In addition to general statements about South Africa's economic power, Moscow has noted specific efforts to protect itself against all possible contingencies. One Soviet review emphasized that South African agricultural production has doubled since World War II and satisfies 90 percent of the country's foodstuffs needs.[105] Moscow's principal foreign affairs journal in July 1979 reported that the RSA was "pre-

[103]Gorodnov, "Soweto—Grief and Anger of South Africa," *Aziia i Afrika Segodnia,* No. 6, June 1977, p. 20.

[104]Tatiana Krasnopevtseva, "Military and Economic Potential," *Asia and Africa Today,* No. 2, February 1979, p. 22.

[105]Yastrebova, "RSA—Place D'Armes," p. 29.

paring itself for prolonged opposition" to which end it "is feverishly storing up oil, increasing the potential of its military industry." In making this effort the article stated the RSA feared "that under the pressure of world public opinion the Western powers will be forced if not to stop, then to limit its support."[106]

Perhaps Moscow's most far-reaching admission of South Africa's strength was implied in the 1977 Soviet campaign against RSA acquisition of nuclear weapons, though the campaign culminated in claims by Moscow that it had forestalled nuclear tests and the acquisition of such weapons by the Republic of South Africa. The campaign was touched off by a TASS statement on August 8, 1977 which warned that "according to information reaching here" (i.e., Moscow), "work is presently nearing completion in the South African Republic for the creation of the nuclear weapon and preparations are being held for carrying out its test." Speaking in the name of "leading circles of the Soviet Union," TASS called on all U.N. members and the "international public" to undertake "most urgent, effective efforts" to prevent such RSA action. TASS charged that "if the racialist Pretoria regime obtains the nuclear weapon, it would create a direct threat to the security of the African states, lead to sharp escalation of instability and tension in the south of Africa, would increase the military threat for all of mankind" and "would have most serious and far-reaching aftermaths for international peace and security."[107]

Concurrently Brezhnev sent messages along similar lines to several Western leaders. Presumably to underscore that Soviet concerns were more than propagandistic, Moscow did not publicize Brezhnev's messages. When, following demarches to South Africa by the U.S. and other Western countries, South African officials gave assurances that the RSA did not have or intend to develop nuclear explosive devices, Moscow took full credit for the outcome. Thus *Pravda* in January 1979 said that the TASS statement, "together with protests from the world public, forced the racists to defer their plans."[108]

Nevertheless, Moscow sought to keep alive a sense of alarm about South African intentions regarding nuclear weapons. The above-noted

---

[106]Borisoglebskii, "Liquidation of the Strongholds," p. 29.
[107]*Pravda*, August 9, 1977.
[108]V. Yordanskii, "Southern Africa: Pandering to the Racists," *Pravda*, January 31, 1979.

254

Pravda piece asserted that the South African nuclear testing center in the Kalahari had not been dismantled and that the RSA was speeding up construction of a plant to produce enriched uranium at the rate of 250 tons a year. Another article stated "there is much indirect evidence that South Africa is on the threshold of obtaining the nuclear weapon."[109]

Earlier, the Soviet media had expressed considerable skepticism about South African assurances on nuclear weapons. *Pravda's* weekly foreign policy review on August 28, 1977 said that despite the RSA's assurances as announced by President Carter the previous week, "many observers doubt its veracity." TASS on August 30 emphasized a statement by South African official Owen Harwood reiterating South Africa's right to develop nuclear weapons. Two months later, *Pravda* reported statements by South African Prime Minister Vorster and Defense Minister Botha denying that they promised the United States never to explode any nuclear devices.[110]

Although the Soviet media did note Western demarches to South Africa, the bulk of Soviet comments were either critical or skeptical. Radio Moscow on August 23, 1977 dismissed Western diplomatic efforts as an attempt "to make it appear that the NATO countries are not privy to the racists' achievement of a nuclear potential and the TASS statement's warning really worries them." However, this and many subsequent Soviet commentaries charged that Western aid to South Africa in the nuclear field made it all possible.

What Moscow's reaction would be if South Africa did in fact detonate a weapon was left open in Soviet pronouncements. Apart from TASS' generalized warnings of the dangers which would follow such South African action, one Soviet article limited itself to the assertion that "the appearance of nuclear weapons in the hands of the Republic of South Africa would undoubtedly damage the efforts of all progressive forces for the creation of the necessary preconditions for stable peace."[111]

---

[109]Krasnopevtseva, "Military and Economic Potential," p. 22.

[110]TASS, "Racists Dash for the Bomb, " *Pravda,* October 31, 1977.

[111]Yu. Tsaplin, "Dangerous Schemes," *Sotsialisticheskaia Industriia,* August 23, 1977.

Meanwhile, the issue appears as part of the general Soviet effort to portray South Africa as a threat to peace requiring the rest of Africa to rely on the USSR for protection and designed to cast further suspicion on Western ties with Pretoria. Thus, the initial TASS statement put South African nuclear weapons development in the context of the overall equipment of the South African armed forces with "the latest military equipment" and its ability to obtain military aid from NATO and Israel despite U.N. decisions.

Along the same lines, it should be noted, the top Soviet leaders themselves have been emphasizing in articles and messages that the very existence of South Africa is a source of danger to the rest of the continent. Thus, Soviet Foreign Minister Gromyko wrote in the Soviet theoretical magazine *Kommunist:* "The inhuman policy of apartheid presents a threat to the independence and free development of the African countries and peoples. It is fraught with dangerous consequences for peace in Africa and throughout the world."[112] Soviet Premier Kosygin's message to an anti-apartheid conference in 1977 said that "the existence in southern Africa of colonial racist regimes relying on the support of imperialism's aggressive forces poses a serious threat to the peoples' security."[113] The Soviet government statement of June 23, 1978 flatly stated that "the racist regime in Pretoria . . . by itself presents a threat to international peace." This line takes on added significance in the light of the USSR's developing doctrines on intervention which assert its right as the custodian of world peace to move anywhere it chooses in support of governments or movements that are battling "imperialism."

---

[112]A. Gromyko, "The Leninist Peace Strategy: Uniting Theory with Practice," *Kommunist,* No. 14, October 1976, p. 29.
[113]*Pravda,* June 18, 1977.

CHAPTER ELEVEN

Conclusions and Implications

SOVIET ADVANCES IN AFRICA confront the West and Africa itself with a challenge of new dimensions.

The essence of the current situation has been enunicated by Soviet Central Committee official Karen Brutents. The Soviet relationship with underdeveloped areas in the past, Brutents asserted, "was largely a matter of *defense* of the first socialist revolution against imperialism, whereas today it is a question of carrying on the *offensive* against imperialism and world capitalism as a whole in order to do away with them."[1] As far as Africa specifically is concerned, the Soviet journal *USA* in January 1980 stated:

> Despite all efforts undertaken by the United States, the main tendency consists in the gradual weakening of the positions of the leading Western powers on the continent. With the material and moral-political support of the socialist community, the African peoples are inflicting one defeat after another on imperialism. Events in Angola, and then in the region of the African Horn, showed that the West as a whole and the U.S. in particular can no longer impose according to their discretion a solution of the problems of developing countries.[2]

[1]K. Brutents, *National Liberation Movements Today,* Vol. I (Moscow: Progress Publishers, 1977), p. 16.
[2]M. L. Vishnevskii, "Washington's Policy in Africa and American African Studies," *USA: Economics, Politics, Ideology,* No. 1, January 1980, p. 118.

The New Dimensions

The interventions in Angola and Ethiopia, first of all, gave new substance to Soviet claims and self-perceptions as a super-power with a global reach. When Gromyko in 1969 and Brezhnev in 1970 expostulated that no world problem could be solved without taking into account the USSR and its power, they were speaking in more of a political than a military context. And though Soviet military spokesmen shortly afterward began to ascribe an external role to Soviet armed forces going beyond the defense of the USSR and its allies, the farthest the USSR had gone in practice before Angola was verbal threats, military aid programs and maneuvers, and limited military participation by air force contingents in Egypt in 1970–71. Indeed, just before the Angolan intervention, a Soviet book on Africa had argued that in the case of such countries as Tanzania and the Congo, "their significant distance hampers the socialist states in rendering military aid in case of imperialist aggression."[3]

But since Angola and even more so since Ethiopia, Moscow's perceptions of its own capabilities has changed drastically. Writing in 1977, Karen Brutents emphasized that "the socialist community has become a factor which exerts a direct influence on a global scale, making itself substantially and frequently even crucially felt in virtually every key area of the world and on all the major international issues."[4] Two years later, a key Soviet journal was presenting as a fact of international life "an enormous increase" in the capability of the Soviet Union and its allies "for immediate intervention, particularly by means of rapidly moving large military units and armaments over large distances."[5] And in fact, the scale of the armaments it flew into Angola and Ethiopia, and the secrecy and speed with which it did so, reflected the impressive dimensions already attained by Soviet airlift capabilities with more to come.

Coupled with growing Soviet logistics capabilities, the availability of large Cuban expeditionary forces gives the USSR a potent new instru-

[3]N. I. Gavrilov, G. B. Starushenko, eds., *Africa: Problems of Socialist Orientation* (Moscow: Nauka, 1976), p. 11.

[4]Brutents, *National Liberation Movements Today*, p. 290.

[5]M. Maksimova, "The World Economy, the Scientific and Technological Revolution and International Relations," *Mirovaia Ekonomika i Mezhdunarodnye Otnosheniia*, No. 4, April 1979, pp. 23–24.

mentality for extending its influence in Africa. A comparison between the size of the Cuban army and those of almost every state in Africa underscores this potential. According to the London International Institute for Strategic Studies (IISS), as of 1980 Cuba had at its disposal armed forces totaling 189,000 as well as another 90,000 reserves and 113,000 in paramilitary forces. The Cuban army accounted for 160,000 of these forces, 22–23 percent of whom were in Angola (20,000) and Ethiopia (16,000–17,000).[6] The CIA estimates that Cuba had a total of 38,650 troops and military technicians in the Third World in 1978, about 24 percent of its army.[7] According to the IISS, in 1978 the total armed forces of possible key targets of Zaire and Zimbabwe-Rhodesia were 20,500 and 21,500 respectively. Most other countries have even smaller forces, so that unless other forces become involved (from the West or South Africa), the Cubans, aligned with the Soviets, have the potential to play a decisive military role in any single case.

The Will and Right to Intervene

The interventions in Angola and Ethiopia meant that the USSR, with African acquiescence, established its right and willingness to use its expanded power in Africa. Soviet justifications on Angola and Ethiopia, and later in Afghanistan, in effect extended the "Brezhnev doctrine" to include regimes beyond the Soviet bloc.

For the benefit of non-communist world opinion and the legalistically minded, Moscow has stressed that its own intervention and that of Cuba came at the request of legal governments in Angola and Ethiopia. However, beyond that, these interventions are depicted as shining examples of "proletarian internationalism" in action on behalf of a beleaguered leftist state or a leftist armed movement.

After the Soviet invasion of Afghanistan, candidate Politburo member Boris Ponomarev justified it and all previous Soviet interventions, as well as others to come, in far-reaching terms:

> The devotees of scientific socialism have no intention of denying their spiritual closeness to the progressive forces in Asia, Africa and Latin

[6]*Air Force Magazine,* December 1979, pp. 117–118.
[7]CIA, *Communist Aid to Less Developed Countries of the Free World, 1978,* ER 79-10412U, September 1979, p. 4.

America. Sympathy with fighters for true freedom is natural for Marxist-Leninists and internationalists. Where such forces exist and are struggling, they have the right to depend on our solidarity and support.[8]

And, according to Soviet foreign affairs journal *New Times,* if the USSR does not respond to the needs of such forces it would be failing in its "internationalist duty."

> What is the international solidarity of revolutionaries? Does it consist only in moral and diplomatic support and verbal wishes for success, or does it also consist, under justified, extraordinary conditions in rendering material aid, including military aid, all the more so when it is a case of blatant massive outside intervention?
> The history of the revolutionary movement confirms the moral and political rightness of this form of aid and support. . . . To refuse to use the potential which the socialist countries possess would mean in fact avoiding fulfilling an international duty and returning the world to the times when imperialism would stifle any revolutionary movement with impunity as it saw fit.[9]

From the Soviet perspective an inestimable gain has been African willingness first to invite the Soviet-Cuban forces in and then to accept the legitimacy and results of their intervention. Leftist forces which establish any kind of foothold domestically presumably can feel confident that they can count on Soviet and Cuban military aid, and that if the issue is put in terms of principles—such as defense of territorial integrity from either domestic or foreign foes—it can get continental acquiescence if not approval.

Both in Angola and Ethiopia, Moscow by its actions hammered home the point that it is better to be aligned with the USSR than the U.S. When the Soviets were aligned with Somalia over a five-year period, they, as one Western analyst put it, "demonstrated a will and capacity to arm Somalia to a greater extent than the United States did for Ethiopia" over a twenty-five year period.[10] Indeed, it was this imbalance which stimulated Somalia to invade Ethiopia in July 1978. When the USSR switched from Somalia to Ethiopia, it applied the same principle again:

[8]*Kommunist,* No. 1, January 1980 as cited by TASS, January 10, 1980.
[9]Editorial, "Communists Are in Solidarity with Afghan Revolution," *Novoye Vremia,* No. 3, January 1980, p. 3.
[10]Steven David, "Realignment in the Horn: The Soviet Advantage," *International Security,* Fall 1979, p. 73.

By comparing the U.S. policy of *cautious restraint* to the Soviet policy of *opportunistic adventurism* in the Horn, and by examining the resulting advantages (in terms of arms and direct military support) bestowed on the Soviet clients, the reasons for the American expulsion from the area and the attractiveness of a Soviet orientation for many third world countries become evident. For it is hard to avoid the central political lesson that has emerged: alignment with the Soviet Union proved demonstrably superior to alignment with the United States.[11]

The USSR has also out-maneuvered and out-done China on the African continent. In Angola, Moscow decisively moved ahead while Peking floundered. And it induced a change in position on the part of previously pro-Chinese states as Mozambique, Tanzania and Zambia. The Chinese opposition to the Soviet-supported winners in Angola and Mozambique, and its support for Zaire and other conservative states have been used by Moscow to undermine Peking's revolutionary credentials, leaving Maoist groups few and far between and with little influence. Although Chinese economic activities in Africa are in certain respects more significant than those of the USSR,[12] Moscow does not appear particularly disturbed. According to *Kommunist*, "considering the potential which China now has and will have in the coming decades, Africa cannot rely on it as its basic source of aid and as a main partner in trade and economic cooperation."[13] Most important, *Kommunist* argued, the objective "need" to confront imperialism "does not allow the African countries and peoples to break with their natural ally, world socialism, and above all, the Soviet Union, as the Maoists would like them to do."[14] In other words, Moscow anticipates a continued ability to outbid the Chinese on the military issues which it foresees occupying the Africans in the future.

This Soviet focus on military issues ties in, of course, with the fact that the crucial element in Soviet decisions with respect to Africa has clearly been and remains the forced withdrawal of Western power from

---

[11]*Ibid.*, p. 69.

[12]According to CIA data, Chinese aid to Sub-Saharan Africa between 1954 and 1978 totaled $2.4 billion, the USSR only $1.1 billion; Chinese credits to Africa as a whole exceeded those of the USSR to 27 countries, the USSR exceeding the PRC in only 10 cases (CIA, *Communist Aid, 1978*, pp. 7–8).

[13]Yu. Alimov, L. Fedorov, "Self-Exposure of Maoism in Africa," *Kommunist*, No. 14, September 1979, p. 109.

[14]*Ibid.*, p. 110.

the continent. Central Committee official Ulianovskii, writing on the Third World as a whole in 1978, stressed that "the closing down of a number of foreign military bases in their territories was a substantial achievement of the countries in the process of liberation."[15] In Africa, these included U.S. bases in Libya, Ethiopia, and Morocco as well as French, British, Belgian and Portuguese bases in the territories under their control. At the end of 1979, the U.S. no longer had any bases left in Africa; the U.K. had defense arrangements only with Kenya; France had agreements on defense and military cooperation with but a few of its former colonies. It is less than coincidental that the step-up in Soviet efforts in Angola came after Portugal's decision to withdraw totally and in Ethiopia after the U.S. withdrew the last remnants of its personnel from Kagnew.

Making Gains Irreversible

The ability to apply on a continuing basis major elements of Soviet and Cuban power on the ground in Angola and Ethiopia adds another dimension hitherto not present in Soviet efforts to make its influence permanent and its gains irreversible on the African continent. As late as 1978, a leading Western analyst on African affairs was suggesting that "the Soviet encounter with Africa is much more likely to continue to be marked for some time by shifts of 'alliances' rather than to produce a solid base of Soviet influence, let alone control." Therefore, he suggested, "the best one can do is delineate those situations in which African interests seem to converge with Soviet interests" and those "in which African interests seem to provide an opening for the USSR."[16] In contrast to this view, however, the indefinite presence of Cuban troops in Angola and Ethiopia sharply reduces the chances that these countries can emulate Egypt or Somalia in straying from the fold. Like the Soviet troops in Eastern Europe and more recently in Afghanistan, the Cuban troops and their Soviet backers seem likely for the indefinite future to serve as the final arbiters of internal affairs in these countries.

[15]Rostislav Ulianovskii, *National Liberation* (Moscow: Progress Publishers, 1978), p. 308.
[16]Colin Legum, "The African Environment," *Problems of Communism,* January–February 1978, p. 13.

For this reason alone, but also because of the Soviet display of power and will, the USSR has necessarily become a permanent feature on the African scene. Moreover, the signature of the friendship treaties with Angola and Ethiopia provides a political and juridical basis for this role, the full import of which was reflected in the use the USSR later made of its comparable treaty with Afghanistan.

While it has the leverage, especially that given by the presence of Cuban troops, Moscow is determined to press its advantages. A striking measure of Moscow's expectations is its confidence that it can induce the ruling groups in Angola, Ethiopia, and other radical African states to transform themselves into Soviet-type parties which, under Moscow's guidance, will establish roots throughout their societies and move steadily toward the establishment of "socialist" states inoculated against Western influence and tied enduringly to the USSR. Anatoly Gromyko even compared prospects in Africa with the process which had marked the establishment of Soviet satellites in Eastern Europe. According to Gromyko, "in a number of countries which have embarked on progressive social changes, attempts were [being] made to use the system of a People's Democracy (already tried and tested in some countries of Eastern Europe and Asia), i.e., a state in which the administration of the country and power is in the hands of the working class and all working people."[17] Soviet attention to these trends is so keen, another Soviet author declared, because "it concerns the natural allies of the socialist countries in the anti-imperialism struggle."[18]

It is also so keen, it might be noted, because of Soviet consciousness of past reverses and of such continuing problems as the insurgencies in Ethiopia and Angola with a possible adverse impact on Cuban staying power. However, for the time being, Moscow and its clients appear completely confident that they can bring these insurgencies under control. Nor is there any evidence as of early 1980—more than four years after their entry into Angola, and after two years in Ethiopia—that maintaining their troops has become a problem for the Cubans. Domestic difficulties which came sharply to the surface in Cuba in late 1979 have been attributed entirely to domestic causes. The African adventures, far from causing trouble, have evidently been a source of pride

[17]Nikolai Kosukhin, "Revolutionary Democracy: Its Ideology and Policies," *Social Sciences,* No. 4, 1979, p. 51.
[18]Radio Salisbury, December 23, 1979.

which Havana was able further to underscore by its assumption in 1979 of the three-year chairmanship of the nonaligned movement.

Prospects Ahead

Even before it has completed consolidation of its positions to its full satisfaction, the USSR is in a well-placed position for further moves in Africa. In Angola and Ethiopia it has acquired potential staging areas and possible new proxies to supplement the Cubans. How this works has already become evident in operations in Ethiopia. Whereas during the first Cuban action in Angola, Moscow and Havana had only a limited staging area in the Congo and had to ferry major additional forces directly from Cuba itself, during the Ethiopian adventure large Cuban contingents were already on hand in Angola for transfer to that front.

From the Soviet point of view, the ability to use African forces as new surrogates would offer further obvious advantages, provided these forces proved, like the Cubans, dependent on the USSR militarily and responsive to Soviet guidance politically. Mengistu in Ethiopia has several times spoken about the time when his country can emulate Cuba on the international scene. After the London agreement on Rhodesia in December 1979, Mozambique President Machel aknowledged for the first time that Mozambique forces had been involved in fighting in Rhodesia.[19] Soviet uneasiness about Tanzania's direct involvement in the overthrow of Idi Amin stemmed entirely from its apprehension that Western influence might be enhanced by Tanzania's action and not from the fact of the intervention itself. One can envisage a future situation in which a "socialist-oriented" state—with Moscow's blessing and support—will attempt something comparable individually or as part of a group of such states purporting to act as a peace-keeping force. Indeed, in January 1980 contingents from Guinea, Benin and the Congo—three states considered by Moscow to be socialist-oriented—did in fact move into Chad, in accordance with an agreement reached by Chad's neighbors in Lagos, Nigeria in August 1979. While in this specific case, these forces may not be able to affect

[19]Radio Salisbury, December 23, 1979.

the outcome of the internal squabble, the precedent is one which can well serve Moscow or its African clients in the future.

As in Angola and Ethiopia, endemic African problems are likely to provide virtually endless new opportunities for future Soviet-Cuban involvement on the continent. Both of these states exposed the fragility of the national entities which replaced the colonial era—in Angola's case because of tribal and regional divisions which transcended the formation of a cohesive nation and state; in Ethiopia's similar divisions compounded by the presence of companion nationalities on the other side of Ethiopia's borders. The problem of tribal and regional divisions has also already involved major civil strife in Nigeria, the Sudan, Zaire, Burundi and Cameroon, and lesser quarrels in other countries. The revival of these conflicts, in Zaire, for example, or in a newly independent Zimbabwe, could lead to a situation in which a "national liberation" or "progressive" faction might ask for "fraternal" help from the USSR.

The complicated cross-border ethnic mosaic which marks the African scene is replete with existing or potential irredentist movements in which one or another party might seek outside involvement. In the wake of the Ethiopia-Somalia conflict, one Soviet journal noted the strengthening in the postcolonial era of "separatist and irredentist moods" on which are "overlaid territorial boundaries inhabited by individual nationalities—the ethnic boundaries, which are especially characteristic of the African continent."[20] In particular, this article cited the overlapping of the Mande people across the boundaries of Mali, Guinea, Guinea-Bissau, Senegal, Ivory Coast, Gambia, Upper Volta and Mauritania; the Fulbe in Nigeria, Niger, Upper Volta, Cameroon and Benin; the Bakongo in Angola, Zaire, the Congo and Gabon; the Somali in Somalia, Ethiopia, Djibouti and Kenya. Another article suggested that 20 African states were relatively homogeneous, with the rest divided internally to varying degrees and often including peoples which belong to broader ethnic or linguistic groups.[21]

This is not to say that the USSR will not move with a certain amount of caution. A review of the Angolan and Ethiopian cases and the abor-

[20]A. Kazanov, "Problem of Inter-State Conflicts in Africa and Events in the Horn of Africa," *Aziia i Afrika Segodnia*, No. 7, July 1978, p. 21.

[21]Yu. Kobishchanov, "Africa: Ethnic Variety or Unity in Diversity," *Mirovaia Ekonomika i Mezhdunarodnye Otnosheniia*, No. 7, July 1978, pp. 137–144.

tive intervention in Zaire indicates that Soviet decisions to intervene were not made lightly. A careful estimate evidently was made in all three cases of the balance of forces on the ground as well as the degree of likelihood of military reactions by the West or political reactions by the rest of Africa. The supplicants of Soviet and Cuban aid in Angola and Ethiopia had a degree of legitimacy—as an OAU-recognized liberation movement in the first, and as a full-fledged government in the second—lending in turn a degree of legitimacy to Soviet-Cuban actions. By contrast, the "liberation movement" claimed to be operating in Zaire appeared too weak to lend credence to any calls for intervention.

Moscow clearly has far from written off the anti-Soviet influence of nationalism or the continued leverage remaining in Western hands, especially in the economic field. The USSR evidently has neither the inclination nor the ability to assume a dominant economic role in any given African country as it has assumed in Cuba. Thus, Anatoly Gromyko contended that "Africa remains a scene of tense struggle between the forces of national liberation and progress on the one hand, and the forces of imperialism and reaction on the other," with "economic levers" playing "a leading part in the policy of neocolonialism."[22]

Moreover, Moscow still shows sensitivity over the possibility of reactions by the West Europeans, as distinct from unilateral U.S. reactions. A Soviet article in November 1978, for example, stressed the importance of Africa as a source of raw materials and investments for Western Europe.[23] The upsurge of Soviet warnings about Western sponsorship of pan-African forces or mini-blocs after the Zaire events suggested the kind of action which most arouses Soviet apprehensions. By the same token, it is this very vulnerability which leads the USSR to keep up constant pressure in the name of economic independence and, where opportunities arise, with Soviet aid in the name of the struggle against imperialism. Moreover, Moscow also sees in increased action by the West opportunities to raise the specter of colonialism. For a number of years, the radical states of Africa have been able to set the

[22]A. Gromyko, "The Present Stage of the Anti-Imperialist Struggle in Africa," *Social Sciences*, No. 4, 1979, pp. 32–33.

[23]L. Aksiuk, "Africa's Mineral Resources in the Raw Material Policy of Imperialism," *Aziia i Afrika Segodnia*, No. 11, November 1978, p. 15.

tone in all African conclaves, especially in the OAU. Given a solid bloc of "socialist-oriented" states, the Soviet position in this respect presumably will remain assured for some time to come. To be sure, the second Zaire episode did lead some Africans, for example the Nigerians, to urge the Soviets not to overstay their welcome in Africa. However, the Nigerians also were careful to praise the USSR for its past aid to African liberation.

Whether constraints operate in the future will, of course, depend on the circumstances. In the cases of Czechoslovakia in 1968 and Afghanistan in 1979, the USSR answered calls which no government voiced and invented legal justifications for intervention after the fact. Each successive intervention presumably raises a louder alarm in the West and in Africa, but by the same token each ends with a strengthened starting point for the next action. Moscow has not let setbacks—in Ghana and Mali, Egypt, the Sudan and Somalia—deter it from actions elsewhere or from seeking to recover ground lost.

Whatever caution Moscow may still see fit to observe in particular situations, there can be little doubt that as a general matter it will continue in a relentless effort to dislodge the West from remaining positions in Africa. And it seems evident that failure of the U.S. to react in Angola and Ethiopia, as well as Soviet perceptions of a general decline in U.S. strength and resolve, will tend to weigh increasingly against caution and in favor of boldness.

A constant in Soviet strategy in the future will evidently be to continue to foster polarization on all levels and in all directions. Within particular states, the USSR aims to encourage radical regimes to pursue ideological goals both domestically and in foreign policy which will separate them from the West and optimally keep them in conflicts with it. To take advantage of its own major asset, both the threat and the real possibility of Soviet and Cuban military action, Moscow's preferred scenario will likely be one of military confrontation involving front-line states seeking Soviet aid against regimes aligned if possible with South Africa and which the West for one reason or another finds it difficult to support. In focusing on issues of this kind, Moscow also has in mind making it more difficult for any African state to pursue a moderate or pro-Western policy. While many African leaders are uneasy about becoming involved in the global East-West conflict, precisely that involvement constitutes the key element in Moscow's approach to the countries of the continent, individually and collectively.

Moscow's Regional Strengths and Problems

Because of its past successes, the USSR as of the beginning of 1980 had advantageous positions in at least three major areas of the African continent.

In North Africa, although the Soviets did not possess the leverage they had gained elsewhere on the continent, their military relationship with Algeria and Libya gave them a strong voice in two major conflicts in the region: the Western Saharan issue and the ongoing civil strife in Chad. Moscow remained to some extent restrained in the first by its economic ties with Morocco and in the second by the preponderant role played by France. Nevertheless, with respect to the Western Sahara, it had bridged the contradictions in its position by supporting the Algerians, Libyans and Polisario Front in fact and by adopting an ambiguous public position professing concern for Morocco as well. If pressed to a choice, Moscow would doubtless consider that the political impact of a defeat for a pro-Western regime in Morocco, both on the Near East and Africa, would far outweigh the phosphate deal with that country, which could then presumably be retrieved under a successor regime.

In the Horn of Africa, the USSR in 1980 was already well placed through its influence in Ethiopia to pursue a variety of objectives. While much of Soviet and Cuban military aid was geared toward the continuing struggles in Eritrea and the Ogaden, the Soviet presence automatically served other purposes. The combination of its position in Ethiopia and southern Yemen has measurably enhanced the USSR's threat to Saudi Arabia and Egypt. Although Soviet gains in Ethiopia were achieved at the expense of the loss of its naval base in Berbera in Somalia, eventually this may be replaced by Soviet facilities in Ethiopia, e.g., Assab and Massawa. And the possibility of course remains that through a change in regimes in Somalia, Moscow can regain the Berbera base. In any event, with its facilities in Aden, the USSR sits astride the exit from the Red Sea. Thus, the Ethiopian venture has markedly strengthened Soviet capabilities throughout the Near East.

It has also put Soviet relations with Ethiopia's immediate neighbors, especially the Sudan and Kenya, into a new context. Ethiopia's ties with the USSR undoubtedly played a significant role in inducing the Sudan in 1979 to modify its previous hostility to the Soviet Union. The signature by Kenya of a freindship treaty with Ethiopia along with a mutual defense pact in January 1979 stemmed from Somali territorial claims against both, but it has also given the USSR new leverage in its relations with Kenya which had been extremely cool since 1965 when the Kenyan government turned back a shipload of Soviet arms and an accompanying military mission.[24] By the same token, the USSR has also retained considerable leverage for use against Somalia. Although hopes for the overthrow of the Siad Barre regime, which Castro once hinted at were not fulfilled, the alliance between Ethiopia and Kenya clearly represents one element of pressure, along with Western reluctance to build Somalia up to the point of a second round against Ethiopia. Further and potentially of great importance, while Ethiopia and the USSR at the height of the conflict with Somalia in 1978 denied that Ethiopian (presumably along with Cuban) forces would cross the border into Somalia, sporadic warnings by Mengistu that the Somalis retain hostile intentions and support hostile actions against Ethiopia has left open the option for cross-border actions against Somalia.

In southern Africa—the third major area of Soviet involvement— Soviet ties with Angola and Mozambique as well as with the other front-line states continue to give it significant leverage in connection with the uneasy settlement in Rhodesia and the continued uncertain situation in Namibia. And in the offing, Moscow has new opportunities arising to come to grips with the major locus of independent power on the African continent, the Republic of South Africa.

To be sure, Moscow in 1980 faced what appeared to be a possible disruption of its preferred confrontation scenario in Rhodesia and Namibia. Compromise political solutions, which Moscow stridently opposes, appeared to be emerging in both, which by definition would mean something less than a complete polarization of forces not only within Rhodesia and Namibia but in relations with their neighbors. Even the first fragile shoots of peace in Rhodesia-Zimbabwe in December 1979 brought an end to sanctions, the opening of Rhodesia's borders with Zambia and Mozambique, and the exodus from the latter two of thousands of refugees who had burdened their economy. If front-line situations finally should come to an end, there presumably

[24]Robert Legvold, *Soviet Policy in West Africa* (Cambridge: Harvard University Press, 1970), p. 262.

would be an end to the front-line states' seeking constant and massive influxes of Soviet military aid, let alone Cuban military forces.

Well aware of this possibility, Moscow's first line of attack was an effort to denigrate the settlement process every step of the way. In the case of the Rhodesian settlement signed in December 1979, this meant continuous emphasis on alleged British perfidy in connection with the elections planned for February 1980. Moscow quickly began agitation that anything less than a victory by the Patriotic Front and especially by Joshua Nkomo would prove such perfidy. Whatever the outcome of the elections in Rhodesia, Moscow made clear it would continue to invoke the South Africa issue which it well knows could recall the pretext for Cuban intervention in Angola. According to *New Times* in January 1980, the West favored a negotiated solution in Rhodesia because it realized that the "game was lost" otherwise and was "afraid that with a victory of the partisans there would arise a new 'radical' state which almost inevitably would enter into a confrontation with the racist RSA."[25] Thus, the West and South Africa were said to be seeking to assure the victory of Bishop Muzorewa, who, according to *New Times,* received "millions of donations" in campaign contributions from South Africa "to which he travels virtually every month." However, *New Times* conceded a Muzorewa victory was not predetermined, in which case "no provocations [from South Africa] are to be excluded." According to the article, the tribal divisions on which Pretoria was allegedly counting might not work out because the idea of national unity transcending tribal loyalties had taken deep root during the guerrilla struggle. "The South African authorities," it said, "do not hide their intentions to interfere in Rhodesian affairs in case north of the Limpopo River there appears, as they express it, 'an unfriendly black state.' "[26]

While Moscow has been cool to Nkomo's major Patriotic Front rival, Robert Mugabe, it publicly welcomed his victory in the February 1980 Rhodesian elections and his invitation to Joshua Nkomo to participate in the government. Initial Soviet broadcasts to Rhodesia urged the new government to adhere to radical programs, and a number of Soviet commentaries warned about the possibility of South African

[25] V. Sidenko, "At the Last Boundary," *Novoye Vremia,* No. 3, January 1980, p. 13.
[26] *Ibid.,* p. 15.

intervention either at the invitation of disgruntled Rhodesian whites or because of direct South African dissatisfaction with the results of the elections. Moscow was thus establishing its own classic scenario for future involvement in Rhodesia.

As in the case of Rhodesia, Moscow also indicated its intent to hamper a settlement in Namibia to the extent possible. Until a settlement is reached there, Angola in effect retains a direct boundary with South Africa and the Soviet-Cuban tandem a continuing justification for the maintenance of Cuban forces in Angola. Within Namibia, as in Rhodesia, Moscow presumably will insist that only a SWAPO victory is acceptable and will seek to hold the SWAPO leadership to the radical measures it has pledged.

Moscow's probable aim, in case settlements take hold in Rhodesia and Namibia, will be to bolster these two along with Mozambique and Botswana as the new roster of front-line states directed for the indefinite future at the ultimate target, the Republic of South Africa. This was already evident in the emphasis during Angolan President dos Santos' visit to Moscow in December 1979 on Mozambique's continued "internationalist obligations." The Soviets can be expected to try to induce newly independent states of Zimbabwe and Namibia—with the encouragement of the rest of Africa—to take up the fight against South Africa even at the expense of their internal development. This would serve two purposes: to promote the radicalization of the new front-line states and to put a premium on their relationship with the Soviet Union. In this connection, it is worth recalling Aleksandr Bovin's statement that armed struggle in southern Africa "promotes the authority of those who support the struggle" and that "if southern Africa gains freedom as a result of armed struggle, it will adopt firm anti-imperialist positions."[27] This same Bovin, in the wake of the Rhodesian agreement of December 1979, remarked that the agreement, whatever its final outcome, "makes the problem of Namibia and the problem of the main stronghold of racism and apartheid, the Republic of South Africa, more urgent and more acute."[28]

In sum, Moscow can be expected to take the position that settlements in Rhodesia and Namibia leave only one major issue in south-

[27]A. Bovin, "Washington and Pretoria," *Izvestiia*, July 13, 1976.
[28]Moscow Television Service, January 6, 1980.

ern Africa, the Republic of South Africa, requiring a special effort by the rest of Africa and its "natural ally," the Soviet Union. It can also be anticipated that Moscow will take the position that the successes achieved in Rhodesia and Namibia came only as a result of armed struggle and that this remains the only feasible way to change the system in South Africa. As in the previous struggles, Moscow will not be seeking compromise solutions but will favor the most extreme "war aims" which will increase the pressure on moderate African forces throughout the continent and enhance Soviet leverage for aligning itself with black Africa and confronting the West with agonizing choices between its interests in South Africa and the rest of the continent.

Thus, while the Soviets make clear their preference for revolutionary as against political settlements in Rhodesia and Namibia, they evidently anticipate that whatever happens in these areas they can still use them as a cutting edge in their drive for dominance in the whole of southern Africa. For one thing, they will surely go all out to induce them to adopt a "socialist-orientation" course on the order of at least Mozambique and, hopefully from their standpoint, even Angola. And to this end they will certainly make full use of the great leverage they have among radical elements to shape to their liking internal developments. Meanwhile, they clearly intend to use the developing situations in Namibia and Rhodesia, whatever their nature, in combination with their power and influence in Angola and Mozambique to mount continuing direct and indirect assaults on the Republic of South Africa. Indicative of Moscow's expectations is the assertion of Anatoly Gromyko, who can be taken to have unusual insights into Politburo thinking, in a book published in late 1979 to the effect that: "The peoples of South Africa were entering the '80s with real chances to finally conquer racism in the foreseeable future" with Zimbabwe and Namibia on the verge of independence and the "movement broadening against apartheid in the main bulwark of the racists—the Republic of South Africa."[29]

Although well aware of Western misgivings about the apartheid system, Moscow regards South Africa as an integral part of the West in the context of the East-West struggle. Soviet spokesmen constantly em-

---

[29]See B. Asoyan, "The Crisis of Racism is Irreversible," *Novoye Vremia,* No. 5, February 1980, p. 24.

phasize that the South African economy is closely geared with the West. Also, Moscow clearly recognizes the growing strategic importance of South Africa to the West in face of the expanding Soviet naval deployments in the Indian Ocean and the mounting Soviet threat in the Persian Gulf. No let-up can be expected in the continuing Soviet campaign to isolate South Africa, with constant attention to divisions already apparent between the West, especially the U.S., and the South African leadership.

Also, whatever changes that South Africa may make in its racial policies, Moscow will be unendingly critical of the results and will seek to take advantage of them to foster the revolutionary transformation of South Africa and its total removal from the Western system. Consciousness of South African power and of the possibility that the West, and particularly the U.S., may come to see it as critical to their overall strategic interests, will probably constrain the USSR and its clients in their choice of tactics, but increasing Soviet self-confidence and the changed situation along South Africa's border make almost certain a sustained and greatly intensified effort to undermine and ultimately to eliminate that power as one of the few cornerstones remaining in support of the U.S.-Western global strategic edifice.

It is beyond the scope of this study to discuss Western options to meet Moscow's mounting challenge in Africa, and with this the Soviet challenge for global hegemony. The purpose is to make clear that this challenge has achieved new dimensions and that the problem the West faces has profoundly changed. Whatever their intentions, the Africans have let the Soviet camel (or bear) into the tent to a degree where previous expulsions offer no precedent or comfort. And the United States and the West generally have looked the other way while this has happened.

Even if Africa has appeared as less important to the West than other areas, it has in fact become vital in every true sense of the word because of its economic and geopolitical relationship to areas whose crucial nature is not disputed, notably the Near East and Western Europe and even Latin America. And while African nationalism and economic aspirations continue to provide the West with some leverage, continuing preoccupations in Africa with local security problems, persisting political and economic weaknesses, the anticolonial heritage still identified with the West, the emotionally loaded racial issue com bined with the increase in Soviet power and the continued will and demonstrated capacity of Moscow to use it in Africa, give the USSR formidable advantages. The West can step aside or hope that long-range trends will somehow operate against the Soviets only at its own peril.

Index

Africa: and East-West struggle, 257, 261–262, 267, 273–274; general Soviet views and aims, 1–5, 8, 257–264, 267; nationalism, 97–100, 266; possible proxies, 264; resources, 266; role of Cuban forces, 262; Soviet versus Western aid, 19, 61–62; tribalism, 103, 265. *See also* Brezhnev, Castro, China, Cuba, detente, Gromyko, Kissinger, major Soviet articles, national liberation, socialist orientation, Soviet Union, United States

Algeria, 3, 69, 73, 75, 76, 77, 78, 80, 85, 89, 97, 106, 130, 268. *See also* Western Sahara

Amin, Idi, 15, 68, 71–73, 264

Angola: Chapters 2 and 7, pp. 4, 9, 33, 74, 76, 79, 81, 82, 84, 85, 86, 90, 91, 97, 98, 104, 111, 113, 156, 157, 158, 160, 161, 172, 199, 206; African reaction, 15–16, 61; Alves coup, 122–123; and African liberation, 17–18, 163, 224, 257; and Ethiopia, 33, 41, 51, 55, 264; and Zaire, 51–53, 55–56, 62–63; as civil war, 14, 22; as Soviet victory, 26; coalition government, 18; consolidation of Soviet position, 118–131; Cuban intervention, Chapter 2, pp. 9, 12, 16, 21, 22–24, 27, 30, 46, 118, 180, 199, 259, 264; Cuban postwar role, 118, 122–123; Cuban withdrawal, 17, 128–130; Dos Santos visit to USSR, 130–131, 197; FNLA (National Front for the Liberation of Angola), 11, 12, 14, 15, 19, 24, 180; ideological status, 120, 122, 124; impact on South Africa, 199, 223, 224, 225, 244; linkage rejected, 49–50; MPLA becomes vanguard party, 123–125; MPLA ties to USSR, 11–14, 19–21, 118, 119–120; Nascimento visit to USSR, 118–120; Neto, Agostinho, 51, 55, 62–63, 113; 118, 124; Neto visits to East Europe, 157; Neto visits to USSR, October 1976, 120–122, 176; Neto visit to USSR, September 1977, 41, 126; Neto visit to USSR, April 1978, 53, 127; Neto (death) September 1979, 130; recognition of, 15, 16; relations with Zaire, 51, 53, 62–63; security problems, 125–130, 263; Sino-Soviet rivalry, 27–29, 121, 180; South African involvement, 16, 22–26, 28, 29, 127–129, 131, 224, 225; Soviet aid, 11–13, 19, 24–25, 29, 75, 78, 119–120; Soviet-Angolan agreements, 118–119, 122, 130–131; Soviet-Angolan Friendship Treaty, 26, 27, 99, 120–122, 184, 223, 263; Soviet-Angolan party ties, 120; Soviet-Cuban denials of involvement, 20; Soviet postmortems, 17–18, 27–31; UNITA (National Union for the Liberation of Angola), 11, 12, 14, 15, 19, 24, 180. *See also* Africa, Brezhnev, Castro, Gromyko, Kirilenko, Kissinger, major Soviet articles, Rhodesia

Benin, 74, 75, 79, 81, 86, 90, 97, 104, 264, 265

Botswana, 68, 89, 180

Brezhnev, Leonid I., 40, 53, 120, 121, 136, 183, 253, 258; congratulates Mengistu, 49; on African upsurge, 4, 5; on bloc-Third World ties, 116; on commitments to Angola, 126; on detente and struggle, 8, 31; on Ethiopia-Somalia, 35, 41; on Ethiopian victory, 143; on Mozambique,